THE
EVERYTHING®
GOLF
BOOK

The Everything® Series

The Everything® Baby Names Book
The Everything® Bartender's Book
The Everything® Bicycle Book
The Everything® Cat Book
The Everything® Christmas Book
The Everything® College Survival Book
The Everything® Dreams Book
The Everything® Etiquette Book
The Everything® Games Book
The Everything® Home Improvement Book
The Everything® Pasta Cookbook
The Everything® Study Book
The Everything® Wedding Book
The Everything® Wedding Checklist
The Everything® Wedding Etiquette Book
The Everything® Wedding Vows Book
The Everything® Wine Book
The Everything® Golf Book

THE
EVERYTHING® GOLF B**OO**K

Essential rules, useful tips, amusing anecdotes,
and fun trivia for every golf addict!

Rich Mintzer and Peter Grossman

Adams Media Corporation
Holbrook, Massachusetts

An Everything® Series Book.
The Everything® Series is a registered trademark of Adams Media Corporation.

Published by Adams Media Corporation
260 Center Street, Holbrook, MA 02343

ISBN: 1-55850-814-7

Printed in the United States of America.

J I H G F E D C B A

Library of Congress Cataloging-in-Publication Data

Mintzer, Richard
The everything golf book / by Rich Mintzer & Peter Grossman
p.   cm.
ISBN 1-55850-814-7 (pbk.)
1. Golf. I. Grossman, Peter. II. Title.
GV965.M479   1997
769.352—dc21   97-28415
CIP

The authors gratefully acknowledge the following for its contribution to this book: *Basic Golf* by Thomas
D. Fahey. Copyright ©1995 by Mayfield Publishing Company. Reprinted by permission of the publisher.

Product or brand names used in this book may be trademarks or registered trademarks. For readability,
they may appear in initial capitalization or have been capitalized in the style used by the name
claimant. Any use of these names is editorial and does not convey endorsement of or other affiliation
with the name claimant. The publisher does not intend to express any judgment as to the validity or
legal status of any such proprietary claims.

INTERIOR ILLUSTRATIONS BY BOB BRANGWYNNE AND BARRY LITTMANN

*This book is available at quantity discounts for bulk purchases. For information,
call 1-800-872-5627 (in Massachusetts, 617-767-8100).*

Visit our home page at http://www.adamsmedia.com

CONTENTS

PART ONE:
THE BIG PICTURE OF GOLF

CONTENTS

PART TWO:
PLAYING AND WINNING

PART THREE:
GOLF IN THE UNITED STATES

PART FOUR:
THE CREAM OF THE CROP

PART FIVE:
BUT WAIT, THERE'S MORE

ACKNOWLEDGMENTS

Rich: I want to thank Carol, Rebecca, and Eric for their patience and my parents for their support. Also, thanks to Kathi, Jennifer, Stacy, and especially Dave for helping out during computer emergencies.

Peter: I want to thank The Sedona Group for their love and support, Robert Grossman for his incredible generosity, Dennis Schneider for his friendship and resourcefulness, Marty Trachtenberg for his patience, knowledge, and unique insights, and my parents, Carole and Ed, who give their love freely and continue to encourage my goals and dreams.

For future golfers, Sam and Max.

We'd both like to thank Laura Morin, wherever she is, and Pam Liflander who took over the huge task of editing this monster. We also want to thank Sheree Bykofsky for bringing us this project.

Special thank-yous to all the people who helped and contributed, including Chad Ritterbusch, publicist extraordinaire for the American Society of Golf Course Architects and some of its members, including Rees Jones and his staff; Dr. Mike Hurdzan; Alice and Pete Dye; Jay Morrish; J. Michael Poellot and his entire company; Cabell and Joyce Robinson; and Robert Cupp.

Also, we must thank Andy and John Mutch, Nancy, and everyone at the USGA Golf House in Far Hills, New Jersey, for letting us use the facilities and for giving us so much valuable information. Thank you to the National Golf Foundation; PGA; LPGA; Nancy Rush at Cotton & Company; Dr. Frances Meritt Stern; The Golf Range & Recreation Association; The Japan National Tourist Organization; The British Tourist Office; George Lewis and the Golf Collector's Society; The College Golf Foundation; Brian Peterson at Golf Week; John Marshall; the always helpful Judy Anderson of Anderson Consulting on Long Island; John Gordon of The Gordon Group in Ontario, Canada; whose help was invaluable; Jeff Bryant at the USTGA; Joanne Masor; Michael Richman; Ron Rothenberg; Norman Bey of BeyFit; Jami Bernard; Sara K. Vogeler of the Neuro-Muscular Center in New York; Richard Miller; Herb Grossman; Paul Grossman; and Carol Mintzer for editing on her lunch hours.

And finally, thank you to all those who make golf the unique, marvelous "slice" of life that it is.

INTRODUCTION

GOLF ON THE RISE

Golf is indeed the fastest-growing game on an international level. From the old course in St. Andrews, Scotland, to new courses built on, around, and through everything from volcanoes to landfills, the game is growing by leaps and (out of) bounds.

In the United States alone there are over twenty-five million golfers, playing over 15,000 courses. Back in 1970, there were eleven million golfers swinging away on just under 11,000 courses. Perhaps one interesting barometer of the game having grown "legs" in America is that the average golfer walks some twenty-eight miles a year on the courses.

Since golf came to America in the late nineteenth century, it has quietly become a staple on the American scene. Without the high-gloss profile of some of the team sports, golf has worked its way into the American lifestyle, with golfing condos and communities putting ardent players at home with the game, and spectacular vacation resorts flanked by lavish, sprawling courses.

THE CHANGING FACE OF GOLF

Once considered the game of the wealthy, golf is changing its image. Exclusive clubs are no longer the mode of the day, as architects are building courses for the public. Over the past five years, more than 75 percent of the new courses opened in the United States have been for the public. Daily-fee golf courses have sprung up to meet the steadily increasing demand.

Golf-course architecture has become big business, and architects are in heavy demand. Courses cost an average of $3 million to build, but that didn't stop a farmer and his family in the Midwest from transforming some of their property into a course for about $800,000. Nor did it stop course builders in the Nevada desert from building an over–$50 million resort course/extravaganza. Country clubs, meanwhile, are now home to a never-ending parade of tournaments of companies, charities, civic groups, and any other organization or association that has caught on to the new golfing craze.

Daily-fee golf has brought the sport to the masses, and high school, and even grade schools now teach golf to students. Collegiate golf is becoming very popular and highly competitive as well. Golf schools, camps, and academies are teeing off all over the place as golf-related complexes featuring state-of-the-art video technology and computerized simulation of the great game pop up in cities as well as outlying regions. There is even night golf!

From the immense golf library at the Golf House and golf museum of the United States Golf Association (USGA) in Far Hills, New Jersey, to the multi-tiered driving ranges of Japan, golf is everywhere. Golf has, in its usual quiet manner, become one of "the things to do" in the '90s, with everyone from Michael Jordan to Madonna trying to sink a putt. Jordan, knowing the value of the game, has even opened the Michael Jordan Golf Center in, where else, Chicago. Celebrities have not only played the game for years but have become part of it, sponsoring tournaments. Bing Crosby, Bob Hope, and Dinah Shore are among the best-known for having their names associated with the game. Nearly all U.S. presidents have played since the nineteenth century, and for vice presidents it has become part of the job description. Off the celebrity trail, corporate golf is a way of life for company executives coast to coast, with nearly every major corporation having or sponsoring a tournament.

Also of significance is how golf has worked its way into the media. What was once a last resort when baseball and football weren't being aired, golf now has prime weekend sports coverage of PGA, LPGA, and PGA Senior tournaments. Golf in films and TV is nothing new, however, from *I Love Lucy*, with Ricky and Fred teaching Lucy and Ethel a mock version of the game in an effort to discourage them (they could have simply taken them to Augusta for their first time out) to the recent film *Tin Cup*, numerous television programs and movies have featured golf in a variety of often comical manners.

While the choice of golfing apparel hasn't necessarily improved for some of the players or fans, the world of golf has expanded into a prime spectator sport. Stadium courses have opened up a wide range of seating options, but major tournaments are still very hard to get tickets for as the demand grows rapidly.

WHY DO WE PLAY GOLF?

Golf is a game that gets into one's soul. It is a personal test, pitting you against your environment. No matter how many players one is competing against, in golf the player is always competing against himself or herself. It is a personal experience and an ongoing challenge to improve.

The majesty of the course makes golf seem implausible. But once you begin to bring the course under control, even if you're shooting a 125, you are still beginning to conquer it. The vastness of the course, and being able to conquer it, is, according to psychologists, one of the lures of the game.

Another attraction of golf is nature. Some of the most phenomenal views and breathtaking scenery can be seen from golf courses. But beyond the views is the idea that you can step away from the real world, particularly for city dwellers, and cloak yourself in natural green surroundings. Psychologists and golfers agree that golf can take your mind away from the rest of the world. On the other hand, it is a place where business can be transacted in a more relaxing, tranquil setting.

As for the game itself, it has been referred to as a game of great frustration and futility. Golf is not easy to master. Yet, once you sink your first 30-foot putt or clear the lake and go from the tee to the green on a par three, you will marvel at your success and talk about it for days, weeks, or years. You will have conquered something that seems so vast, so much larger than yourself.

The game is so attractive because of its unique combination of mental and physical skills. It is appealing because it is a game anyone can play. You do not have to be fast, have great physical strength, or be particularly tall or short. The game is a matter of strategy and ability, and anyone can learn the basics. That opens the game up to mass appeal. As the game evolves from the country-club set to the daily-fee and public courses, the financial considerations are finally beginning to disappear.

Another reason for the love of the game is its history and nobility. Kings, queens, presidents, the stars out in Hollywood, and the jet setters have played golf for ages.

There is something special about taking part in an activity that has such a rich and varied history.

INTO THE FUTURE

As we zero in on the new century, golf-course designers and architects are focused on keeping courses in line with environmental concerns. They are in the process, along with the USGA, the Audubon Society, and other environmental groups, of changing the stigma that golf is bad for the environment. Wildlife habitats are becoming part of, not par for, the course. The idea of building a new course is also more environmentally sound than putting up yet another shopping mall.

The future will also see golf continuing its transition, from outer space (via Neil Armstrong) to Cyberspace, thanks to a more proficient, new brand of hackers. Computer Web sites are numbering in the thousands, while indoor golfing facilities are using technology to measure the speed of your swing, trajectory of your shot, and so on. Every aspect of the game and its equipment have been carefully studied and sculptured to meet the high standards of the game. Interestingly enough, while the game forges ahead with new and innovative equipment, it holds true to long-standing traditions. The USGA, the R&A, purists, architects, and golf lovers hold fast to the idea that while the game moves forward, it must preserve a legacy and maintain the traditional boundaries and guidelines established so long ago.

One of the most unique aspects of golf is that it is not easily mastered. A tour professional may be holding a trophy one week, while struggling to qualify the next. This elusive, unconquerable quality of golf, complete with the majesty and magnificent beauty of so many outstanding courses, puts the game in a class or world of its own. Golfers say there is nothing quite like being out on the course. It's you versus nature, and you're always at the mercy of the vast course that surrounds you.

When you're out on the golf course, it is a different world. The air is clear; the sounds are those of nature; and the world is a calmer place on the golf course, no matter how frustrated one gets.

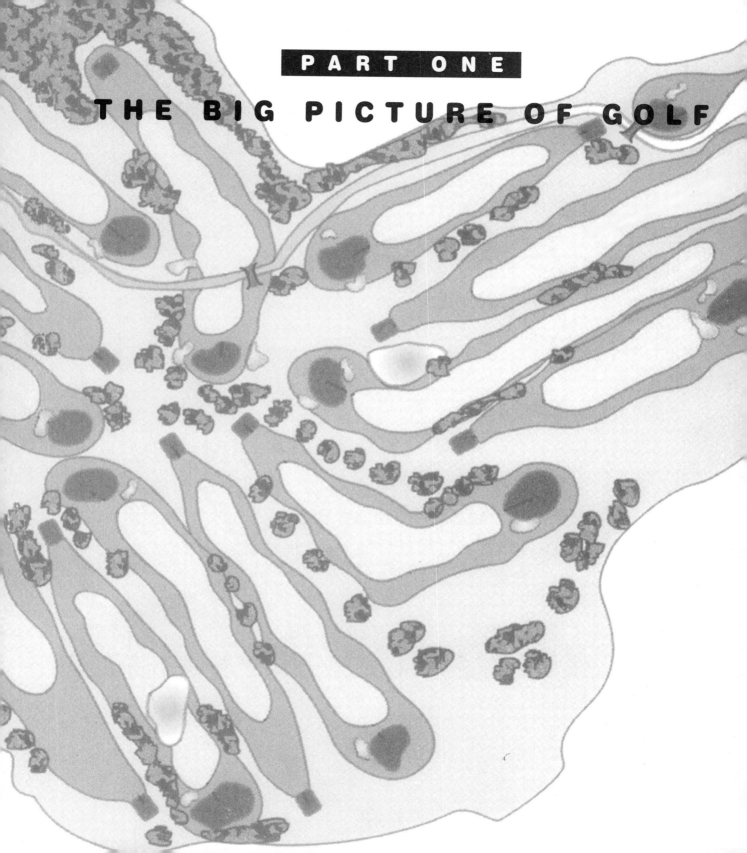

GOLF HISTORY

The origins of the game, not unlike many a modern scorecard, are widely disputed. A host of ancient games resembled golf in some manner, with a club of some sort striking a ball. The Romans played a game called *pagancia*, using a leather ball stuffed with flack. In England a similar game was played in the fourteenth century called *cambuca*. *Pall mall*, or *jeu de mail*, also involved hitting a ball with a stick and was played by the Italians and later the French in the seventeenth century.

Perhaps the oldest resemblance to golf came from Holland in 1296, where four holes were played in a game that also involved a ball and a stick of some sort. Belgium holds the distinction of creating golf in the form of a game called *chole*. A derivation of hockey, this game was played in Flanders, Belgium, and dates back as far as the 1350s. Many of the oldest games, however, appear from old drawings to be more closely related to hockey, as they involve several players and one ball, and are played in the ice or snow.

Another resemblance to golf came from Scotland, where in the early fifteenth century a newer version of the game of *chole* was introduced. It was this game that, over the next twenty to thirty years, is said to have emerged into what we know as golf.

However golf began it was soon put to a halt, at least in Scotland. Golf, along with football, was banned in the late 1450s in Scotland because it was interfering with archery practice, a key element to military training for the war with England. King James II banned the game, as did James III in the 1470s and James IV in the 1490s. Finally, in 1502 the trend came to an end and the ban was lifted. King James IV then purchased clubs made

from a bow maker in Scotland. This purchase of clubs set the stage for golf's return to popularity in Scotland.

In the 1550s the archbishop of St. Andrews issued a decree that gave the locals the okay to play golf on the links at St. Andrews. By 1567, Mary, Queen of Scots, had taken up the game, becoming the first known female golfer.

Golf continued to grow in popularity throughout England and Scotland. In 1618, King James VI even allowed the public to play golf on Sundays. Also around this time a new ball, the feathery, made from two pieces of leather stuffed with boiled feathers, became popular. (The ball would remain in vogue for over 200 years.) Soon links courses started to appear in other parts of Scotland, with holes ranging from 100 yards to a quarter of a mile in distance.

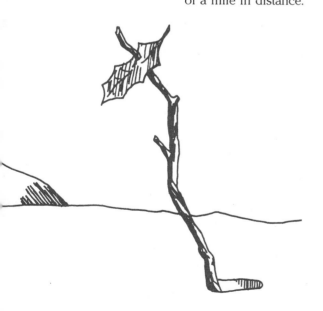

Point of Interest: In 1641, King Charles II is playing golf at Leith when he receives word of the Irish Rebellion, which marked the beginning of the English Civil War. He finishes his round of golf.

CLUBS AND COMPETITIONS

In 1682, Leith, Scotland, played a role in golf history by hosting the first recorded golf match, which pitted the Duke of York and John Paterstone of Scotland against two English noblemen. The Duke of York brought a man along to carry his clubs for him, the first evidence of a caddie.

Since the game had become a popular pastime throughout Britain and Scotland, it was only fitting that a club be formed strictly for the purpose of golf. Thus the Honourable Company of Edinburgh Golfers was formed. An annual competition was started, with a silver cup given to the winner. The first such winner was a fellow named John Rattray.

Not to be outdone, golfers at St. Andrews in 1754 purchased a silver cup, held an open championship, and gave the cup to the winner, Bailie William Landale. With championship matches becoming fashionable, there arose a need for standardized rules and regulations, so the golfers at St. Andrews printed the first codified rules of golf. By 1760, stroke play became accepted for such tournaments. (Up to that point only match play had been used.)

In 1764, St. Andrews had 11 holes, which when played in both directions equaled a 22-hole course. They decided to combine the first four holes into two, making a 9-hole course, or eighteen when played once out and once back. The golfers at St. Andrews did not realize that their little decision would become the standard for generations to come.

In 1767, a score of 94 by James Durham set the St. Andrews record. That score would stand, amazingly, for the next eighty-six years! Meanwhile, Leith, always competitive with St. Andrews, erected the first golf club house in 1768.

By 1783, Glasgow was among those offering a silver cup for competition winners. In the New World, America requested and received a shipment of 96 clubs and 432 balls from Great Britain in 1743. It was not until 1786, however, that the South Carolina Golf Club was formed in Charleston, the first golf club outside the United Kingdom. The Savannah Club would follow

in 1795, but golf would not come to prominence in the United States for another 100 years.

BALLS, BOOKS, AND OTHER BREAKTHROUGHS

Nearing the middle of the nineteenth century, a major breakthrough in golf equipment made a significant impact on the game. The guttie or gutta percha ball was created and replaced the long-time favorite, the feathery. The ball was less expensive to produce, could be made more quickly, and could fly much farther, adding another twenty to thirty yards to a drive than that of the feathery.

The new ball was made from a rubberlike tree sap that was more resilient than the feathery. Originally, the guttie had a smooth cover, but golfers found that when the cover was nicked or scraped, the ball's aerodynamic properties were changed. This was the start of a myriad of cover patterns that are still emerging today.

In 1856 an important rule change was instituted that said a ball must be played as it lies in match play. Although ignored by many a casual golfer, the rule was an important one that is still part of tournament play.

As golf was beginning its emergence as the world's most popular game, the first of millions of how-to books was published in 1857 by H. B. Farnie called *A Keen Hand*. The top professional golfer of the era was Allen Robertson, while George Condie was regarded as the top amateur by virtue of winning the first Amateur Championship at Perth. Open to both amateurs and professionals, the British Open began its long and storied history in 1861.

GOLF IN AMERICA

As for golf in the United States, it would begin its rise in the 1880s. Early courses included Oakhurst in West Virginia in 1884, the Dorsett Field Club in Vermont in 1886, St. Andrews in Yonkers in 1888, and the Middlesboro Club in 1889. By 1894 there were over seventy golf clubs in America. During the 1890s the first public golf course was opened at Van Courtlandt Park in New York City, and the famed Shinnecock Hills Golf Club was founded, also in New York.

Pretty soon amateur championships were being held at several clubs. Two clubs, in fact, proclaimed

to have the official amateur champion. On December 22, 1894, in an effort to establish a central body with uniform rules and regulations, the United States Golf Association (USGA) was formed. Five clubs would make up the original USGA, including the Chicago Country Club in Wheaton, Illinois; The Country Club in Brookline, Massachusetts; The Newport Golf Club in Newport, Rhode Island; St. Andrews Golf Club in Yonkers, New York; and Shinnecock Hills Golf Club in Southampton, New York.

Now that they had become the official governing body of golf in the United States, the USGA could host national tournaments. Newport Country Club had already staged a twenty player event, which eight players finished, taking four attempts at the course. St. Andrews, in Yonkers, had held their own tournament as well. In 1895, the first official U.S. Open was played in Newport, Rhode Island. Postponed from September to October, so as not to interfere with the yacht races, the championship was won by Horace Rawlings. It was the first of what would become the premier event in American golf for years to come.

LADIES GOLF

In the 1890s ladies golf in the British Isles was on the rise. By 1893, the British Isles Golf Union, the first official women's golf organization, had been formed. Margaret Scott won their first Open Championship.

The U.S. Women's amateur event was also decided in

1895. Thirteen ladies played 18 holes at the Meadowbrook Country Club in Hempstead, Long Island. Mrs. Charles S. Brown claimed the first victory with a score of 132. Women's golf had already taken shape in the United States. Just a year after the formation of the women's golf union in the British Isles, the Morris County Club in Morristown, New Jersey had the distinction of being the first club founded entirely by women. The course had cleverly named holes such as Hoodoo, Blasted Hopes, and Sunset.

THE GAME GROWS IN THE STATES

Nearing the turn of the century, men, women, and even college students were getting into the act. In 1897 Louis Bayard Jr., won the first ever NCAA Championship. And, if no one knew what was transpiring in the world of golf until that point, they were able to read about it by the end of 1897 when *Golf* magazine was published for the first time.

The keys to the growing success were the advent of new equipment, the popularity of competitions, and the design of many new

courses. Golf architect Donald Ross, from Scotland, was one of the premier golf architects of the time, designing over 200 courses, some of which are still in existence today. Equipment previously imported from Great Britain was now being made primarily in the United States. Hickory for shafts emanated from the Tennessee Hickory Belt, while persimmon and dogwood were also used for club making.

As golf flourished along the East Coast, slightly more inland major technical accomplishments were taking place. Workers at the BF Goodrich Company in Akron, Ohio, adapted the art of winding rubber thread under tension on a solid rubber core. They utilized this newly founded creation to invent the rubber golf ball. The new ball was livelier than the popular gutta percha ball and could be mass produced more easily. By the year 1900 golf balls could be produced in factories instead of shops. Golf balls became a big industry, and as the equipment became more easily accessible, the number of golfers rose rapidly in the United States.

By 1900, Coburn Haskell patented the rubber-cored ball, which ushered in the modern age of golf and led to standardizing the size and weight of the ball. Within a year, Walter Travis won the U.S. Amateur Open, Sandy Herd won the British Open, and Laurie Auchterlonie won the U.S. Women's Open, all with the Haskell ball. That satisfied doubts of golfers worldwide, and the ball became the standard of the game. The golf ball would evolve over the years thanks to scientific advances. Materials would be added, including balata, surlyn, and lithium. Balls were constructed in one-, two-, and three-piece constructions, but the golf ball designed by Haskell is still basically the same today.

Also at the turn of the century, a dentist in Boston, Doctor George Grant (the first black graduate of the Harvard School of Dentistry) would invent the first wooden golf tee. In upcoming years, American inventors and golfers with extra time on their hands would create over 150 different kinds of tees, including plastic and copper ones. Along with new tees would come new ways to grip a golf club. British golf star Harry Vardon, who had come over on a very successful exhibition tour in 1900 and won the U.S. Open and British Open, would go on to immortality by establishing the overlapping "Vardon" grip, a standard grip for many golfers.

On the equipment front, not to be outdone by American ingenuity, an Englishman, William Taylor, would create the first dimple pattern for golf balls in 1905. Thousands, if not millions, of patterns would emerge over the years since Taylor's original dimpled ball.

As is always the case, when something is made that works someone will try to top it. In 1906, Goodrich decided to market their latest creation, the Pneu-Matic golf ball,

a very lively ball featuring a rubber core filled with compressed air. The problem was that in warm weather the ball was prone to explode. This didn't sit well with the golfing community, and production of the ball was stopped.

While the equipment was changing, new courses were coming into play. In 1901, Donald Ross built the first of many Pinehurst Resort courses at the Carolina Hotel, which would become one of the most highly rated resort courses in the world. Two years later, Oakmont, a legendary course designed by Harry Fownes, opened in Oakmont, Pennsylvania. Over the next several years, course building would become a very significant and lucrative endeavor, as hotels and country clubs realized the value of a neighboring golf course.

TOURNAMENTS AND CHAMPIONS

As golf continued to grow in popularity, the number of tournaments and prize money also grew. By 1908, Mrs. Gordon Robertson became the first female golfer to turn pro. One year later, the USGA ruled that caddies, caddymasters, and greenskeepers over the age of sixteen were considered professional golfers. That rule would be drastically altered in years to come.

As the equipment evolved and rules were restructured to fit the many new advancements, championship play became more popular. The British golf scene was dominated by John Ball, who won eight consecutive British Amateur Championships. Meanwhile, championships and matches were taking place all over the world, and in 1913 the first international professional match was held between the United States and France.

In 1916, to help organize and standardize the professional golf tournaments popping up at numerous clubs, the PGA of America was formed. The organization had eighty-two charter members, and the first PGA Championship was held in Bronxville, New York, and won by Jim Barnes. Within a decade, tournaments were being held coast to coast, with Florida, Texas, and California getting into the act.

Just as fast as golf was sweeping the international scene, so was World War I. The First World War soon put the British Open, the U.S. Open and the PGA Championship on hold for several years, and slowed the production of golf equipment, as military equipment became a prime concern.

AFTER THE WAR

By the Roaring Twenties the progress of golf was back on track. The Walker Cup Matches were initiated, and the Olympic Club in San Francisco and Winged Foot in New York were first opened. Both would become landmark golf locales. Courses were now part and parcel of forty-five states across the country.

While courses were opening up from coast to coast, equipment continued to advance with new technology. Changes occurring in equipment between World Wars included the switch from wooden to steel shafts, persimmon and laminated club heads, and deep-grooved irons which were later banned in 1929 by both the USGA and the R&A. Even the U.S. Department of Agriculture got into the swing of golf, developing what is known as creeping bentgrass for putting greens. By this time, American manufacturers of golf equipment were relying more heavily on science and mathematical precision to create matching sets of clubs than on visual judgment and the feel of the club. The USGA and R&A were kept very busy, trying hard not to let any such changes ruin the tradition and integrity of the game.

It was also in the 1920s that golf clubs were no longer referred to by name, and were replaced by the series of numbers still used today. And who was playing with these new "numbered" clubs in this era? The one and only Bobby Jones, a player who would change the face of the game. From 1923 through 1930, Jones won thirteen national championships before retiring from competitive golf in 1930 at the age of only twenty-eight. Jones won everything in sight and heightened the interest in golf as a spectator sport in America. Jones won the U.S. and British Amateurs and the U.S. and British Opens all in one year, one of the most outstanding feats in all of sports history. Perhaps his most significant distinction was his ousting of the British from dominance in the game in America. Until that time British players such as Horace Rawlings, Joe Lloyd, Fred Herd, Willie

Smith, and Harry Vardon were the stars of the game.

The battle between the United States and Great Britain would heat up and a biennial tournament would be initiated in 1927 to decide the champion. Billed as the United States versus Europe, the Ryder Cup got under way, with Walter Hagen captaining the American team for the first seven years. The United States would go on to dominate the Ryder Cup with captains that would include Jack Nicklaus, Arnold Palmer, and Sam Snead.

As the Depression grew near, golf clubs were still springing up, most notably at Cypress Point in California and in Palm Beach, Florida, where the Seminole Golf Club first opened its doors. Out west, the Los Angeles Country Club staged the first L.A. Open, the third-oldest PGA tournament still in existence today. They offered a $10,000 purse, which at that time was equivalent to the purses of today's tournaments.

Through the '30s the PGA saw the tour money rise to over $130,000, and sponsors like Hershey Chocolate began their association with the tour. Celebrities soon became part of the golf scene, as the Bing Crosby Pro-Am kicked off in 1937 in San Diego. In 1938 charities linked up with golf as well, with the Palm Beach Invitational becoming the first tournament to make a major charitable contribution of $10,000.

THE MASTERS AND THE WAR BEGIN

In 1934, Bobby Jones began a little tournament for a few of his friends. The tournament would evolve into the Masters Tournament, one of the most prestigious of the game. Jones played in the first several as a courtesy to his guests. Unlike many tournaments that would find new homes every year, the Masters would remain in Augusta, Georgia.

Just as the USGA ruled a limit of fourteen clubs per golfer, equipment production was once again slowed to a halt. World War II reared its ugly head, and many PGA touring pros found themselves joining the military. Major tournaments were halted as the world focused on the events in Europe.

In the years following the war, golf found itself back on track rather quickly. The first U.S. Women's Open was played, and was won by Patty Berg. Golf was first seen on local television, as the U.S. Open was broadcast in St. Louis. There were no slow-motion, stop-action replays of every swing, but bringing the game to television increased golf's popularity.

In 1950 the Women's Professional Golf Association was replaced by the Ladies

Professional Golf Association (LPGA), beginning a new rise to prominence of women's golf in America. Patty Berg was the initial president, and by 1952 there were twenty-one tournaments on the LPGA tour. Besides Patty, who split her time between the LPGA administrative work and her own successful career, other top women golfers of the early '50s including Babe Zaharias, Marilynn Smith, Peggy Kirk, Louise Suggs, and Betsy Rawls established a first-rate core of lady professional golfers.

Meanwhile on the men's tour, players like Byron Nelson, Bobby Locke, and Ben Hogan were among the giants of the sport, while Al Brosch shot a 60 at the Texas Open to set a new PGA record in 1951.

Throughout the 1950s more and more people were becoming interested in the game. Magazines and books were regularly keeping the public in touch with what the pros were doing and included tips on how to play. The game was not only for country clubbers, but was promoted for all to enjoy. In fact, Tommy Armour's *How to Play Your Best Golf* became the first golf book to make the bestseller list. In 1954 the U.S. Open was televised nationally for the first time, followed in 1956 by the Masters and in 1957 by the weekly series called *All Star Golf*.

The 1960s saw tremendous growth in the popularity of PGA events and ushered in the era of Arnold Palmer. Palmer would win the 1960 Masters and U.S. Open, and the 1961 and '62 British Opens. While Palmer was on his way to becoming the new superstar, the long overdue color ban was lifted

Mercury seven . . . On May 5, 1961, Admiral Alan B. Shepard Jr., piloting the Freedom 7, became the first to rocket into space. Less than a decade later Shepard was one of three to command the Apollo 14 to the surface of the moon. He carried a special shafted 6-iron club and two golf balls. The club featured an aluminum/teflon shaft that was adapted from a tool designed to scoop lunar rock samples, and the entire instrument weighed only 16.5 ounces. Shepard was the first to take golf to a new frontier.

from the PGA constitution in 1961, allowing Charlie Sifford to become the first black golfer to compete in a PGA-sponsored tournament in the South.

Elsewhere, Gary Player would become the first foreign-born player to win the Masters, and some kid named Nicklaus would break into the professional ranks in 1962, notching his first professional win at the U.S. Open. Meanwhile, by 1965 Sam Snead would amass an incredible eighty-one tour victories. There was a growing interest in becoming a professional golfer, and for the many professional hopefuls the PGA set up their qualifying school at the National Golf Club in Palm Beach Gardens.

By the start of the '60s the LPGA tour money reached $200,000, and in 1963 the LPGA made it to television with the U.S. Women's Open Championship. It was also in the early '60s that Kathy Whitworth embarked on the first stretch of what would amount to an incredible eighty-eight LPGA titles.

Throughout the decade the LPGA continued growing in stature and received more coverage by the sports media. A Hall of Fame was established, and by the end of the '60s, prize money was up to $600,000 in a total of thirty-four tournaments.

As the '60s unfolded, professional and amateur golfers set a host of astounding new records. Bill Burke shot an amazing 57 at Normandie Country Club, a new low for an 18-hole course. Arnold Palmer won the 1965 Masters with a record 271, and three years later became the first player to surpass $1 million in career PGA earnings. An amateur golfer named Norman Manley became the first player to score consecutive holes-in-one on par-four holes at the Del Valley Country Club. But as if all the excitement of golf around the world wasn't enough, Alan

Shepard would round out the '60s by hitting two legendary shots with a 6-iron on a course called Fra Mauro Country Club, not a country club at all, but actually a little place on the moon.

BACK ON EARTH

As the '70s progressed, so did the game. The graphite shaft was invented; Lee Elders became the first black golfer in the Masters; and Jack Nicklaus won his fourteenth major PGA championship to surpass Bobby Jones. By the mid-1970s the PGA was indeed a profitable big business, with total revenues of nearly $4 million. Lee Trevino, Hale Irwin, Tom Watson, and Johnny Miller rose to prominence in the sport, and the number of tournaments grew steadily, as did the number of sponsors and purses. In 1978 the first Legends of Golf was played in Austin, Texas, and would become the precursor to the PGA-sanctioned Senior Tour. Judy Rankin became the first LPGA golfer to surpass $100,000 in income in one season, and Nancy Lopez won five tournaments in a row.

The '80s offered a whole new type of club. Golf's first oxymoron came in the form of metal woods introduced by a company called Taylor Made. Back on the spectator scene, the Players Club at Sawgrass opened and became the prototype for other "stadium" courses, designed to allow greater visibility for spectators. Despite the lack of vendors hawking peanuts, popcorn, and golf tees, the stadium courses were a major success. While spectators were getting a closer, better look at the action, golfers who kept playing into their 50s, 60s, and beyond now had the Senior Tour, which was introduced by the PGA with two events.

On the women's circuit, Kathy Whitworth became the first female golfer to surpass $1 million in career earnings. Tour money was over $4 million, and in 1982 the entire four rounds of the Nabisco Dinah Shore tournament was televised. Pretty soon, the number of lady golfers trying to become professionals would have the LPGA incorporating an all-exempt qualifying system. Corporate sponsorship now became a staple of women's golf, and the prize money and number of tournaments continued to grow. Beth Daniel, Betsy King, and Patty Sheehan were among the pros leading the way.

In the '80s, money in sports began to take off dramatically. In 1986 the Panasonic Las Vegas International offered the first $1 million purse. By 1988 Curtis Strange became the first golfer to exceed the $1 million mark in one season, and thirty players competed for a $2 million purse in the first Nabisco

Championship, which would later become The Tour Championship. As the purse money and player earnings grew, so did the charitable contributions by the PGA and LPGA, which exceeded $200 million in the 1980s alone.

As the '80s wound to a fruitful conclusion for the LPGA, prize money topped $14 million and the LPGA Urban Youth Golf Program and LPGA Girls Golf Club were established to fortify programs for girls interested in golf.

As the '90s ushered in the era of astounding (even obscene) money in professional sports, the Shadow Creek Golf Club hired Tom Fazio to design a course in the Las Vegas desert that would cost somewhere in the area of $50 million. *Golf Digest* ranked the course in their top ten in 1994, outraging those who didn't like the idea that money could buy you a highly rated course.

The 1990s also sparked more and more tournaments, as companies from coast to coast vied to sponsor a golf championship event of some type. The PGA-sanctioned Nike Tour, which began in the early '90s as the Hogan Tour; the Futures Tour for women; the U.S. Golf Tour; and others were establishing a training ground for the future professionals. On the professional front, the LPGA initiated a Ryder Cup tournament of its own, the Solheim Cup, a biennial event pitting the United States against Europe, and between 1990 and 1995, the PGA donated over $130 million to charity.

As always new and inventive equipment continued to appear on the golf scene, then in the form of oversized metal woods. The clubs sold like hotcakes, as golfers were enthusiastic about their better chance to find the sweet spot.

By the mid-1990s golf was all over the place. Companies routinely held golf outings for their clients and offered incentive golf packages for their best employees; golf tours took travelers across Europe and Asia; and an all-golf channel debuted on cable, providing twenty-four hours of golf information. Super stores sold golf equipment at an astounding rate; golf courses covered what were once landfills; and nearly all PGA and LPGA tournaments were covered on television. By 1995 there were over 25 million golfers in America, playing nearly 500 million rounds of golf a year. WOW!

Then in 1996 and 1997, as if the sport wasn't growing quickly enough, Tiger Woods gave golf another giant shot in the arm. The young phenom won four of his first twelve events as a professional, including his first major, the 1997 Masters. An impressive 40 percent of all televisions in the United States were tuned in to the last day of the Masters to watch Tiger as he set the record for lowest winning score (-17), largest winning margin (twelve strokes), and a host of other categories.

As golf heads toward the new millennium, the PGA is at the forefront of sport at a professional level. Timothy W. Finchem, commissioner as of 1995, looks to strengthen the PGA from a business perspective and continue to expand the tour on an international level. Television revenue continues to rise steadily, and with the likes of young players like Tiger Woods, the PGA and golf in general is very sound heading toward the year 2000 and beyond.

LPGA HALL OF FAMERS

1951	Patty Berg
1951	Betty Jameson
1951	Louise Suggs
1951	Babe Didrikson Zaharias
1960	Betsy Rawls
1964	Mickey Wright
1975	Kathy Whitworth
1977	Sandra Haynie
1977	Carol Mann
1982	JoAnne Carter
1987	Nancy Lopez
1991	Pat Bradley
1993	Patty Sheehan
1995	Betsy King
+1994	Honorary member, Dinah Shore

Most Victories—Career
Kathy Whitworth   88
Mickey Wright   82

BALL STORY

Here are some more details on the evolution of the golf ball as we know it today.

Feathery balls traveled farther when they were scuffed. Later golfers roughed up the surface and added considerable distance to the balls' play.

The rubber core ball started the new era of ball manufacturing. Between 1902 and 1905 there were ninety-seven patents issued for new balls. There were forty-one during that time period issued in the United States, but none would match Haskell's rubber-core gem. The new ball would turn par fives into par fours, and everyone liked the idea of getting closer to the green.

New developments in golf balls in the era from 1910 to 1915 included:

- A ball with four tiny steel balls inside, fixed in a plain rubber center, surrounded by rubber thread, wound tightly, and covered with composition.
- A ball with four tiny, loose steel balls inside.
- A ball with a rubber core and mercury in the middle.
- An American creation called the pneumatic ball, filled with compressed air and a composition cover. This was originally developed as the pneu-matic ball in 1906 and later developed again between 1910–1915 as the pneumatic ball.
- A ball with a center of water.
- A ball with a center of jelly or soft soap.
- A ball filled with an incompressible fluid such as glycerine.

By the 1930s all golf balls had dimples. By the 1960s, 336 manufacturers had produced a variety of patterns, shapes, and sizes to promote a more effective air follow around the ball in flight. The result was greater consistency in flight and ability to design customized trajectories.

THE ABRIDGED
"OFFICIAL RULES"

Until 1951, the United States Golf Association (USGA) and the Royal and Ancient Golf Club (R&A) of St. Andrews, Scotland, governed the rules of golf as separate entities. Each had a somewhat strained relationship with the other. Fortunately, for our sake, the USGA and the R&A now work closely together to refine and govern the rules of the game. The rules of golf are updated by the USGA every four years and are decided by a committee of four to fourteen people who serve for two years.

GOLF'S MOST COMMON RULES

The USGA publishes a 144-page book entitled *Rules of Golf*, and to reproduce it here would be akin to trying to play all eight Pinehurst courses in one day. The USGA also publishes a six-panel card entitled "Golf Rules in Brief." It is from that publication that we have adapted most of the rules in this section.

Some of the rules discussed distinguish between match play and stroke play. Match play is a game for twosomes where

each hole is a separate contest within the round. The player with the most holes won in this type of game wins the *match*. Stroke play (also known as medal play) is individual play. Here, the player with the lowest score for the entire round wins.

It should be understood that the following adaptation is designed to explain some of golf's most common rules and is not sanctioned by the USGA. This is strictly the author's adaptation. So without further ado, here's the dirt, or should we say the divot, on golf's adherent guidelines.

BEFORE TEEING OFF

Make sure your ball is identified with some sort of marking. If you can't identify your ball during play and you discover that someone in your group has an identical ball, then your ball is considered lost and that means you lose a stroke. See the Dropping In section later in this chapter.

You or your caddie are allowed to carry between one and fourteen clubs on the course. If you go for the maximum, have your chiropractor's number handy.

In the "Hey, what's that?" category, you may not use an artificial device or unusual equipment to measure distance or conditions. Leave your binoculars at home. If you are unsure what is considered artificial or unusual, contact the USGA.

GRIPPING

When gripping the club, plain gloves may be worn. Resin or drying powders may be used too, as well as a moisturizing lotion if you desire. Tape, gauze, even a towel may be applied to the grip to help your stroke, as long as the grip itself isn't specifically molded for your hands.

ADVICE

As far as advice goes, keep in mind that everyone plays differently and advice is rarely appreciated unless a pro is giving it to a player who is taking a lesson. During a game, the only person you can ask advice from is your partner or your caddie. That goes for giving advice too.

PRACTICE SWINGS AND STROKES

Practice swings are allowed, but not practice strokes. You can't hit the ball and then exclaim, "That was just practice!" While playing you may take as many practice swings as you want. Keep the game moving; one must play without delay. Any excessive delay in play (overdoing the practice swings, crying, etc.) is considered a delay of the game and incurs a penalty stroke.

READY TO PLAY

On the first tee, the players draw (or determine by lot if a draw is not available) to decide the order of the participants.

Place your tee within two club lengths behind the front edges of the tee markings. If you tee off outside this area during match play, the opposition may, and rightly so, ask you to replay the stroke. If you do this during stroke play, you are penalized two strokes and then must play within the proper tee settings. In other words, this is not the place for creativity.

During a *match*, after teeing off, the ball farthest from the hole is played first. When the next hole is ready to be played, the winner of the previous hole tees off first. If a player for any reason plays out of place anywhere through the course, opponents can rightfully ask this individual to replay the stroke.

During *stroke* play after teeing off, the ball farthest from the hole is played first. The player with the lowest score of the previous hole tees off from the next hole first. In the event of a tie on the hole, the honor for the next tee goes to the player who teed off on the previous hole. Note that in stroke play playing out of turn is generally not penalized.

NOW THAT WE'RE IN PLAY

Strike the ball from where it has landed, or as it's generally known, where the ball lies. For the most part, you are not allowed to move the ball without incurring a penalty stroke unless a rule permits so. You are allowed to move the ball without penalty if it lands in casual water (golfspeak for puddle). The same goes if another player has inadvertently moved your ball. Here, no penalty is incurred if you place the ball back in its original spot.

You are not allowed to improve your lie while on the fairway. If you find your ball in a spot where your swing is interrupted by a tree branch, you may not alter this object in any way. Nor may you press anything down. You may remove an object if it interferes with your stance, but only if that object is removable (i.e., don't ask the greenskeeper for explosives to remove this annoyance). If your ball lies in a bunker or water hazard, you are not permitted to touch the ground in the bunker or water hazard before the downswing.

A ball is to be struck with the clubhead. Pushing it or scraping it is not considered striking the ball. If your club hits the ball more than once in a single swing, that stroke is counted plus a penalty stroke.

In match play, if you strike the wrong ball you lose the hole. If this occurs in stroke play, add on a two-stroke penalty and then play the correct ball.

THE PROOF IS IN THE PUTTING

Once on the green, lift the ball and place a marker where it lies. During this time you may clean the ball or replace it. It is your turn to putt when your ball is farther away from the cup. If you putt the ball and it does not drop into the cup and other players are farther out than you are, lift your ball again and mark its lie until it's your turn to putt again. Keep in mind that the only time your ball should be on the green is when it's your turn to putt.

Pressing anything down in the line of your ball to the hole is not permitted. However, if there is an old hole mark/plug in the line of putt, you may repair it. Removal of objects in the line of the putt is also allowed by using your hand or your golf club. Using a leaf blower would be a tad overdoing it. Testing the surface of the green by scraping or rolling the ball on its surface is not permitted.

In match play, if all the players are now on the green and for some odd reason your ball strikes the flagstick, you lose the hole. In stroke play, if you hit the flagstick, you incur a two-stroke penalty. So, pull the flag out of the cup, and place it far away from the hole.

In match play, the ball must be played until the player sinks it, unless the competition acknowledges that the putt could be made, allowing the player to move on to the next tee. Every player must hole out in stroke play. No conceding of strokes is allowed.

THE ROVING BALL

Whether accidental or not, if your ball is moved by you, your partner, or your caddie, or if it moves after addressing it (you're already in your stance and ready to strike the ball), you must add a penalty stroke and replace the ball where it was. If the ball was moved by anyone else, restore the ball to its original site without penalty. There is also a

THE RULES DON'T FORESEE EVERYTHING

The USGA's main goal is to maintain the skill and challenge of the game. From time to time it adjusts its rules or makes a new one. For instance, though metallic clubheads were allowed, inserts such as copper, graphite and aluminum were not. The rule was changed to conform with the times and now a player is allowed to have an insert in a club. Titanium or oversized clubs are allowed as long as they retain the strength at the base of the club. At one point in time the USGA had no official ruling on how long a golf club should be until someone submitted a six-inch putter called the "kneel and pray putter" to the USGA for approval. No doubt a smile or two came across the faces of the USGA committee, but the situation had to be addressed. Hence the USGA ruled that a golf club must be no less than 18 inches long.

penalty for moving a ball when searching for a covered ball in a hazard or casual water.

In match play, if your ball is moving and it's stopped by you, your partner, or your caddie in any manner, you lose the hole. During stroke play you are penalized two strokes and the ball is played where it landed.

If your ball is in motion and it's stopped by someone else, play the ball where it lands without penalty to you. In match play if your competition or his caddie has interfered with the ball, you can play the ball where it has rested or replay it. If you're playing a stroke game and you're on the green and the ball is deflected by someone other than yourself or your caddie, you need to play the ball again.

If your ball is moving and is stopped in any manner by another ball in play or at rest, play your ball where it lands. During a match, the player is not penalized. In a stroke game, you are penalized two strokes if your ball and the other ball were on the green before your swing.

DROPPING IN

Any time a ball is lifted its position needs to be marked and the ball must be replaced. Some of the reasons for dropping are when a ball is lost, lands in water, or is hit out of bounds, or when a player declares his lie unplayable. To drop a ball in play in the fairway, put the ball in your hand, stand straight up and hold the ball out to your side at shoulder height, then drop the ball. If you are dropping a ball that was in a hazard, it must be dropped back into the same hazard,

otherwise you lose an additional stroke. If you drop a ball and it hits a player, his partner, a caddie, or any equipment, the ball needs to be redropped. No penalty is incurred, just wrath.

If a dropped ball rolls in, or in and out, of a hazard, finds its way onto the putting green, winds up out of bounds, or is in a position where it is interfered with, the ball must be redropped. Interference includes obstructions, abnormal ground conditions, or an embedded ball. A ball also must be redropped if it lands more than two club lengths from its originally marked spot. If the redropped ball lands in any of the spots mentioned above, replace it where it originally struck the part of the course when it was redropped. *Note*: A redropped ball cannot lie closer to the hole from where it was removed.

INTERFERENCE

Interference occurs in a myriad of places on the links. If your ball is in the way of another player, you may lift it if it will assist that player. Consequently, you may request that any ball interfering with your play be temporarily removed so that you may continue.

Any natural loose impediments such as rocks, stones, and leaves that are not a solid part of the course but are interfering with your play may be removed. However, if your ball is touching a loose impediment, you must play it as it is. If you move a loose impediment within a club length of your ball and your ball moves, unless it was on the putting green, you must put the ball back in the same spot and receive a penalty stroke.

OBSTRUCTIONS

Unlike interference, an obstruction is a man-made object. However, objects such as fences, stakes, or immovable man-made articles displaying out-of-bounds lines are not considered obstructions.

Obstructions that are movable may be moved. If your ball moves while you move this obstruction you can replace it without being penalized. If you're on the green, you may move any obstructions that are in your ball's line.

Aside from your ball being in a water hazard, you may drop your ball a club length away from an immovable obstruction that blocks your stance or swing. Again, if your ball is in a bunker, you've got to drop it in the bunker. As always, when dropping a ball, you cannot drop it closer to the hole. A lost ball due to an immovable obstruction (this does not include a water hazard) may be replaced at the point where the ball disappeared without penalty.

UNUSUAL COURSE CONDITIONS

If your ball winds up in casual water or in the midst of ground being repaired, or a strangely possessive animal has run away with it, you may drop a ball without penalty within one club length of the closest point of relief not closer to the hole. If a club length isn't good enough, you may drop a ball in a place closest to the point where it was lost and where you can take a full swing. Under penalty of one stroke, you may drop the ball behind a water hazard and take the shot again. If you're on the putting green, place the ball in the nearest position that allows you a full stroke without interference. And no, you cannot place it closer to the hole.

If your ball is lost under abnormal ground conditions (except for the possessive animal or a water hazard), you may drop the ball at the point where the ball crossed into that area and that allows you a full swing.

WATER

If your ball encounters water that isn't so casual (you've given it a bath via a small lake known on the course as a water hazard), you may drop the ball anywhere behind the water hazard as long as it is in line with where the ball took a dive without its scuba gear. You may also replay the shot, or drop the ball on the other side of the water hazard in line with where the ball took a drink. Of course, there's a one-stroke penalty for all of the above.

23

THE USGA

According to the latest estimations, there are 25 million golfers in the United States and every one of them owes it to themselves to visit the USGA Headquarters and Museum. Located in the sweeping hills in the middle of New Jersey, it has the largest public collection of golf art, memorabilia, and books in the world.

A favorite for visitors is the most unique golf club ever used by any earthling—the club used on the moon by Alan Shepard on his Apollo 14 mission. This amazing display has been recently upgraded and includes footage from NASA showing Shepard swinging away.

There's also a room solely dedicated to Bobby Jones that includes many of his trophies and personal items in a warm, welcoming setting, reminiscent of the era in which he was a champion. Upstairs there's a time-line display showing the beginnings of the game and how it evolved from a man hitting a ball with a stick to the present-day game. Check out the featheries and gutta perchas.

The library at the museum stocks several thousands of books relating to golf. There's also a gift shop where you can purchase quality clothing and memorabilia, including quality items for the U.S. Open, a tournament the USGA conducts along with the Women's and Senior's Opens.

The main function of the USGA is to uphold the traditions of the game and, with the Royal and Ancient Golf Club in Scotland, to write and interpret the rules of golf.

The USGA has its own Testing Center stocked with state-of-the-art scientific-research technology to test golf clubs and balls for accuracy and conformity to the standards set forth under USGA rules and regulations. The USGA started making equipment rulings as far back as 1908 and has records that go back as far as 1934. They have about 9,000 clubs, which they have ruled upon, in the basement, under lock and key.

Having modernized, the USGA now keeps a detailed computer listing just in case anyone wants to know about the eligibility of a club. A golfer

THE USGA

is welcome to call and give them the product name, the company name, and the description, and the USGA will let them know if it is an acceptable club.

Balls cannot exceed 1.68 inches in diameter, weigh less than 1.62 ounces, fly further than 280 yards (plus a 6 percent test tolerance on the USGA range), and go faster than 255 feet per second. Laser beams placed at several points on the ball's path are used to analyze a golf ball's spin rate, launch angle, and velocity. The lab also analyzes clubhead mechanics, shaft mechanics, impact, and biomechanics (the role the golf swing plays), and has an area devoted to growing and testing grass and sod.

The USGA, however, does not publicize their findings. "It's all confidential information," explains research expert John Mutch. "Manufacturers submit their products . . . they spend a lot of money on research and development and we keep everything confidential. We communicate with the person who submitted it." If the balls conform,

the USGA does list them in their conforming golf-ball booklet, which is published twice annually. Manufacturers can either put the balls on a three-year list or a five-year list, whichever they prefer. Only balls in that book can be used, as a condition of play. The U.S. Open, all the USGA events, PGA Tour events, and most club events follow the conditions adhered to in the book.

Anyone can become a member of the USGA and support the great game of golf on all fronts. Membership includes a monthly subscription to the <u>Golf Journal</u>, substantial discounts at the gift shop and from the catalog, and a copy of the <u>Rules of Golf</u>. Memberships start at a very reasonable $25. Higher membership rates include tickets to the U.S. Open.

The United States Golf
  Association
Headquarters and Museum
Far Hills, NJ 07931
1-800-345-USGA
http//www.usga.org

PROVISIONAL PLAY

Your ball is out of bounds or lying at the bottom of an artificial lake whose beauty you had until recently admired. It is simply lost. At this point you may take a provisional stroke, but only after you've asked in a polite but not pleading way to do so. If the other players agree, drop the ball where you believe the ball was last seen and swing away. You must, of course, take a penalty stroke for this. If by chance your original ball is found after you've taken the provisional stroke, you must play the original ball and disallow the previous stroke and penalty.

MISSION: IMPOSSIBLE

There are those occasions where a ball simply is not playable due to a myriad of situations. In this case, you may drop the ball within two club lengths, but not closer to the hole, and play it from there. You may, if you desire, play the ball again from its original spot. Is there a one-stroke penalty for any of this? You bet. Let's face it, this is a game that can make even the most stolid person whine.

POPULAR GOLF GAMES AND THEIR RULES

BLIND BOGEY

In this game, each player does his or her best to come closest to a score that has been pulled out of a hat. Try not to get carried away with this, however. If none of the players scratch (shoot par), don't place the number 68 in the bowl. Start with higher numbers.

CHAPMAN (SIMILAR TO PINEHURST)

Each player on a two-person team hits a tee shot. They then each play a second shot using their partner's ball. At this point, they select the best ball, and the player who did not hit plays, alternating shots until the ball is holed.

FOUR BALL

In this game the better ball of two players is played against the better ball of the two players who oppose them.

MEDAL PLAY

This game is used on the PGA tour and is for any number of players. The lowest score for the round wins. This game can also involve Nassau bets. If the abilities of the players vary, handicaps should be incorporated.

NASSAU

This is a very popular game for twosomes and foursomes. The Nassau format can be either match or medal play. A $3 Nassau is in reality three bets: one for the front nine, one for the back nine, and one for the entire eighteen holes. Each bet is $3. Foursomes playing Nassau actually would be two-person teams playing a best-ball format in match or medal play. However, most Nassau games are played in the match-play format.

ODD/EVEN (ALSO CALLED FOURSOMES)

Here, two players play one ball and alternate hitting shots. One player tees off at the odd-numbered holes and the other at the even-numbered holes.

PINEHURST

Similar to Chapman, each player drives a ball from the tee and the players alternate from there until the ball is holed. In Chapman, both players hit each other's second shot and then alternate till the ball is holed.

ROUND ROBIN

This is a great game for four players whose abilities vary. Two-person teams play a low ball or a low total game to ascertain the winning team of each hole. During the game you change partners every 6 holes, so by the end of the round, everyone's been paired once. Because partners switch every six holes, you can have three separate bets.

SCOTCH FOURSOME

This game has partners who alternate hitting the same ball. This scenario continues on to the next tee regardless of who sank the previous hole's putt.

SCRAMBLE

Used for many tournaments, the players, usually a team of four, tee off at the hole as they normally would. After the initial tee off, the team decides which is the best-hit ball and everyone on the team plays from that place. This repeats for each shot until a ball is holed.

SKINS

Here's a game for three or more players. A specific bet is agreed upon for each hole (usually all holes are the same amount). The lowest score on each hole wins a designated bet. If a hole is tied for the low score, the bet for that hole is carried over to the next hole. If a player wins the next hole and it includes a carryover, that player wins two skins. If several holes in a row are tied, the value of the next skin increases accordingly. If two players tie, everyone ties. This allows any player to win the next skin regardless of how a player performed on the previous hole.

THREESOME

A game where two players in a threesome play the same ball, alternating strokes between them, while the single player plays against them.

THE RULES OF GOLF CIRCA 1744

According to the Honourable Company of Edinburgh Golfers, here are the initial rules of golf as they appeared in 1744, all thirteen of them. If you can decipher half of them, congratulations. If not, you'll just have to settle for an 800 on the SATs.

"Articles and Laws in Playing at Golf 1744" as they appear in the English of the time.

1. You must Tee your Ball, within a Club's length of the Hole.
2. Your Tee must be upon the Ground.
3. You are not to change the Ball which you Strike off the Tee.
4. You are not to remove Stones, Bones or any Break Club, for the sake of playing your Ball, Except upon the fair Green, and that only within a Club's length of your Ball.
5. If your Ball comes among Water, or any wattery filth, you are at liberty to take out your Ball and bringing it behind the hazard and Teeing it, you may play it with any Club and allow your Adversary a Stroke, for so getting out your Ball.
6. If your Balls be found anywhere touching one another you are to lift the first Ball, till you play the last.
7. At Holling, you are to play your ball honestly for the Hole, and not to play upon your Adversary's Ball, not lying in your way to Hole.
8. If you should lose your Ball, by its being taken up, or any other way you are to go back to the Spot, where you struck last, and drop another Ball, And allow your Adversary a Stroke for the Misfortune.
9. No man at Holling his Ball, is to be allowed, to mark his way to the Hole with his Club or anything else.
10. If a Ball be stopp'd by any person, Horse, Dog, or any thing else, the Ball so stopp'd must be played where it lyes.
11. If you draw your Club, in order to Strike and proceed so far in the Stroke, as to be bringing down your Club; if then, your Club shall break in any way, it is to be accounted a Stroke.
12. He whose Ball lyes farthest from the Hole is obligated to play first.
13. Neither Trench, Ditch or Dyke, made from the preservation of the Links, nor the Scholar's Holes or the Soldier's Lines, Shall be accounted a Hazard. But the Ball is to be taken out Teed and play'd with an Iron Club.

John Rattray, Capt.

GOLF ETIQUETTE

Etiquette and integrity are at the very heart of golf. As with the rules, there is enough golf etiquette to fill a book—and such books have been written. You'll discover that most golfing etiquette addresses slow play, the most common complaint from golfers. If every golfer practiced proper etiquette on the course, slow play would be virtually eliminated. Etiquette separates the knowledgeable from the rank amateur.

Generally, etiquette is what you *should* or *should not* do, while the rules are what you *shall* or *shall not* do. Here are some highlights of golf protocol:

ETIQUETTE ON ETIQUETTE

If someone in your group is not familiar with golf etiquette, teach them. It will benefit both your game and that person, and help the game move faster.

FORE!

Probably the most considerate thing you can do during a round is to yell "Fore!" A dimpled projectile traveling at over a hundred miles an hour can really do some damage to muscles, bones, and eyes. If you hear this utterance expelled from someone's lungs, proper etiquette is to take cover as best you can. Most choose to hit the deck.

COMMUNICATION DEVICES

Avoid bringing beepers, pagers, or cellular phones onto the golf course. If you must do so, turn them off while on the course. Also, if your watch beeps, remember to turn it off at the starter's desk. Having these things go off

whether accidentally or intentionally when a player is swinging is considered very rude. You may find yourself talking on the phone and not be aware that you are within earshot of the person currently playing. Enjoy the course and the scenery; let the office survive without you.

MOVING RIGHT ALONG

As previously stated in the rules, golfers are obligated to keep the game moving. Play without delay. Once all the players have sunk their putts, place the flag in the cup, and move on quickly.

IT WENT THAT'A WAY

Watch your playing partners hit the ball. This way you can help them locate it if need be. This too results in faster play. Also, do not look for your ball or someone else's ball for more than three minutes.

CLOTHING AT THE CLUB

If you're going to a club, call ahead to find out what the dress code is. Generally tee-shirts or halters are not allowed on the grounds. If you're not sure of the dress code, a collared shirt is always appropriate. Some golf clubs don't allow shorts either, so pants are always appropriate.

NO SHIRT, NO SERVICE

Men, no matter how hot it gets on the course, you should never remove your shirt. Ladies, avoid this too.

OH, YOU KIDS

If small children are accompanying you out on the course, that's fine. However, make sure that a chaperon accompanies them. Children, being who they are, can interfere with many a golfer's game.

CHEATING

Cheating is very easy to do during a golf game. One can write down a 5 on the scorecard instead of a 6, or move the ball to improve the lie without recording a penalty stroke. However, there are times when someone cheats without knowing it. With all the rules golf has, it's no wonder. If you spot someone cheating, whether intentional or not, the best thing to do is take care of it right there. Needless to say, you should handle this with your most diplomatic balm. Politely informing a player of their infraction at the time of its occurrence gives the player an opportunity to correct his or her temporary lapse.

PREGAME

TIMING

Arrive at the course on time. Tee times are tight. Don't hold up the rest of your two-, three- or foursome. If for some reason a partner is late, notify the starter so he/she can adjust the tee-off times.

IT'S TIME TO CHANGE

At most clubs, locker-room facilities are available. If you need to change any clothing before playing, do it there. Even if you're only changing shoes, please do it in the locker room, not in the parking lot or on the course.

BAG THE PRO SHOP

If you bring your clubs/golf bag into the pro shop, unforced Jerry Lewis–type errors await you. If you do bring your bag into the shop, the salesperson will make it loud and clear to you to remove the bag from the premises. Park your bag in the area allotted for bags before you venture inside.

UP IN SMOKE

If you need to smoke out on the links, ask your playing partners if it's okay to light up. Most of the time they'll say it's fine with them. It's simply good form to ask first. Also, remember to keep the course clean. Do not leave cigarette butts on the grounds, and refrain from putting them out on the green.

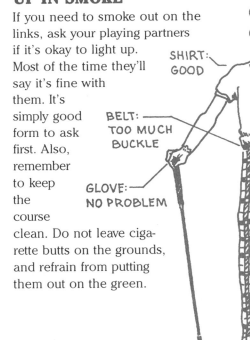

SHIRT: GOOD

BELT: TOO MUCH BUCKLE

GLOVE: NO PROBLEM

HAT: ONLY IN SCOTLAND

WATCH: WEIGHT IMPEDES THE SWING

SLACKS: AN OVERSTATEMENT

FOOTWEAR: ONLY IF YOU PLAN TO SPEND A LOT OF TIME IN THE SAND

AT THE TEE

GREETINGS

Be the first to step up and introduce yourself to new playing partners.

WHO GOES FIRST?

In friendly play off the first tee, decide amongst yourselves the order of play. If ladies are playing in a mixed group, they should be asked to play first. For more serious play you may draw straws. Some prefer to flip a tee. Proceed by throwing a tee in the air and let it land inside the circle of the players. Whoever the tee is pointing to is out. For instance, if you're playing with a foursome and the tee is flipped, whoever it points to first becomes the last to tee off; when the tee is flipped again, whoever the tee is pointing to is out again, and they become the third person to tee off, etc.

Sometimes after players have teed off they stare and moan at the ball they've hit. It is not necessary to wait for them to get out of the box. Have a tee in your hand and step up. It is not rude to do so even if you're out of order. This action also lets the player know that they're slowing things up and that they should be aware of their behavior. Remember, the game is not to be rushed, but it is to be played in a timely fashion.

WHICH TEE MARKER IS FOR YOU?

Tee markings allow golfers of different abilities to play together. It is quite common for golfers in the same group to play from different tees. Players should use the tee most suitable to them. If you're a beginner, tee off from the tee marking that's closer to the hole. Some of the newer courses have as many as five tee stations, starting with beginner and advancing to expert. A general rule of thumb is that red tees are designated as the ladies tees; the white tees are for the average player; and the blue markings are for advanced or experienced golfers. Men who are beginners should generally tee off from the white tees.

STAND OFF

When a player is teeing off, the others in the group should be standing together outside of the markers and off to the side to avoid being a distraction. Standing behind a player who's teeing off is akin to reading over someone's shoulder. It is rude and should not be done. If you have to ask if you're in the way, this too is a distraction. Use your common sense.

SEEKING AUTOGRAPHS AT A TOURNAMENT

A good time to ask a player for his or her autograph is after the player has had a chance to relax after the round. Let him/her wind down and perhaps have a drink. After they've done that, many return to the practice area. This is a good place to get their signatures.

Refrain from asking a pro for an autograph right after he/she has finished the hole. This is a time where they must focus solely on their games. Any diversion from that focus is not appreciated. Let them proceed to the next tee quickly without shoving a pen in front of them.

Use your good judgment and refrain from asking for an autograph when someone is eating dinner or in the bathroom.

The best way to get an autograph is to call or write the PGA or the LPGA. These organizations will send you a list of addresses where you can write to players and ask them for their John Hancocks

LPGA
2570 Volusia Ave., Ste. B
Daytona Beach, FL 32114
904-254-8800

PGA TOUR AT SAWGRASS
112 T.P.C. Blvd.
Ponte Verda Beach, FL 32082
904-285-3700

KEEP IT DOWN

Respect your fellow players. Talking, moving, or even standing close to a player while playing is poor judgment, not to mention potentially dangerous. You should refrain from whispering when a player is at the tee taking his or her practice swings and is ready to hit away. If, inadvertently, you have in some way disturbed the golfer during his or her swing, apologize. If you don't, the rest of the game will be filled with unnecessary tension.

ON THE FAIRWAY

COOL YOUR JETS

Sometimes we're anxious to tee on the next hole as soon as we finish the previous one. You might even feel tempted to move along the group ahead of you while they're taking their second shot out on the fairway. Try to refrain from such behavior. The group ahead of you is most likely doing their best to move along too, so wait until they're out of ball-striking distance.

THE DIRT ON THE DIRT

Proper play includes taking divots. In fact, if you're not taking them, you're probably not swinging very well. If you've just sent a chunk of real estate the size of Rhode Island into the next fairway, please pick it up and put it back. Replacing divots is one of the cornerstones of proper golf etiquette. Replacing divots is also essential to maintaining the course. Would you want to

play on a course riddled with holes? Of course not. Chances are you wouldn't want to find a great shot of yours nestling in one either. Riding carts often provide a small shovel and a bucket of sand to assist you in repairing a divot. Please use it. If you happen to see another hole in the earth nearby, it's a good idea to fix that one too.

CARTING ABOUT

If you're driving a cart on the course, do not pull up behind the player. Just as when standing at the tee to watch a fellow golfer swing, park alongside the golfer, but far enough away to avoid being a distraction.

Riding carts and pull carts should never encounter the green. The "carpet" is usually softer than the fairway and is very susceptible to damage. Pull carts, like shopping carts, can at times have minds of their own. Whether you rent a pull cart or use your own, make sure it's stable so your bag doesn't accidentally topple over, spilling your clubs and distracting a player's swing. Carts also tend to squeak, so check to make sure that an annoying sound is corrected by you or at the pro shop. Make sure your cart is generally in good shape, and that everything is tightened. If not properly maintained, cart wheels have been known to fly off and speed away from the golfer. If this happens, say on the second tee, you'll be lugging the wheel, the broken cart, and the bag for another seven holes.

Etiquette suggests placing your pull cart or riding cart right alongside where you will build your stance. This way, after you hit the ball, only a step or two is required to move on to your next shot, hence, keeping play moving.

Some golf courses make riding carts adhere to what's called the 90° rule. This means that carts must stay on the cart path and that the cart must be pulled up parallel to where the ball is. You cannot take the cart out onto the fairway to the ball. If you are unsure of which golf club to use, simply take more than one club to where your ball is. Having to go back and forth between the cart and the ball slows play tremendously.

If you are allowed unrestricted cart movement on the course,

HOW MANY PRACTICE SWINGS ARE ALLOWED?

Practicing your swing is meant for the driving range, practice green, and lessons. It is not meant to be perfected on the golf course. In fact, except for the tee, taking practice swings when it was your turn to hit was not always allowed by the *Rules of Golf*. However, no such rule exists today, so technically there are no limits on how many practice swings you're allowed to take. For the most part, when it's your turn to hit, one or two should be enough. The longer you stand over your golf ball trying to set up the perfect swing, the tighter your body gets.

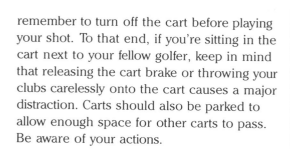

Your mind starts to go around in circles and becomes deceptive. This results in slow, tedious play. In fact, when many pros step up to the ball, they do not take practice swings because they're fined if they slow up the game. Pros are limited to forty five seconds to hit their shot from the time they reach their ball and the group in front of them is out of hitting distance. The key is to practice your swing while others are practicing theirs. When it's your turn, be ready and hit away, or as the case may be, putt away. If for some reason you find yourself taking more than two practice swings, make up for the time by moving more quickly on

remember to turn off the cart before playing your shot. To that end, if you're sitting in the cart next to your fellow golfer, keep in mind that releasing the cart brake or throwing your clubs carelessly onto the cart causes a major distraction. Carts should also be parked to allow enough space for other carts to pass. Be aware of your actions.

the course. If you're waiting to play because the group ahead of you is still in range, you can take as many practice swings as you like.

WATCH WHAT YOU SAY

It's okay to point out the makeup of a hole. It's another thing to say something like "Watch out for the pond on your left, or the hazard on the right." It is rude to alert a fellow golfer about impending trouble and is never appreciated. If someone offers you unnecessary advice, be tactful and tell them that you appreciate their words, but would prefer not to be helped.

UMBRELLAS

If you're using an umbrella, remember that it can make a lot of noise when it is opened and closed. Be careful not to do either when a player is about to hit away.

WHEN A TIE OCCURS

If you find yourself in the same position away from the green with another golfer, decide among yourselves who should shoot first. The same goes for being on the green. See the Who Goes First section in the earlier part of this chapter if more than one player ties on a hole.

TAKING MULLIGANS

Dropping a new ball after making a poor shot and not taking a penalty stroke is known as a Mulligan shot. Even though the Mulligan is occasionally taken during friendly play, it is illegal according to the *Rules of Golf*. The truth is Mulligans are a tremendous waste of time and are a major contributor to slow play. Some folks feel they deserve to take Mulligans every time they hit a poor shot, and the average golfer can hit many of them. Buck up and take responsibility for your game and your swing. If you feel the desperate need to hit the ball again, do so and take the stroke. This will soon cure your desire to take a Mulligan.

THE FLYING CLUBS

We can all get frustrated on the course. Our rage can occasionally result in throwing our clubs. This is considered very bad form and you can injure your fellow players. If for some reason you find yourself hurling clubs, throw them forward; that way at least you can pick them up on the way to your ball and not slow the game down.

THE NEXT TEE BOX

As you approach the green by foot or riding cart, find the next tee box. It's a good idea to place your clubs or cart in that area and then arrive at the green. After everyone has holed out they can go straight to the next tee and tee off without having to go backward or sideways to find their carts and clubs, making for faster play.

If your ball isn't quite on the green, you can do two things: play the shot first then bring your clubs to the tee and return with your putter, or bring your clubs to the next tee and carry back your putter with the club you'll use to get onto the green. Be careful here: When two clubs are out of the bag, it's easy to lose one.

PLAYING THROUGH

Playing through is allowing the group of golfers behind you to play ahead of you, and it is the right thing to do. However, if there were any situation in golf where generally civil folks lose it, this is it. Egos tend to clash when a good group of golfers catches up to an average group. The average group tends to feel inferior, while the better group tends to feel superior. Both are wrong. Letting faster players play through is the right thing to do, and those that are playing through should see it as a courtesy, not an entitlement.

Playing through can occur under a variety of circumstances. As stated, some foursomes play faster than others and can encounter a group at the tee with no one on the green in front of them. If twosomes are on the course, more than likely they're playing faster than foursomes and they would like to play through too. (Twosomes should pair up on the course whenever the opportunity presents itself.) A good place to play through is at the turn after the first nine holes have been played. Par threes, since they are shorter, are also a good place to play through. Under these circumstances the slower group should hit away, walk to the green, mark their balls, and indicate to the next group at the tee to begin.

Once a group is offered the opportunity to play through, they should say thank you and start to play. Any bags, tees, carts, or clubs belonging to the group that is letting the group behind them play through should be removed promptly. The group playing through should not take Mulligans. If a ball is lost, they should not take a long time to look for it.

If a course is particularly crowded and players are waiting to tee off at every hole, playing through will not speed things up, and therefore this courtesy should not be extended.

ON THE GREEN

BAGS, CARTS, CLUBS

Before stepping on the green, leave your bags and carts outside on the skirt (fringe) of the green. On many occasions you can even take your bag or cart to the next tee and then bring your putter with you back to the green and proceed.

TAKE IT EASY

The green is more fragile than the rest of the course. Please treat it so. Walk softly, never run. Remember to pick up your feet so as not to leave long, dragging cleat marks on the carpet.

REPAIRING BALL MARKS

When a ball lands on a green it often makes a deep indentation known as a ball mark (this is not to be confused with marking your ball). This indentation needs to be repaired by the golfer who hit the ball. This is done with a golf tee or a ball repair tool. Depending on how the ball lands, it is sometimes difficult to spot this mark. Once it is discovered, take the repair tool or the tee and gently dig around the mark and manipulate it until it becomes even with the ground. Then take your putter and tap down on it to make sure it is firmly in place. If you see other ball marks on the green, repair them too, if time permits.

TENDING THE PIN

If you're playing without a caddie, the player with the ball closest to the cup tends the pin. Do not automatically remove the pin from the cup, as some may prefer it left in to help them locate the cup. If the pin is in the cup, remove it once the player putts. Do not wait for the ball to get near the cup. To tend the pin correctly, hold the shaft at arm's length. If it's windy, steady the flag. Also be aware of shadows. Make sure that your shadow is on the same side as the pin and the flag. Also make sure it's

not on the putting line. If the player about to putt requests the pin be pulled, do so, remembering not to yank it out but to slowly turn it and pull it out gently. If no players want the flag stick in the cup, lay it down on the fringe or skirt of the green, not on the green itself.

The first person who holes out should be the one to retrieve and replace the flagstick after the last person sinks his or her ball. This allows the last person putting to move on to the next tee box without having to find the flag, pick it up, and place it back in the cup, which would obviously slow the game down.

CLUBS

Refrain from letting clubs drop on the green. The "carpet" is very sensitive. Dropping a club on a green can cause unnecessary indentations that will need to be repaired.

THE LINE OF PUTT

Once the ball is on the green, there is an imaginary line that leads from the ball to the cup. Stepping on it is akin to punching the player in the face. Granted, you may at times feel like doing that, but hold off until you're in a boxing ring.

HOLING OUT

After sinking the ball into the cup, please remove it promptly. Although more than one ball can fit into the cup, it's bad form to leave it there. Many golfers are a superstitious lot and having more than one ball in a cup can set them off. Please respect them.

After everyone has holed out, place the flag carefully in the cup using two hands. This makes for less wear and tear on the cup, resulting in less maintenance for the course.

SUPPORT CLUB

You may have seen a pro on television after sinking a putt leaning on top of the putter grip for support while removing the ball from the cup. As much as you might like to copy the pros, avoid doing so in this case. Leaning on the putter pushes the carpet down around the tin, causing an unnecessary break and changing how a ball will roll on the green. Breaks on the green should only be created by the course architect or Mother Nature, not the player.

SCORING

Whether the last hole was good or bad, we all tend to be anxious to write down our scores and move on to the next tee. Refrain from placing your score on the card until you arrive there.

BUNKERS

ENTERING AND EXITING

Most bunkers are sand traps, sometimes referred to as "the beach." Bunkers however are a bit more fragile than the sand on the shore and should be treated as such. The lips and the rims of bunkers can be easily damaged, so enter and exit the sand trap from the low sides. Though you may be tempted, never jump in or climb up the wall of a bunker.

WHERE TO STAND

If your fellow golfer is playing from the bunker onto the green, chances are some of you are already on the green. This is not an opportunity to line up and practice your putt. This is one of the tougher shots of the game, so there's no need to increase distractions. Stand out of view and let the person in the bunker take his or her shot.

RAKING THE SAND

Locate the rake before you enter the bunker. Once you have hit your sand shot, retrace your steps and pick up the rake outside of the bunker. Retrace your steps once more and rake backward to the fairway. Leaving the bunker in a different direction than you came in makes for more footsteps to be raked over, hence slowing down the game. Always leave the rake outside the bunker.

CRASH GOES THE WINDOW

Occasionally things might go badly for you on the course. Say you've just sliced your favorite dimpled projectile through a window in a house on the edge of a course. Not only would the rules demand you take a stroke, but it would be poor etiquette for you to swing from the homeowner's dining room carpet. Technically, when a homeowner purchases a house at a golfing community, they assume the risk. They understand that there's a chance a ball may dent a shingle, crack a window, or wind up in a soufflée, and they'll have to pay for the repairs. Homeowners also recognize that they need to install some sort of protective device to stop such things from happening.

However, that's not always the case. There have been cases where course owners have had to pay for the damages. Etiquette-wise, the right thing to do is to buck up and come clean to the homeowner and offer to pay for replacement of the window.

POSTGAME

AFTER THE ROUND

When the round ends, extend a warm handshake to your playing partners. This is especially good if you've had a poor round. It ends the game on a positive note. Whether your round was good or not so good, if you've taken a caddie with you, tip him or her well.

RENTED EQUIPMENT

If you have rented equipment, clean off the clubheads and return the clubs to the pro shop or rental facility. If you have rented a cart, return it to where you picked it up or ask an attendant where it should be returned to.

CLEANING UP

Clean your golf shoes of grass and dirt after you have finished playing. Remove your shoes before entering the clubhouse, bathroom, or any dining facilities.

Take a shower once you've finished the round. If you're unable to do so, wash your face and hands. It'll make you feel good, and if you're having lunch, you'll look much more presentable.

FINALLY . . .

A good sport who's had a great round buys lunch.

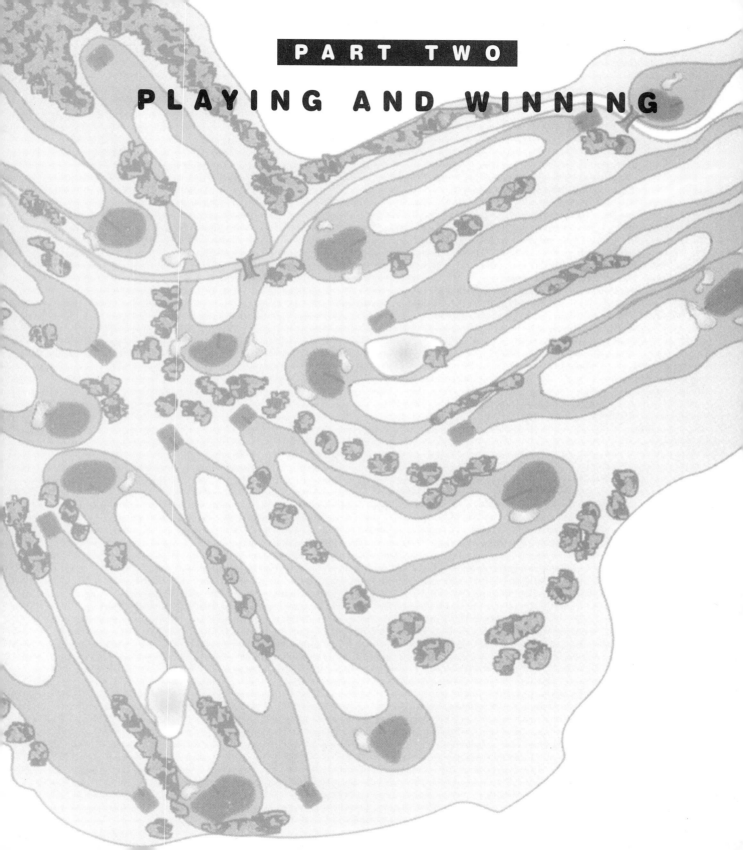

PART TWO
PLAYING AND WINNING

GOLF EQUIPMENT

Though the game of golf really hasn't changed too much over the past several hundred years, materials to play the game certainly have. Woods are no longer made of wood. Most irons are no longer forged in mills. Putters can now be adjusted by removing material to find a desired weight. Golf balls have changed several times, starting off as boiled feathers bound by leather, then as tree-sap solids, and now tightly wound strings of rubber with or without liquid cores surrounded by different kinds of plastic with an array of dimple designs.

Women's clubs are different from men's clubs in their weight, strength, and size of the grip. They come in both petite and regular sizes. Shaft weight and composition also play a role.

Below is some of the equipment you'll need to play the game, not all of it is essential, but you'll want to have most of the following in your bag, cart, or pockets: golf clubs; golf balls; golf bag or other carrying harness; tees; golf shoes (one can play without them, but it's not suggested); golf hat, golf cap, or visor; golf glove (this isn't essential, but most golfers use one); small towel that attaches to the golf bag; comfortable, loose clothing; green-repair tool (it's easier than using a tee); water bottle (to

1st TEE

keep you hydrated); Band-Aids; and a small first-aid kit. Suggested items to keep in a golf bag are: sunscreen, lip balm, bug repellent, aspirin, small jewelry pouch, lightweight rainsuit, snack bar or raisins, sweater, extra pencil, and ball marker (a dime can be substituted). Not necessarily needed, but good to have on hand are: pull cart; covers for your woods; golf umbrella (a very large umbrella); money, if you're making a small wager or two; spike wrench to keep the spikes on your shoes tightened; and, current USGA rulebook.

One thing you should leave at home: your ego. Practically everything about the game comes in conflict with your ego, such as rules, etiquette, and if wagering, the possibility of not winning the bet. Even when you're in the clubhouse, getting on

someone's case for making a poor decision is generally not appreciated—just as bragging about a great shot or game isn't either. Appreciate the praise without asking for it. The bottom line is to just get out there and enjoy.

GOLF BALLS

Today there are basically two types of golf balls: Surlyn and Balata. Balata is a plastic substance, and it encases a golf ball made of a liquid core surrounded by wound rubber. Balata's soft plastic exterior is prone to cuts and nicks that inhibit a ball's trajectory. The Surlyn ball has a solid core covered with a tough plastic cover. Surlyn's advantages are that it flies farther, lasts longer, and is cheaper than a Balata ball. Balata's advantage is that it has more back spin, hence more control. For many, the higher price one pays for that advantage is worth it.

Which ball should one go with? Surlyn (distance) or Balata (control)? It's one's own personal preference. Some golfers claim the control factor of the Balata is overrated, while the Surlyn doesn't really achieve that much more distance. Others will swear by each ball's performance. All will probably tell you that it's your swing that's most important—and that would be right. So, splurge a little and purchase a sleeve of both and see how you feel about each.

GOLF-BALL COMPRESSION

Golf balls are available in compression ranges from 80 to 100. Some say striking a 100-compression ball is like hitting concrete, while striking an 80-compression ball might feel like slamming a slug. "Feel" is a big deal in golf, as you will see it mentioned much in this chapter and others. Most golfers find themselves in the middle of the compression scale, going with a 90-compression ball. All we know is that there's a great rush through your body when you hit a great ball solidly. There's nothing else like it. It should also be duly noted that it is untrue that the higher the compression, the farther it will fly.

GOLF CLUBS

CASTING CALL

Clubheads come in two varieties: cavity back and forged. Most amateurs and some pros use cavity-back irons, so called because there is a cavity in the back of the clubhead.

Cavity-back or investment cast irons are also known as perimeter-weighted or heel-toe weighted irons. These clubs are made with a manufacturing technique known as casting. Casting metal is a process in which metal is poured into ceramic molds and allowed to harden, and has been around since the late 1800s. Applying this manufacturing technique to golf-club composition didn't come into use until the 1950s. This process distributes the weight around the perimeter of the iron, generating a larger sweet spot and thus resulting in a more forgiving club.

Irons used to be forged in mills, like chains. The metal or steel was pounded into the shape of the club and was finished by milling, grinding, and drilling. Some irons are still actually manufactured that way, and they are called forged or blade clubs. This club is popular with pros and low handicappers.

Manufacturing "woods" in the same way as "irons" soon followed. While the wood clubs were usually molded from pieces of wood, layered together like a French pastry (layers of maple wood were used for this and were shellacked), or were shaped from a block of persimmon wood (a tropical evergreen tree) or ash, metal woods were soon "cast" by the same manufacturing technique used to produce perimeter-weighted irons. The metalwood is often filled with what are called inserts. These inserts include graphite, titanium, plastics, Kevlar, or a combination thereof to balance the club and distribute the weight around its perimeter. A "sole," usually made out of metal is then attached to the bottom of the clubhead.

Manufacturing clubs in this manner puts weight in the clubhead, allowing the golfer to hit with more power as well as a larger sweet spot. The sweet spot that used to be the size of a dime in a normal wood or iron, is now the size of a quarter in the casted clubs.

Club makers are now producing forged irons with cavity backs. Although casting has made golf a lot more enjoyable for most of the golfing population, what it sacrificed for many was the "feel" of the club. The cast clubs simply didn't feel solid enough for many pros and those who used muscleback (blade) clubs before casting became popular. Now, that has all changed.

The hybrid clubhead, with its larger blade than that of the muscleback and its perimeter-weighting, is slowly growing in popularity. Because it is expensive to manufacture these hybrids, be prepared to shell out more than you'd normally pay for either a cavity back or forged club.

THE SHAFT AND THE HOSEL

Shafts are made from many materials such as graphite, aluminum, or stainless steel. Some shafts are even made of very hard plastic. Golfers and golf manufacturers claim that the combination of flexibility at certain points, and stiffness at other points on the shaft

makes a better club. Others claim that such flexibility is detrimental to the club and your swing. As in many aspects of the game, make the choice based on what you like and feel.

The hosel offset, or offset, is the hollow part of the clubhead where the shaft is inserted. It is placed at different angles for each club. For metal woods, the shaft is placed at an angle, putting you farther away from the club than you would be with an iron, which has a closer angle. This is done because, over the centuries of golf playing, it has become common knowledge that these angles are optimum for the best possible playing. The chances of your finding a metal wood with a short shaft, angled close, are slim to none, and vice versa for irons. Some manufacturers have even eliminated the hosel all together and have put that weight into the clubhead, claiming that it helps golfers hit better.

THE CLUBS

Let's discuss the clubs in the order they are used when starting from the tee. Metalwoods are made for distance; irons and wedges are for accuracy; and the putter is the club used to sink the ball in the cup once on the green. The numbers on clubs indicate relatively how high and how far a ball will be hit when the club is used. For instance, a club with the number 1 will hit a ball low and far; a club with the number 9 will hit the ball high and relatively short.

A standard set of clubs available from manufacturers includes the following eleven clubs: 1, 3, and 5 woods, and the 3, 4, 5, 6, 7, 8, 9, and the PW (Pitching Wedge) for irons. Then there's the putter, making a total of 12. Additional clubs such as a 2- or 4-wood, or a 1- or 2-iron or a Sand or Lob Wedge can be added to give more versatility. But remember, fourteen is the maximum amount of clubs you are allowed to carry on the course.

METALWOODS

1-wood, driver, big dog

The driver is generally used to strike the ball from the tee, though some substitute it for a 2-wood out in the fairway.

Average distance: 225 to 250 yards

2-wood, brassie

Close to the driver, the brassie is often used in the fairway, as it achieves more loft than a driver. However, one can use it from the tee as well.

Average distance: 200 to 225 yards

3-wood, spoon

This club is used on the fairway and the tee. If you're debating between distance and accuracy in the fairway, the spoon is a good compromise. At the tee, the spoon is a good club to use when you desire to hit a high ball with the wind at your back. Here you'll get more accuracy than you would with the driver, and probably get good distance.

Average distance: 190 to 220 yards

4-wood, cleek

This club, with its small head and shallower face, gives you more loft than a spoon. The club is popular for use in bad lies where you need a long shot with a greater arc to get the ball up and out of trouble.

Average distance: 180 to 210 yards

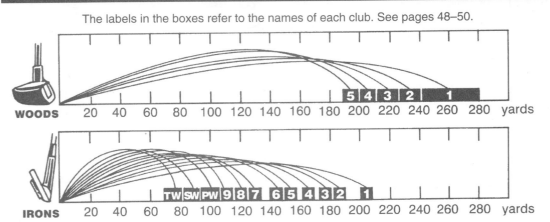

An Average Golfer's Distance Using Irons and Woods

The labels in the boxes refer to the names of each club. See pages 48–50.

WOODS   20 40 60 80 100 120 140 160 180 200 220 240 260 280   yards

IRONS   20 40 60 80 100 120 140 160 180 200 220 240 260 280   yards

5-wood, baffy

A versatile club, the baffy can be used in the fairway or the rough. The head of the 5-wood gets a ball up quickly and achieves more loft than the previously mentioned clubs. Women often find this club a favorite, as it fits them well.

Average distance: 170 to 200 yards

6-wood

The 6-wood gets a ball up a little higher and is pretty much used under the same circumstances as the 5-wood.

Average distance: 150 to 190 yards

7-wood

This wood is becoming more favorable than the longer 1-, 2-, 3-, or 4-iron.

Average distance: 140 to 180 yards

IRONS

Irons are generally classified into three categories. The 1-, 2-, and 3-irons are considered long irons; the 4-, 5-, and 6-irons are medium irons; and the 7-, 8-, and 9-irons and wedges are designated as short irons. These categories reflect the length of the shafts on each of the clubs.

1-iron, driving iron

Hardly around anymore, most club producers don't include it at all in a standard set. This club achieves very little loft when it strikes a ball. A good use for it would be when wanting to keep the ball low while hitting into some sort of gale-force wind.

Average distance: 180 to 220 yards

2-iron, midiron

This versatile club is not easily mastered by the beginner. It is usually used on the fairway for long shots, and like the 1-iron, can also be used from the tee. Under certain conditions it can be used in the rough. The midiron, however, has been replaced by a club you should already have in your bag, the 5-wood.

Average distance: 160 to 190 yards

3-iron, mid-mashie

Commonly used for long shots, it is much easier to handle and master than the 2-iron. The mid-mashie provides better accuracy and a higher loft.

Average distance: 150 to 180 yards

4-iron, mashie iron

The mashie iron is often used from the tee on par 3 holes. It's good for shorter shots on the fairway, in the rough, or for bad lies. It can punch a ball out of difficulty while keeping it low to gain some decent distance.

Average distance: 140 to 170 yards

5-iron, mashie

In the rough, off the tee on the occasional par 3 hole, or on the fairway, this club hits the white, round projectiles long and high. Although it's generally used for distance, the ever-popular mashie is also good for punching a ball up onto the green from 50 yards out.

Average distance: 135 to 155 yards

6-iron, spated mashie

Another iron for a good pitch-and-run, the spated mashie gets the ball up high from situations where you need some distance and better accuracy. It's good in tall grass and has been known to be used in the sand trap when distance is essential.

Average distance: 110 to 135 yards

7-iron, mashie niblick

The backspin and loft the mashie niblick delivers makes this the favorite club for many golfers. Its combination of control, loft, and distance can be used to send a ball over a treetop or two. The backspin holds the ball well on the green once it lands. It is also used when just off the green and a nice chip shot onto the carpet is needed.

Average distance: 95 to 125 yards

8-iron, pitching niblick

Like the 7-iron, the pitching niblick is good for getting the ball over hazards and bunkers. It shoots a bit shorter than the 7, and can bring the ball up higher. Use it for pitch shots from the fairway as well.

Average distance: 80 to 115 yards

9-iron, niblick

The club face on the niblick has a lot of loft. Its heavy head is good for use in the damp sand, tough rough, and thick grass. It's also good from the fairway if you don't need the distance of an 8-iron.

Average distance: 80 to 105 yards

WEDGES

Pitching wedge

Though the PW can be interchangeable with the 9-iron, it can provide greater control when pitching up to the green, from say 50 yards away. Many also use this wedge when confronted with sand.

Average distance: 80 to 105 yards

Sand wedge

Making its way into many golf bags, this wedge is used for pretty much the name says, digging you out of "the beach." Its heavy head and broad flange can practically backhoe your ball out if it's buried deep in the bunker. This club, when used properly, gives the ball a very high, soft landing. Occasionally the SW has been used to pitch from the fairway or the rough.

Average distance: Just enough to get you out of trouble, give or take 50 yards

Lob wedge, third wedge

Also finding its way into many golf bags, this club, with its severe loft angle, can be used on the fairway, deep in the beach, or in the rough. It will hit a ball a little bit higher than a sand wedge.

Average distance: Like the sand wedge, approximately 50 yards

THE PUTTER

Used on the green to sink your ball into the cup, the once simple putter is now available in enough designs to make your head spin. Originally, there were six kinds of putters.

Going by names like Calamity Jane, Blue Goose, Type Mallet, Schenectady, Cash-in, and the simple Mills, they all essentially performed the same way. Even the BullsEye, which was introduced in the 1930s, had the same design in mind: the weight of the putter was dead center, the so-called "sweet spot." Hit the ball dead center and the ball would roll in the direction you aimed for. Strike the ball just off center, even one degree, and you'd probably find yourself having to putt again.

It was during the 1960s that a man named Karsten Solheim introduced the Ping putter and changed everything. Solheim designed the Ping so that the weight was distributed evenly from the heel of the putter to its toe. This way, the putter was much more forgiving. If a golfer missed the dead center of the putter head, there was still a good chance that the ball would still go fairly straight. Today, practically every club designer has a heel-toe weighted putter, and it's the preferred choice for most golfers. Jack Nicklaus used a heel-toe weighted putter to win the 1986 Masters Tournament.

Putters now come in all sizes and shapes. There are oversized putting heads, long shafts, and a combination of the two. There are even interchangeable "performance faces" such as ceramic, balata, graphite, and aluminum that are designed for use on greens of different speeds. The BullsEye design is still around today for those who prefer not to use a heel-toe weighted putter. Again, "feel" plays a big

JACK NICKLAUS

In 1986, Jack Nicklaus used a heel-toe weighted putter to win the Masters Tournament. He said the club worked well and that he enjoyed using it. Naturally, this was a great coup for the folks who designed and manufactured perimeter-weighted putters. A player of Nicklaus's stature would surely encourage many to purchase such a putter. However, after the win, the Golden Bear returned to using a standard putter because he believed the perimeter-weighted putter could be deceiving. Because the heel-toe putters were more forgiving than standard putters, one could, Nicklaus believed, hurt one's putting. This was because, even if you didn't hit the ball dead center, your shot would still turn out well, and that did not help one become a better golfer. Nicklaus's words couldn't have been truer, but the rest of us who aren't playing the circuit or have no aspirations to, will probably keep on playing with a perimeter-weighted putter.

part here. It's one of the great things about golf, freedom of choice.

STUFF TO PRACTICE WITH

The golf world is filled with gadgets that promise to help you with your game. Many of them are successful, thanks to good marketing, but that's about as far as it goes. Below are some items that have been proven to actually help you practice.

THE MEDICUS

This practice club has an adjustable tension hinge in the shaft that breaks if the golfer isn't swinging correctly. The advantage here is that the golfer gets instant feedback. The club is available in a 5-iron or Driver.

Available through GolfSmith (800) 456-3344 or your local golf shop.

IMPACT TAPE, HIT & TELL DECALS, AND LABELON TAPE

These devices are simple and inexpensive. They are so simple, in fact, that all you do is place them on your clubface and hit away. After you've hit, check out the marking left by the ball to see whether you've hit the ball dead center on the sweet spot or off to the left or right.

Available through just about any golf catalog.

THE MIYA COMPUTER PUTTER CHECKER

On this lightweight device, beams of light detect the angle of the putter face and the sweet spot position as you hit the ball. The beams of light give an immediate readout on a small screen, showing you how you swung your putter. If your stroke isn't up to par, the Miya gives off a brief beep. However, if you swing correctly, you get rewarded with a long beep. You can use the Miya with any putter, indoors or out, and it can operate without a ball if necessary.

Available through Miya Epoch: (213) 320-1172

WIFFLE BALL GOLF BALLS

If you use your yard for a practice range, the Wiffle company makes it easy. Like their famous baseballs, the Wiffle golf ball is made of light plastic, is hollow, and is filled with holes. The ball is regulation size and looks like the offspring of a regular-sized Wiffle ball. It is true that you could put out a window or an eye with these balls, but if you use some discretion, you'll be able to avoid such mishaps.

Available from Sporttime: (800) 444-5700

THE KERDAD GOLF SWINGER

Here's an odd-looking tool that works great and has been helping golfers from all over the globe for the past twenty-five years. The Swinger has a grip and a shaft, and is weighted at the bottom to feel like a clubhead. Instead of a clubhead, there's a mechanism at the end of the shaft that clicks. When you swing correctly, the mechanism clicks at the bottom of the downswing, then resets itself after you follow through.

The Swinger is convenient for indoor practice. It comes in two weights—21½ ounces and 26½ ounces, and is a compact 25 inches long.

Available from Kerdad: (415) 352-8662

THE ORIGINAL SHAG BAG

Shagging balls was revolutionized by this device. Its long aluminum tube placed on a golf ball it sucks the ball into the tube, where it stays until another ball finds itself inside the tube and gets pushed up. Eventually the balls enter a canvas bag, allowing you to empty it wherever you want to play them again. The device holds up to ninety golf balls.

PURCHASING GOLF CLUBS

The best way to purchase clubs is to actually hold them in your hand and use them. To narrow things down a bit and get a feel for what you want, club makers are making demo clubs and full sets available to pro shops so that you can actually take them out on the links and play with them. What's even greater for the

golf shopper is that these clubs can be fitted especially for you. You don't have to take something off the rack that's made for the general public. Following are some of the more well-known companies and what they're doing to get their clubs into your hands.

Callaway Golf (800) 228-2767

Popular Clubs: The Big Bertha line of woods, known for their bore-through and no-hosel design

Comments: Callaway's on the road forty to fifty days during each playing season, stopping at clubs and practice ranges around the country. They make irons and metalwoods in every shaft, steel, and graphite composition. Demos include men's and ladies' clubs. If you're left-handed, fear not, there are clubs here for you too.

The Company Suggests: Keep an open mind when you come to a demo day. It's possible that what worked for you at one time may not this time. Flexes in shafts and different lofts on new models can feel different than what you're used to.

Cleveland Golf
(800) 999-6263

Popular Clubs: The radical-looking Cleveland 792 VAS and the VAS+

Comments: Cleveland demo tour vans scour the country up to six days a week, focusing on the major metropolitan areas. All vans carry demonstration clubs in every model in both men's and women's sizes.

The Company Suggests: To locate the right shaft flex, compare the demos with the club you normally strike at approximately 150 yards.

Cobra Golf

(800) 223-3537 or (800) THE-KING

Popular Clubs: King Cobra Ti Drivers and the Norman Grind irons

Comments: You can find Cobra demonstration sets at most retail outlets and pro shops. The sets consist of nine irons, three woods, and a loaner bag. As for their demo programs, Cobra has a nationwide network, led by technical specialists and sales associates, that allows you to try every type of club that Cobra offers.

The Company Suggests: There are no "silly questions" when purchasing a club. Talk with the tech reps about how the new styles and materials can be advantageous to your game.

Daiwa Golf

(800) 736-4653

Popular Clubs: Hi Trac MF-100 Irons and Emeritus (Senior) clubs

Comments: Participating pro shops and practice ranges carry demo sets. These sets include eight irons and three woods, including the driver. Emeritus and women's sets are available at some locations. Daiwa also provides a club fitting chart, which you can get directly from them.

The Company Suggests: The best way to decide on a club is after you've tried all of the versions of the club you're interested in.

Founders Club (800) 252-8448

Popular Clubs: The Judge Strong and Tour CB

Comments: Ask about the special demonstration rack. This is probably where you'll be able to get a good idea about all of the Founders clubs. Many pro shops carry a complete set of irons that you can shoot a round with. For the titanium metalwoods, Founders Club has a demo cart filled with all of their styles. Use their easy-to-understand card to find out which club, loft, and shaft flex best suits you.

The Company Suggests: When it comes to titanium metalwoods, it's important to have the spectrum of clubs available to try out. Many of these clubs have longer shafts and higher launch angles.

Ben Hogan Company (800) 88-HOGAN

Popular Clubs: Medallion club line

Comments: This company goes all out to satisfy the golfer's fitting process with the Ben Hogan Precision Clubfitting System. This clubfitting system is handled exclusively by club professionals. After you've been fit professionally, the Hogan company ships your clubs to you within three days.

The Company Suggests: Fitting clubs to golfers is paramount with new equipment. One doesn't purchase shoes that aren't one's size. The same thing goes for equipment. Know your specs and sizes.

Karsten Manufacturing: (800) 4-PINGFIT

Popular Clubs: The famous Ping Eyes, ISIs, and Ping putters

Comments: Karsten Manufacturing is known for its color-coded, custom-fitting display. Demo clubs are available in graphite or steel shafts. The eighty or so styles from the putting line are available to try out as well. As far as demo days go, they're put together by a club professional, so consult with them as to when the Karsten reps will be available.

The Company Suggests: With a little research, check out the clubs you want to buy. Compare what they actually do with what they're advertised to do.

Plop (800) 231-7567

Popular Clubs: Slotz Irons

Comments: Plop recently invested $4.5 million in its Club Heat Telemetry Measuring System. This totally computerized system measures over 1,000 elements of the clubhead during impact, then uses that data to fit their clubs to you. Golfers can test drive 5-, 6-, and 7-irons, as well as the wide variety of putters Plop makes.

The Company Suggests: The prospective Plop purchaser should punch a few mishits on the toe of the demo and notice the feel and direction of the shot.

Ram Golf (800) FX-CLUBS

Popular Clubs: Ram Pro-Set Irons

Comments: Ram products are available for testing through golf pro shops. The company, like many of the others, offers its own fitting system. You can check out the Ram Pro-Set Irons and their Zebra Scoring System products.

The Company Suggests: Go into the demo understanding what your goal is. Do you need more accuracy, more distance, or a club that feels better?

Taylor Made (800) 888-CLUB

Popular Clubs: Burner Bubble Irons and Metalwoods, Champagne Titanium Women's Woods

Comments: 5-irons and metalwoods are usually available to players through participating pro shops. When new products come out, golfers can test out all of the Taylor Made products.

The Company Suggests: Do research. Establish what you want out of a club. Check your information and goals with pros and friends. Do you want higher ball flight with midirons? Perhaps you want to reduce slices with your driver. After that, narrow your search down to, say, three companies and devote some good time to testing them all.

Titleist (800) 225-8500

Popular Clubs: The DCI line, both black and gold; special designs for women and seniors.

Comments: A hefty portion of Titleist's promotional budget is devoted to getting Titleist brands into customer hands. Their campaign includes twenty-five-minute lessons with a pro who matches the right club to the player's swing. Titleist also sends out their top professionals to demonstrate their full line of DCIs.

The Company Suggests: There are three major factors to game improvement. Here they are in order of importance: get professional instruction, practice, and buy better equipment that fits you.

Tommy Armour Golf (800) 723-4653
Popular Clubs: The Tommy Gun and the 855/855-S Series
Comments: The Tommy Armour Dynamic Fitting System is available through participating golf shops. This system incorporates the centrifugal and rotational forces encountered when swinging. The company is also out there over 200 days a year, giving demos nationwide.

The Company Suggests: When going to a demo day, it serves the customer best to test the clubs out with a Tommy Armour representative, using their Dynamic Fitting System.

Top-Flite (800) 225-6601
Popular Clubs: Top-Flight Tour and the Intimidator (driver)
Comments: Top-Flite's five tech vans, equipped with their latest fitting technology, conduct over 1,000 demos throughout the country at golf courses and driving ranges. The company also has a number of clubs available for

prospective customers to test at more than 4,000 on- and off-the-course retail stores.
The Company Suggests: Know your game, including aspects like your current swing speed. This helps the company help you find the best shaft and club for optimum play.

Wilson (800) GO-WILSON
Popular Clubs: The Staff line, Invex woods, and Ultra line
Comments: Wilson uses its Dyna Fit system of club fitting at over 800 golf pro shops. To get new clubs into golfers' hands the company also conducts 500 demo days at driving ranges and golf courses throughout the country. Wilson's thoroughly trained technicians conduct these demo days to fit you properly.
The Company Suggests: Bring your clubs with you to the demo days to compare them with the clubs you are interested in trying out. Take some time to try out different models with different shafts.

CUSTOM-FIT CLUBS

Another alternative to name-brand clubs are custom-fit/custom-built clubs. Their advantage is that they're specifically built for you and not derived from specifications for average golfers. Custom-fit/custom-built clubs can be less expensive than name-brand clubs, but their resale value, because they are custom built for you, will most likely be on the low end. To find a custom clubmaker, speak to your local pro or inquire at a pro shop. After you've gotten some names, call the

Professional Clubmakers Society (PCS) at (800) 548-6094 in both the United States and Canada. The PCS certifies clubmakers and can tell you if a manufacturer received a Class A clubmaker certification.

After you've checked out the custom clubmaker's certification, call them and ask questions, such as how long they've been building clubs, what kind of training the craftspeople have, and if you can speak to some of their customers about their experience with the manufacturer. Next, make an appointment at the driving range with the clubmaker. A good custom clubmaker will want to assess your swing and the clubs you currently are using.

BUILD YOUR OWN

If you're interested in making your own clubs and want to get started, check out a catalog from companies such as GolfWorks at (800) 848-8358 or Golfsmith, ask for their Components and Repair Catalog (800) 456-3344. These companies and others like them provide guidance and materials for the serious golfing hobbyist. If you've done your research and are ready to get started, it is advised that you start off by building your own putter. Once you've created a good putter, you can move on to an iron, where shaft lengths and flexibility play a major roll. After you've made an iron or two, you may want to try your hand at a wood, and eventually manufacture a whole set of clubs for yourself.

GOLF PERIPHERALS

BAG IT

Do you want a bag that stands on its own? How about a bag that you can travel across the country with? Or perhaps you'd like a bag that's flexible enough to be two bags in one? Like other equipment, there are an array of golf bags on the market. Things to consider when purchasing a bag include ease of operation, how heavy it is, how you want to transport your clubs, and of course, price. Today, many bags are made of lightweight material like nylon. Some are reinforced with leather or another tough material at the stress points. Inside the bag there are often several compartments to help organize your clubs to make them more easily accessible. Outside of the bag are several pockets for balls, shoes, tees, etc. Staff bags are usually very large bags that allow you to carry most of your house with you and often aren't good for the average golfer. There are, however, mini staff bags which provide all the versatility of staff bags' compartments and accessibility, only in a more compact form.

If you're looking to carry your clubs around the course, look for a light bag called a "stand bag." These bags have shafts that flex out when they're placed on the ground and easily reattach to the bag when the bag is picked up. Some bags even hide the shafts when they're attached to the bag. If you prefer to put your bags in a pull cart or ride around in an electric or gas cart, you can get a bigger bag that's more versatile.

When shopping for a bag, ease of operation is probably the most important factor in deciding on which one to purchase. It's a good idea to pay a bit more money for something that's easy to work with on the course. Grips not only grip your hand and glove, but they also grip other grips. When the grips make contact down in the bag, it can make life a bit frustrating when you're trying to pull them out. Sometimes clubs you don't want can fly out all over the place when you're pulling away or the club you do want gets stuck. To cut down on this craziness, many bags have compartments in which two clubs fit but aren't crowded. These compartments are often lined with a smooth, felt-like material, allowing the clubs to slide in and out easily. Another way to help shaft movement in a bag is to have individual plastic tubes for each club inside your bag.

The latest in golf baggage is a sort of metamorphosis. Unfasten the front end of a mini staff bag and it becomes a completely functional lightweight carry bag. Some even have removable fanny packs.

One thing all bags should have is a cover to protect your clubheads. If it suddenly rains and the bag isn't covered, it can make for a big mess. A cover is also convenient if you travel with your clubs.

If you're traveling with your clubs, there are a couple of options. If you do not want to take your personal bag with you, there are special bags made for traveling and surviving the ravages of airport baggage handling. These are totally enclosed bags with hard plastic covers that have wheels at the bottom, making them easy to walk around with in the airport. These bags are often expensive (upwards of $300) but if you find yourself constantly hoofing it across the country and you want to keep your clubs safe and ready to play with when you arrive at your destination, it's probably worth it. Another option is to put your current bag in a specially constructed case that is made for travel. You simply put your bag and clubs in these cases and close them. They are usually equipped with a handle and wheels, allowing you to manage the bag easily.

The beginning golfer should probably spend between $80 and $150 for a good bag. If you're an average golfer who's out there twice a week, you might want to spend a little more for durability and convenience.

CARTING AROUND

The pull cart, or caddie cart, has been around since the 1930s. The original carts were a bit cumbersome, heavy, and difficult to maneuver. Today's cart is light, easy to use, and folds up, allowing you to put it in the trunk of your car. Carts are most commonly used on public courses, as that's where the demand for them originally initiated. Today most country clubs allow them on the course, unless you're required to take an electric/gas cart. Although golfers can rent pull carts at various public and semi-public courses, purchasing one is a good investment. Look for pull carts that have places to store your golf balls and other equipment for easy accessibility and that may even include a clipboard to write your scores on. New on the horizon are electric pull carts. They are driven much like a power mower or power vacuum cleaner and only require you to steer them.

MARKING YOUR BALL

As discussed in the beginning of this chapter, it's important to mark your ball, even if you have exchanged information with your fellow golfers on who's playing what. A device called the One Stroke Golf Ball Stamp is a handy item that can do this automatically. It's a pre-inked stamp that's specifically designed to mark golf balls. The ink dries almost immediately and can withstand several ball washings. You can order a personal monogrammed stamp using up to five characters, or you can stick with the eight designs that come with the stamper. The device runs approximately $25 for the standard eight characters and $30 for a customized monogram.

GOLF GLOVES

Practically all golf gloves are made of leather. The reason for wearing a glove is to provide a feeling of a surer grip. Not everyone likes to wear a glove, and those that do sometimes remove it while putting. A glove should fit snugly, yet allow for some freedom of movement. Remember, anything restricting your movement is detrimental to your game. For the ladies, there are gloves that have holes in the end of the finger tips that allow nails to protrude through the ends.

SHOE ENOUGH

There are basically two types of shoes for golfers. The more common leather shoe is for normal or rainy days. The other shoe is a lightweight sneaker type. The sneaker types are great for your feet on very hot days and in hot climates. With more courses adopting a spikeless policy, to eliminate spike marks and turf damage, you must now be more aware of what is on the bottom of your shoes. You can replace your existing spikes with Softspikes, specially designed spikes made of plastic or ceramic that cause minimal damage to the course, or go with a spikeless shoe.

Both of these options have improved much to reduce the early criticism that they didn't provide enough traction.

FASHIONABLE AND FUNCTIONAL

Golf fashion has become big business. Top design houses such as Liz Claiborne, Hugo Boss, Tommy Hilfiger, Giorgio Armani, and Ralph Lauren are manufacturing clothing for men and women alike. Even pros like Greg Norman provide fashionable and practical clothing for the course. (Looking good on the course only improves the game and its image.)

Here are a few guidelines for dressing at the course, whether it be a club, public, or semi-public course.

In general, clothing should be nonrestrictive and nonbinding, otherwise your performance on the course will be impeded. Manufacturers of golf clothing understand this and make their sizes a bit bigger and roomier. When choosing clothing, literally put yourself in a stance (sans golf club, please) and swing away. Feel how the shirt, the sweater, and the pants fit. If you're restricted in any way, don't make the purchase.

Some clubs require all players to wear long pants, but for the most part, shorts are allowed. Essential for both pants and shorts are pockets. It is often necessary to carry an extra golf ball, a ball marker, perhaps some tees, or maybe even your glove. For both men and women, shorts should be of the Bermuda type, with a length somewhere around knee length. For women, if you prefer to wear a skirt, go with a "skort," a piece of clothing that combines both shorts and a skirt. Keep in mind that lighter colors reflect the sun while the darker ones absorb the heat. If you're prone to perspiration, it's something to seriously consider.

Often a jacket is needed on the links if you play early in the morning. A lightweight rainsuit is also suggested if you play in areas where sudden cloud bursts are part of the normal weather makeup. Two important things to consider are the breathability of the garment and how your neck feels against the garment when you swing away. A material like Gore-Tex allows the skin to breath while keeping moisture out. If you find yourself having to wear a layer or two to keep warm, look for a garment that wicks away moisture from your body to keep you dry. A material called Polypropylene will do the trick. As far as your neck goes, sometimes zippers and buttons can rub against your skin. Make sure that your jacket doesn't distract your focus on the course.

Hats and caps provide protection from the sun and the rain (according to the *Rules of Golf* you are not allowed to be covered by an umbrella when swinging). The key here is to make sure your hat fits snugly. Some hats provide a band inside made of a material to absorb perspiration, so that may be a consideration as well.

PLAYING THE GAME

THE BEGINNING GOLFER

You've heard your friends rave about the game. You stare in wonderment as they watch it on TV. Perhaps you've heard that much business is conducted on the golf course, or perhaps you want to understand the magnificent obsession of the game. Whatever the case, you're at the point where you're considering learning how to play. Congratulations. Here are some guidelines on how to go about it.

The best way to get started is to head out to your local public course and/or driving range. Rent some clubs and hit a bucket of balls. It is not necessary to dive into the game by purchasing clubs, shoes, and other golf equipment. See how much you enjoy the game before investing a lot of money.

When you get to the range, you'll see people slamming the ball into oblivion with the Driver. As a beginner, it's probably a better idea to start out with a club that's easier to control, like a 9-iron, and work your way down the club numbers. Even though hitting balls from a driving range isn't the same as playing on a course,

you'll begin to get a feel of what it's like to play. Most likely, sometime through the bucket you'll discover that you may need some advice on how to hit the ball. This is where a golf instructor can be very helpful. Novices, amateurs, pros, even instructors, take golf lessons. Why? Because all golfers want to improve their game. Another way a new golfer can learn the game is to take group lessons or classes.

HOW TO FIND A GOOD GOLF INSTRUCTOR

Golf is a game of many different viewpoints. How to swing, how to play, and what clubs to use, are just some of the many elements of the game. So where do we find someone to help us navigate through these elements and achieve our goal of playing and enjoying the game? First, look for an instructor who teaches a class locally. You can find instructors at golf courses, driving ranges, and golf resorts.

Many teachers are certified through institutions like the United States Golf Teachers Association (USGTF), which is affiliated with other teaching associations such as the European, Asian, Spanish/American, and Canadian organizations. Other teachers are certified by the PGA and the LPGA. Some outstanding teachers aren't certified or affiliated with any organizations and go strictly by recommendation.

The USGTF has a seven-day certification program. Prospective teachers must pass a playing ability test, a verbal teaching test, and a written rules examination. They're taught how to teach every aspect of the

game. Many prospective instructors come to the USGTF with a wealth of experience.

To find out how your local pro is certified, call the instruction facility, golf course, or driving range and ask about the instructor's certification. If you happen to be at one of these facilities and are considering instruction, chances are that in the pro shop or near the starter's area, certificates for the instructors are displayed on the walls, much like in a doctor's office.

The next step is to watch a lesson being given by the instructor without being intrusive. This is, at times, a tough and frustrating game, and how an instructor works with a student is one of the keys to good instruction. Is the instructor communicating well with the student? When the student gets upset, how does the instructor react? Do you see the student hitting better? Is the student satisfied with the instruction? Ask the student about the instructor after the lesson is finished. Watch more than one student with the instructor. Observe how consistent the instructor is in his or her manner and teaching methods. As for classes and group lessons, you can do the same thing. In fact, you can ask the instructor to audit the class, that is, to sit in on it to see if you'll like the class that's being offered.

The next step is to speak to the instructor and see how you feel with him or her. A good instructor will ask you what you'd like to accomplish. The teacher will establish whether you're a novice or an experienced player. Some folks like to work on different parts of their game. They want to change their swing; they want to improve their pitching, chipping; etc. On many courses you can have what's called a "playing lesson" in which the instructor accompanies the student on a round of golf. Keep in mind that this can run into a bit of cash, as it takes up much of the instructor's time. The cost of personal hourly lessons varies greatly. It is advised that the beginning golfer check several golf facilities for lesson fees.

Occasionally there are lessons that will help you make quick adjustments to your game, but most of the time this is not the case. Unless you're a gifted athlete or have some innate ability, you will need time to master this game. For most, it takes years to get proficient. As far as quick fixes go, they're usually temporary and not so quick, if they work at all. When an instructor explains that you may need a certain amount of lessons to help you accomplish your golfing goals, chances are the teacher is on the level with you.

Golf is a game noted for its integrity. You'll find that practically all who teach it have a deep love for it and want to share it. They've given up a portion of their lives for the game, or they make a living teaching the game. Most instructors are sincere and devoted to helping you.

After some instruction, students are ready to take their chances on the course. Rent some clubs and head out to the links. If you have friends who play, it's probably a good idea to pair up with them. Chances are they'll be a bit more tolerant of your playing ability than strangers.

For beginners, it is suggested that one play nine holes or a back nine (the second half of a regulation golf course). Back nine's are usually played in the wee hours as the sun is rising. The reason for this is that players who are playing 18 holes are starting at the same time as the players at the back nine, and the chances of their catching up to you are nil. However, by mid-morning, the first foursome on the front nine is already reaching the back, so no new players can start the back nine at that time.

Although some courses designate everyone to tee off from the same point, many courses have three tee markings. White tee markings are for the average golfer; red markings are referred to as the ladies' tees; and the blue markings are designated for the advanced/experienced golfer.

Before heading out onto the course, warm up by hitting a small bucket of balls. It's best to start with a pitching wedge or a 9-iron and work your way up—there's no need to get to the driver before the bucket is finished. You're just warming up. In fact, when you get out on the course, you may not want to hit a driver on the first tee. An easier iron shot might be preferable.

Practicing on the putting green is also a good way to get an idea of how the greens are playing that day. Keep in mind that the practice green speeds may differ from the ones on the course.

ARRANGING A TEE TIME

To reserve a tee time, call the golf course or golf club in advance of your game. Many players call very early in the week to set up a tee time for the weekend. If you don't get through, don't be discouraged, keep hitting that redial button on your phone.

Once you've made the tee time, if for some reason you cannot arrive at the time you've designated, call the Starter at the course and cancel. This saves a lot of aggravation for the Starter and your fellow golfers waiting to play. This is more than etiquette, it's simply common sense and good faith.

Many golfers who play on a regular basis pay an annual fee to a golf course or club and automatically have a specific tee time reserved for them on a particular day during the week. If for some reason they are unable to make this tee time, they need to cancel or they'll be charged an additional fee. Often golfers will cancel, therefore opening up a time for someone calling in who wants to shoot a round. Arrive at the course roughly half an hour before the tee time you've requested.

WHEN YOU DON'T NEED A TEE TIME

If you're playing a back nine, usually there is no need for a tee time. Upon arriving at the course, see the Starter. Your name will be put on a list and you may be paired up to make a foursome.

At many par-three courses and some public and municipal courses, advance tee time reservations are not required. Many of these courses are nine holes. Just ask the Starter to put your name on the list, and wait for an opening.

THE BEST TIME TO PLAY IS . . .

During the week. Weekends are often packed at golf courses. Not crazy about that idea? Call in late to work, get a back nine in, and arrive at work mid-morning. You'll see a world of difference on the course during the week, and a pleasurable one it will be. Another suggestion is to leave work early during the summer and play in the late afternoon.

PLAYING TIPS TO ENHANCE ANYONE'S GAME

A WORD ABOUT THE GRIPS

There are basically three ways to grip the club. The most popular is the Vardon grip, also known as the overlapping grip, in which the pinky overlaps the index finger. In the interlocking grip, the index finger locks in with the pinky. The baseball grip, in which the club is held like a baseball and the fingers don't overlap or interlock at all, is good for players with small hands. Some instructors swear by the grip; others feel students should grasp the club in the manner they feel comfortable with. Whatever style you choose, the grip should be firm but not tight. If you're holding it too tightly, then the rest of your body will be too stiff to swing properly.

KNOW YOUR DISTANCE

At the driving range, learn how far you can hit with each club. This will help immensely when you're on the course. If there is one

tip pros could teach all others, it's this one. The distances given in the chapter on equipment are for the average golfer, however, you may not be average. Once out on the links, you don't want to overshoot the green or come up short. You want to be able to set up your next shot properly. Not everyone is a power hitter like John Daly. Golf at every level is very much a game of finesse.

FIRST SHOT OF THE DAY

When standing over the ball for your first shot of the day, relax. You don't want to kill the ball; you want to finesse the ball out onto the fairway.

ADDRESSING THE BALL

Golfers, like players of other sports, should stand in a ready position. That means standing with your feet shoulder-width apart, legs bent, and arms bent with your hands out front. Generally, the longer the shaft, the wider the stance. Place the sole of the club flat on the ground to find out how far you should stand with it. There's no need to stretch to swing the club or get in very close to it.

KEEP YOUR EYE ON THE BALL

If you hit a ball poorly, it's going to immediately make your life a lot more difficult. Slow play is often attributed to golfers who don't keep their eye on the ball, then insist on looking for it for more than three minutes.

As hard as it may be at times, keep your eyes on the ball until it stops rolling. Judge where it has landed and get there quickly. Look for a marker, a tree, bush, or anything to use as a reference point to help you locate your ball.

MARKING A BALL PROPERLY

Most golfers aren't exactly sure how to do this. Often, golfers try in one swoop to slip the marker under the ball, putting the marker precisely where they think the ball is and lifting the ball at the same time. To avoid making this common mistake, place the marker directly behind the ball, then lift it to clean or replace it. Put it back in front of the marker and remove the marker.

ON THE SCORE CARD

Record how many putts you make on each green when you write down your total for each hole. This will help you get a fix on what you need to improve.

HITTING INTO AND WITH THE WIND

If you're hitting into the wind, take another club number down than you normally would use and swing smoothly (for example, if you would normally use a 5-iron, use a 4-iron instead). Hitting the ball too hard creates more backspin and may cause the ball to go too high, decreasing your distance and perhaps carrying your ball in the wrong direction.

For playing with the wind, you want to keep your ball down too. Hitting it high will make the ball much harder to control. It will go farther, but again, perhaps in the direction you don't want it to travel.

SWINGING AWAY

The key to a good golf swing is to relax and swing easily; there's no need to crush the ball. Many new golfers simply try too hard. The backswing should come up slowly, winding the body tightly like a rubber band, then the downswing begins like a rubber-band uncoiling. This is where the power comes from. As you come down, the big muscles in your shoulders, arms, and legs release, allowing the club to come down and strike the ball. This is not something that needs to be pushed. If you wind up correctly, the clubhead will do the rest when it strikes the ball. This is not to say that the club does all the work. It's simply an extension of your body, specifically, your hands. It's the power in your body that sends the ball to your goal.

HIT DOWN ON THE BALL

Hitting a golf ball is not scooping under it and lifting it into the air. One strikes a golf ball by hitting down on it. This pops the ball into the air and sends it either low or high, depending on what club one uses, how one addresses the ball, what kind of stance one has built, and most importantly, the quality of the golfer's swing.

1.

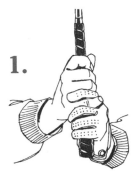

The interlocking grip: The little finger on the right hand interlocks with the index finger of the left hand.

2.

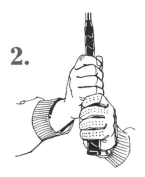

The baseball or natural grip: All four fingers of both hands, lie on the club.

3a. Letting the club lie on the fingers of the right hand, place the little finger of the right hand so it lies on top and between the first and second fingers on the left hand.

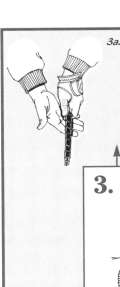

3b. With the heel of the left hand on tope of the club, close your hand. The thumb and forefinger of the left hand should form a "V". The "V" should point to somewhere between your chin and right shoulder.

3.

The overlapping grip: The little finger on the right hand lies on top and between the index and second fingers on the left hand.

3c. The right hand thumb and forefinger should form a "V". The "V" should point to somewhere between your chin and right shoulder.

PLAYING THE LOB WEDGE

Focus on swinging the club in a sweeping motion. If you find yourself in the rough, trying to "dig" your ball out is detrimental. Let this high-lofted club do the work and remember to follow through completely.

THE PITCH-AND-RUN SHOT

This shot is good for when the pin is in back of the green, and is usually used from about 40 feet off the green. The goal is to get the ball rolling to the cup once it hits the green. Stand with your right foot farther from the target line than your left foot. This is known as a "closed" stance. On the backswing, bring the club approximately halfway up. On the downswing, concentrate on rotating your right arm over your left. This puts the toe of the club in the position to give the ball the proper spin. The ball sails up and lands on the green then runs to the pin.

PITCHING THE BALL INTO THE WIND

The object here is to keep the ball low. A good way to do this is to place about two-thirds of your weight on your left foot and play the ball toward the back of your stance. With the clubhead a couple of inches behind your hands, take your backswing. Upon bringing your club down and through the ball, keep the follow-through short and your left wrist steady.

PITCHING TIPS FROM SEVE BALLESTEROS

Whenever you need to hit a super-high, super-soft shot:

1. Choke down on the grip.
2. Stand as far away from the ball as is comfortably possible, with your feet in an open position.
3. Lower your hands dramatically.
4. Set the clubface wide open.
5. Swing down, trying to point the knuckles of your left hand skyward. This will help you slide the clubface underneath the ball and hit it super high.

LANDING THE BALL SOFT ON THE GREEN FROM THE ROUGH

Use a sand wedge and play the ball forward, using an open stance. Turn out the face of the club (opening up the face). Take your backswing and swing down on the ball. This movement will give the ball the proper spin so that it lands softly and will not run on the green.

PITCHING FROM AN UPHILL LIE

Address the ball so that your body is at the same angle as the slope. This gives you a normal, flat lie. From here just swing away as you normally would.

PITCHING FROM A DOWNHILL LIE

In the case of the down hill lie, address the ball so it's closer to your back foot. This allows you to hit the ball correctly.

TO IMPROVE YOUR CHIP SHOT

A common fault in the chip shot is that golfers tend to stand too far away from the

GOLF SWINGS—COMMON PROBLEMS AND REMEDIES

PROBLEM	REMEDY
SWINGING TOO HARD Attempting to initiate downswing with upper body.	Initiate downswing with lower body. • Swing at 80% effort.
BENDING THE LEFT ELBOW Moving the clubhead back with the hands during the backswing.	Don't move the left arm without moving shoulders.
SLICE (CURVED FLIGHT FROM LEFT TO RIGHT OF THE GOLFER) Spin on the ball caused by hitting it with an open clubface. • Swing arc moving from outside to inside during downswing. • Moving head to the right.	Hit ball with more of a closed clubface. Rotate the forearms counterclockwise during downswing. • Initiate downswing with legs. Maintain same swing arc during backswing and downswing. • Keep head still; initiate downswing with the legs.
HOOK (CURVED FLIGHT FROM RIGHT TO LEFT OF THE GOLFER) Moving head to left. • Closing clubface on contact with ball. • Swing arc moving from outside to inside during downswing with closed clubface.	Swing around head and initiate downswing with the legs. • Improper grip. Right hand too far under grip (strong grip); correct grip. • Moving past ball on impact due to improperly starting downswing with upper body; start down swing with lower body.
HITTING THE BALL FAT (HITTING BEHIND THE BALL) Lowering your head during the downswing. • Uncocking wrists too early on downswing. • Shifting weight to left foot on backswing.	Keep knees flexed at constant angle throughout the swing. • Delay wrist release as long as possible. Keep hands ahead of the ball. • Begin backswing with hands, arms, and shoulders as a unit.
TOPPING THE BALL Losing arm extension during the swing. • Lifting head during the swing. • Too much right arm pressure on downswing. • Swaying forward on downswing.	Keep head down and still. • Lead downswing with legs and left side of body. • Swing arc should rotate around the head. • Anchor heel of front foot during the backswing.

ball. To improve your shot, let your right arm bend a bit at the elbow. This will bring you closer to the ball, allowing you to hit better shots.

IF YOUR CHIP SHOTS ARE FLYING OFF LINE

Place two irons on the ground, parallel to each other and about a foot apart. Place your ball midway between the shafts. Address the ball as you normally would. Now, with your clubhead square, swing at the ball. If you find yourself striking the shafts, adjust your swing until you hit the ball without doing so.

IF YOU'RE HITTING YOUR CHIP SHOTS TOO LONG

Hitting long chip shots is often the result of lifting your left heel too high off the ground. This results in picking your club straight up and coming down too hard on the ball. Keep your left foot flat on the ground when executing your backswing.

CHIPPING TIP FROM DAVE PELZ (THE SHORT-GAME GURU)

"Good contact is crucial to good chipping because, after putting, this is the weakest swing in golf. Letting too much grass get between the clubface and the ball will sap that already limited power.

"To encourage crisp contact, place the ball two to three inches behind the center of your stance when you chip. Your stance should be very narrow—the heels only five to six inches apart—so the ball will be off your right (back) ankle. Since I suggest angling both feet toward the target to encourage a slight body turn through impact, the ball will appear to be behind your back foot. Now you can make a normal swing, and your club will descend on the ball with only a minimal amount of grass getting between them."

PREPARING FOR THE BUNKER SHOT

If your ball is in a bunker, take a practice shot or two outside the bunker. The rules of golf do not allow you to make any contact with the sand prior to hitting the ball out. Taking a practice shot in the sand incurs a penalty stroke. Once in the sand, plant your feet well. It's important not to lose your balance.

HITTING THE BALL OUT OF THE SAND TRAP

When a ball is in the sand, it's the sand that takes the ball out. The way to execute this shot is to take a backswing about three-quarters of the way back, then downswing smoothly at about 75 percent of your normal speed. On the downswing, strike an area approximately two to four inches behind the ball, following through as you normally would, letting the sand lift the ball out. It should be noted that this applies to sand traps with soft sand. If the ball is resting on hard sand, then the ball must be struck.

HOW TO HIT A BALL SITTING ON BOTH THE SAND AND THE GRASS

In this case it's best to use a lob (third) wedge. Address the ball with the clubface open. Take the same backswing as you normally would on a bunker shot, but come down a bit harder, hitting a spot in the sand one to two inches behind the ball.

HITTING A BALL THAT'S UP AGAINST THE WALL OF A SAND TRAP

In this situation, it's not always necessary to hit the ball out the side of the bunker. To execute this shot, open the clubface wide and choke down on the club. Take the backswing almost straight up, then on the downswing, while keeping the clubface open, strike the ball. This should pop the ball straight up and in front of you.

HITTING A GOOD CHIP SHOT

Hitting the ball with the bottom of your club, or topping the ball as it's often referred to, commonly happens during chip shots. The reason for this is that the chip is the crucial shot to get good placement on the green. What often happens in this situation is that during the backswing golfers

tend to rise up, and this throws the whole swing off. The solution to this problem is to remember to keep your knees flexed throughout the entire swing. This will cure may chip ills, as you won't lift your body up too soon to see where you've hit the shot before you hit it.

PUTTING PROPERLY

To putt a ball properly, one needs to keep the head and body still and lift the putter like a pendulum. Look at the hole from both sides before putting. This will help you understand which way the ball will break. For putting, only your arms and shoulders should be moving. To help you see if you're moving anything else, lean your head against a wall and perform your putting stroke.

GOLF SCHOOLS

Novices, amateurs, and even pros go to school. Golf schools offer intensive weekly programs, many of which delve into the fundamentals of the long, middle, and short parts of the game, the swing, and putting. Most golf schools assume that you have already been playing the game for a while. If you're a beginner and want to attend one of these schools, inquire if there is a curriculum for you.

Golf schools are generally affiliated with resorts. Many of these resorts are located where it's warm. Those of you who are fortunate enough to live near such a facility won't have to dole over the dollars for accommodations. Those of you who aren't need to consider the extra costs of food, room, and travel expenses just to complete your week or so of intensive training. You'll most likely need at least that much time to improve your game. Of course, going to golf school guarantees nothing. But if you're motivated enough and are able to practice consistently what you've learned in school, you can lower your handicap.

CHOOSING A GOLF SCHOOL

It's important to decide what you want out of a golf school. Schools tend to focus on different areas and philosophies of the game. Do you feel your success on the course depends on your swing? Then, focus on a swing class, or even a school that specializes only in the swing. Perhaps you already feel you have a great swing and want to improve your putting. Then focus on a putting class. Having trouble with your pitching or chipping? Look for a class that improves your short game.

Golf schools are prejudiced about what they teach. For instance, while one teaches thinking, another teaches imagery. Their methods may not jibe with your own instruction experience or with teaching methods used by other schools, which can make golf more complicated.

Your game will improve if you devote a solid chunk of time and effort to it. Whether you can get more bang for your buck at home, or whether combining golf with a vacation is too appealing to pass up, are obviously things you'll have to determine. All package deals are not created equally, so make sure you know what is and what is not included.

POPULAR GOLF SCHOOLS

The Academy of Golf at PGA National
(800) 832-6235
(407) 624-8904 (Fax)
Student/Instructor Ratio: 3:1
Programs: General, short game, full swing, players school, and junior academy
Location:
Southeast: Florida—Palm Beach Gardens
School Highlights: Computer analysis is used to compare a student's swing with the perfect model swing. The program includes free follow-ups of swing analysis via mail-in video. There's also access to continued instruction upon graduating.

Alternative Golf Workshop Inc.

(310) 453-1552
Instructor: Marty Trachtenberg
Student/Instructor Ratio: 4:1
Programs: The Golf Swing
Location:
West Coast: California—Santa Monica
School Highlights: Daily workshops are offered here, as well as private lessons from Trachtenberg. Trachtenberg is affiliated with the famous Bel-Air and Hillcrest country clubs. His success with swing mechanics rates high among many pros. Beginners are welcome.

Arnold Palmer Golf Academy

(800) 729-8383
(813) 973-8933 (Fax)
Student/Instructor Ratio: 4:1
Program: General

Locations:
Southeast: Florida—Orlando and Tampa
Southwest: Nevada—Mesquite
West Coast: Southern California—
  Rancho Cucamonga
Midwest: Missouri—St. Louis
School Highlights: Four topics encompass the academy: The "Scoring Zone," Practicing Like a Pro, Mastering the Fundamentals, and Course Strategy. All instructors are approved by Arnie himself. Palmer's creed is to keep it simple, and that applies to his teachings.

Aviara Golf Academy

(800) 433-7468
(619) 438-7391 (Fax)
E-mail: Kipputt@aol.com
Web site: www.birdie.com/s/kipputt
Student/Instructor Ratio: 5:1

THE SWING: THE FIVE BASIC STEPS TO THE PERFECT GOLF SWING

Program: General
Location:
West Coast: California—Carlsbad
School Highlights: Students study video-taped swings of the best in the business and are video-taped themselves both on and off the course. The staff here works with your swing motion and doesn't try to adhere to one particular formula.

Ben Sutton Golf School

(800) 225-6923
(216) 453-8450 (Fax)
Student/Instructor Ratio: 4–7:1
Program: General
Location:
Southeast: Florida—Sun City Center
School Highlights: Frequented by senior golfers, this specially designed, forty-two-acre learning center allows everyone to practice under real conditions. Sutton's philosophy is that a crucial part of the game occurs during in-between yardages, hence that is where much of the schooling and practice takes place.

Byron Nelson Golf School

(217) 717-0700
Instructor: Mike Abbott
Student/Instructor Ratio: 3:1
Program: Corporate
Location: *Southwest:* Texas—Las Colinas
School Highlights: This facility caters to the corporation. The view here is that the biggest barrier to learning is being embarrassed by one's performance on the links. Corporate folks are immersed in the teaching process and become involved in student-to-student instruction. Video tape analysis is also used.

HANDY TIPS

- Many clubs look alike. It's a good idea to label yours.
- When holding two golf clubs on the green, hand one to someone who can hold it, or place it on top of the bag. If you just lay it down, it's easy to lose the club.
- Keep an extra golf ball in your pocket.
- If you've been paired up with folks you've just met, remember their names.
- Wipe off your clubs after each shot. It's also a good idea to clean your clubs after each round.
- Take your business cards with you. Many connections are made on the course.
- When hitting balls at the driving range, aim for targets.
- Carry breath mints or gum in your golf bag. It'll help you get rid of that early morning breath brought on by either coffee or last night's drinks. (Remember to keep it quiet when you're sucking or chewing; it could disturb your fellow golfer's shot.)
- Playing during non-peak hours saves money on most public golf courses.
- After playing a great round, have a fellow player sign your score card. This validates your score, and it will be a great memento.
- To hit a few during the winter, find a driving range with heated golf tees.
- The 40-to-60 yard pitch shot is often encountered in a round, so practice these shots when you're at the driving range.
- Practice putting. It's easily half the game.

Craftz-Zavichas Golf School

(800) 858-9633
(719) 564-4449
Student/Instructor Ratio: 4:1
Program: General
Location:
Rocky Mountains: Colorado—Pueblo
School Highlights: Founded in 1968, this is one of the oldest schools in the country and was started by Penny Zavichas, whose aunt was the great Babe Didrikson Zaharias. Here, female instructors teach women, and male instructors teach men.

David Leadbetter Golf Academy

(800) 424-3542
(941) 592-1040 (Fax)
Student/Instructor Ratio: 3:1
Program: General, short game, junior, private, playing lessons
Locations:
Northeast: New York
Southeast: Florida—Orlando
Midwest: Illinois
West Coast: California
School Highlights: Leadbetter has the reputation of being one of the finest coaches in the game. His students include Nick Faldo and Nick Price. Leadbetter uses teaching aids he developed himself. Video-taped analysis is utilized at this school as well. There are also two-day retreats in which only six students are allowed to participate.

Dave Pelz Short Game School

(800) 753-9868
Student/Instructor Ratio: 4:1
Program: Short game
Locations:
Southeast: Florida—Boca Raton
West Coast: California—La Quinta
School Highlights: Known the world over as "Professor Putt," Pelz specializes in the short game. In fact, this is the only school that devotes itself exclusively to it. Pelz believes that 65 percent of the game is short play and that, if played right, it results in 100 percent satisfaction. He may have something there.

Dean Reinmuth School of Golf

(619) 562-9755
Instructor: Dean Reinmuth
Student/Instructor Ratio: 4:1
Program: Customized
Locations:
West Coast: California—San Diego
Pacific: Hawaii—Princeville
School Highlights: Famous for teaching Phil Mickelson and Dave Stockton Jr., Reinmuth believes tension is what trips up golfers, so that's what he and his instructors focus on. This school is also known for its bilingual staff and Japanese instruction program, which has made Dean something of a cult figure in Japan.

Fred Schoemaker's School for Extraordinary Golf

(800) 541-2444
Student/Instructor Ratio: 3:1
Program: General
Locations:
West Coast: California—Palm Springs and Carmel
School Highlights: Enjoyment, performance, and learning make up the essence of this school. Since Shoemaker believes that awareness is the key to improvement, he feels the student understands what is wrong with the swing and works with them from that basis.

The Golf Advantage Schools

(800) 759-4653
Student/Instructor Ratio: 5:1
Program: General, junior
Locations:
Southeast: North Carolina—Pinehurst Virginia—Hot Springs

Southwest: Texas—Austin
School Highlights: At the Pinehurst location there are eight championship courses, including, of course, the world-reknown Pinehurst #2. The Virginia site is at The Homestead, and in Austin, the site for the school is at Barton Creek. For juniors a 15 handicap or lower is required to qualify for the school.

Golf Digest Schools

(800) 243-6121
Student/Instructor Ratio: 6:1
Program: General, low handicap, playing, women's, short game, couples, parent/child, corporate
Locations:
Southwest: Arizona—Scottsdale and Tucson
West Coast: California—Carmel and San Diego
Oregon—Bend
Rocky Mountains: Colorado—Vail
Southeast: Florida— Tapron Springs Georgia—Atlanta and Sea Island Virginia— Williamsburg

Northwest: Idaho—Sun Valley
Midwest: Illinois—Chicago
  Michigan—Cadillac
  Minnesota—Minneapolis
Northeast: New Jersey—Galloway
School Highlights: There's something for everyone here. It's great that you can share and learn the game here with your child or vice versa. Program includes video analysis of swing instruction. Emphasis is on drills as a tool for improvement.

Grand Cypress Academy of Golf

(800) 790-7377
Student/Instructor Ratio: 4:1
Program: General, women's, mental game, and juniors
Locations:
Southeast: Florida—Orlando
School Highlights: Having an LPGA Hall of Famer like Kathy Whitworth on your team says a lot about the quality of this school. Computer instruction is used here to compare your swing to the perfect swing.

Innisbrook Hilton Golf Institute

(800) 456-2000
Student/Instructor Ratio: 4:1
Program: General, women's, juniors, playing
Location:
Southeast: Florida—Tarpon
School Highlights: This resort is the largest resort-owned and operated school in the country. There are 63 holes of championship golf here, where the instructors teach four different concepts for each playing level.

The Jimmy Ballard Swing Connection

(800) 999-6664
Student/Instructor Ratio: 5:1
Program: General, private, short game
Locations:
Southeast: Florida—Fort Lauderdale and Melbourne
School Highlights: Ballard's connection theory of the swing in which the player coils behind the ball before releasing the entire body through the shot is taught here. Students observe video tapes of the best ball strikers in the biz to help students comprehend the right positions and motions of the swing.

Jim McLean Golf Academy

(800) 223-6725—Florida
Student/Instructor Ratio: 4:1
Program: General, power school
Locations:
East Coast: New York—New York City (Chelsea Piers)
Southeast: Florida—Miami
Southwest: Arizona—Scottsdale
West Coast: California—Foster City and La Quinta
School Highlights: At McLean's centers, he employs cutting-edge video technology. Emphasized here are attitude, the full swing, the short game, and course management. Dr. Fran Pirozzolo, famed neuropsychologist, is on-staff too, and focuses on the mental side of the game.

THE ART OF THE DEAL

Millions of dollars' worth of business deals are consummated on the golf course. Relationships are formed, and a bond can be built on the course that is unique unto itself. It is you and your client, boss, prospective associate, or future V.P. taking on an "out-of-the-office" activity that transcends the normal boundaries of conference rooms and power lunches.

Like the strategies of the game, business has its long hitters, who will take the daring approach over the trees or gamble on a more risky venture. Golf, like business, also has the more conservative player, who will take the slow-and-steady approach to the game. Similar to the business community, golf also tests your ability to deal with a variety of unexpected situations.

The reasons for combining golf and business range from making a strong first impression to closing a deal. Even Ralph Kramden, on *The Honeymooners* television series, tried to learn the game overnight to impress his boss.

Judy Anderson, author of *Teeing Off to the Green: Using Golf as a Business Tool* and golf/business consultant, has developed several steps to business golf. According to Judy Anderson, "One of the secrets to successful business golf is knowing the difference between golf and business golf. Business golf includes skills, techniques, and politics of conducting business on the course." Here are a few things to consider during a business golf outing:

Step 1: Determine how golf is used in your business, industry, profession, and company.

Certain industries, such as financial services and insurance, use golf extensively. Golf in these fields is an important business tool, so you

THE ART OF THE DEAL

will need to hone your skills or you'll be at a disadvantage. In other industries, an annual outing may be your only business golf opportunity. You'll still want to know the basics of the game, but the novelty of this once-a-year event will often overshadow your particular score.

Step 2: Set Your Objectives. The goal of business golf is developing a rapport and building a relationship. Beyond that, what do you hope to accomplish? Determine whether you are prospecting, entertaining clients, strengthening shaky relationships, or networking.

Step 3: Determine the value and benefit of reaching your goals. If you achieve them, what will you gain? Weigh the value not only in terms of dollars and cents, but also in goodwill and establishing a strong relationship.

Step 4: Review various golf and non-golf options. Is golf the best

way to reach your objectives? Would a business lunch, theater tickets, or some other activity suffice? What makes golf the right option for the right client? If they are intimidated by the game, they might not be in a good position to do business. On the other hand, they may be overly competitive, which can also make doing business more difficult.

Step 5: Determine the cost of each option, considering both time and money. This step will help prevent you from making a decision based on your personal love of golf.

Step 6: Decide on your plan of action. Should you decide on a golf outing, decide which course you'll play, when to play, whom to include in the foursome, nineteenth hole activities, conversation strategy, and follow-up. Then, once you've done your homework to prepare for this business meeting, go ahead and extend the invitation.

John Jacobs' Golf Schools

(800) 472-5007
Student/Instructor Ratio: 5:1
Locations:
South: Alabama—Point Clear
Southeast: Florida—Fort Lauderdale, Vero
  Beach, Orlando, and Marco Island
Southwest: Arizona—Tucson, Green Valley,
  Mesa, Scottsdale, and Litchfield Park
  Nevada—Las Vegas
  Texas—Rancho Viejo
Rocky Mountains: Colorado—Crested Butte
  Utah—Midway
Midwest: Wisconsin—Delvan
Great Plains: Missouri—Osega Beach,
  and Transverse City
Northeast: New York—Margaretville, and
  Hauppauge
  New Jersey—Atlantic City
West Coast: California—Rancho Mirage,
  and Palm Desert
  Oregon—Portland
School Highlights: With more locations
than any golf school in the United States,
the instruction here focuses on the results
of your swing and then focuses on how
to make the changes. The mental game
is stressed as well. Women make up over
40 percent of the newer students.

La Costa Golf School

(800) 653-7888
Student/Instructor Ratio: 1–2:1
Program: Full-day private
Location:
West Coast: California—Carlsbad

School Highlights: La Costa has perhaps
the world's largest collection of video
tapes featuring the best swings in the
game. They believe that simply watching
an individual swing and making changes
needs to be enhanced by these tapes.
With the student ratios being so small,
the student gets very personal attention.
Consistency by the two instructors is
ensured as well.

Mike McGetrick Golf School

(800) 494-1818
Student/Instructor Ratio: 3:1
Program: General, course management,
full swing, short game, juniors
Locations:
Rocky Mountains: Colorado—Englewood
School Highlights: To improve scoring,
the instructors use on-course conditions.
Video-tape and computer analysis is
used as well. All students receive an
instruction manual and take-home video.

Nicklaus/Flick Golf School

(800) 642-5528
Student/Instructor Ratio: 4–5:1
Program: General, parent/child,
women's, couples
Locations:
West Coast: California—Pebble Beach
Southwest: Arizona—Desert Mountain
Southeast: Florida—Palm Beach
Midwest: Missouri—Harbor Springs
Rocky Mountains: Utah—Park Springs
School Highlights: More than 50 percent
of the classes here are taught by Jim

Flick. Nicklaus contributes to the classes as much as he can, depending on his schedule. There are specialty schools here for special-interest groups, including tournament play.

The Phil Riston Golf School

(800) 624-4653
Student/Instructor Ratio: 4:1
Program: General
Locations:
Southeast: North Carolina—Calabash
  South Carolina—Pawleys Island
Great Plains: Kansas—Overland Park
School Highlights: Your swing is video-taped and analyzed. Students can also, after they have completed the curriculum, video-tape their swings and send it in. The instructors will do a voice-over analysis and send it back to the students to make sure they're following what they've learned.

Pine Needles Learning Center

(800) 747-7272
Instructor: Peggy Kirk Bell
Student/Instructor Ratio: 4:1
Program: General, junior, corporate
Location:
Southeast: North Carolina—Southern Pines
School Highlights: This facility combines the course for the 1996 U.S. Women's Open with the world-famous instructor Peggy Kirk Bell. Programs include instruction and competition. Students also get follow-up video-tape feedback. Telephone assistance is available as well.

Rick Smith Golf Academy

(800) 444-6711
Instructor: Rick Smith
Student/Instructor Ratio: 2:1
Program: General, swing, short game
Location:
Great Plains: Missouri—Gaylord
School Highlights: Instruction occurs in the morning, leaving the afternoon for

GROUP LESSONS

Group lessons are a great way to learn and improve your game. Although you may not get the personal attention you'd receive in a private lesson, you can learn much in a group setting. Some group lessons include classroom time. Once you're out on the instructing facility you get to see other students trying to accomplish the same goals as you are, and get to listen to the instructor without feeling you're intruding on the lesson. Many times something the instructor says to another student proves beneficial to you. It's also a great place to establish a camaraderie with your fellow golfers, which can often lead to more friendships, business associations, and future foursomes.

play. Smith, who has coached many pros including Lee Janzen, makes his classes extremely small, giving his students very personal attention.

Roland Stafford Golf School

(800) 447-8894
Student/Instructor Ratio: 2:1
Program: General
Locations:
Northeast: New Hampshire—Francestown
New York—Clymer and Windham
Southeast: Florida—Pembroke Pines, Pensacola, and Tampa
School Highlights: Stafford believes that there tends to be an over-analysis of the swing, resulting in much confusion. He likes to keep it simple, using only a few basics to achieve good swing results.

The School of Golf Exclusively for Women

(800) 457-5568
Student/Instructor Ratio: 3:1
Program: General. Students need to have some golf experience.
Location:
West Coast: California—San Diego
School Highlights: Master and Class A golfer, Shirley Spark has developed the program and oversees all students. The stress here is on swing analysis. Students get to play in a "fun scramble tournament." Video-tape analysis and personalized note books are used to complement post-school training.

Stratton Golf School

(800) 238-2424
Student/Instructor Ratio: 5:1
Program: General
Locations:
Northeast: Vermont—Stratton Mountain
Southwest: Arizona—Scottsdale
School Highlights: Lyford is the only pro in New England to belong to the PGA's Nation Teaching Committee. His program includes video-taping students' swings as well as using stop-action photography. The school is a favorite for beginners.

Sugarloaf Golf School

(800) 843-5623
Student/Instructor Ratio: 4:1
Program: General
Location:
Northeast: Maine—Carrabassett Valley
School Highlights: Here's an opportunity to learn and play at what is considered the best mountain course in the country: The Robert Trent Jones Jr. Sugarloaf Golf Club. Students learn on the course and off, as well as learning about club selection. Flexibility in students' learning curves is stressed here too.

Swing's the Thing Golf Schools

(800) 797-9494
Student/Instructor Ratio: 5:1
Program: General
Locations:
Mid-Atlantic: Maryland—Ocean City
Pennsylvania—Shawnee-on-Delaware
New York—Appalachian

Southeast: Florida—Orlando
School Highlights: The Japanese government's Public Television Network selected the Swing schools to teach their golfers swing fundamentals, utilizing a series of half-hour programs.

PUTTING OVER LUNCH

A great way to do lunch is to putt it away. Carry your putter with you in the car or keep it handy at work. In this world of getting everything done by yesterday, break away from the crowd by taking a putting lunch during your workday. Leave the office cafeteria or the local pizza, fast food or deli joints behind and take your putter with you. It's great to be outdoors and practicing putts in the middle of the day. If you're in a big city and greens are a bit far off, it may be possible to find a golf simulation venue where you can hit away with your clubs. It's a wonderful break from the pressures of the office.

The United States Senior Golf Academy
(800) 654-5752
Student/Instructor Ratio: 3:1
Program: General
Location: *Southeast:* Florida—Melbourne
School Highlights: A minimum of nine holes of golf are played here daily with an instructor. Though the school is senior-oriented, students of any age are encouraged to learn here too.

The Woodlands Golf Academy
(412) 329-6900
Student/Instructor Ratio: 4:1
Programs: General, beginners, advanced, and couples
Location:
Mid-Atlantic: Pennsylvania—Farmington
School Highlights: State-of-the-art, high-tech, computerized equipment is used here to analyze swings. Emphasis is on setting up for the shot, pitching, chipping, putting, and general strategy on the course.

DETERMINING YOUR HANDICAP

The USGA Handicap System is well recognized and widely accepted by golf clubs throughout the country. This handicap system is based on the best ten differentials from a player's last twenty scores.

A differential is determined by subtracting the USGA Course Rating from the

OTHER BUSINESS GOLF CONSIDERATIONS

Once you've planned your golf meeting, you have to know your on-course strategies. Here are a couple of considerations:

1. When do you bring up business, and when do you focus on golf?

The host should know the other party's level of affection for the game. If you are bringing an avid golfer onto the course, their home away from home, they may be thinking you are simply trying to gain a sense of camaraderie. If you plan to discuss a merger on the first fairway, you may not be putting your best cleats forward.

2. Who wins?

If you are simply taking the boardroom meeting and moving it to the course, then the emphasis is on business and no one really cares who wins, or even if you keep score. If, however, you've chosen golf because your "attendees" enjoy a friendly competition, then you must compete. This means selecting a course that is at a level that meets everyone's game. It also means having a foursome that can play together comfortably. Executives, right or wrong, have been known to make determinations about each other by their activities and behavior on the course.

adjusted gross score, then multiplying the resulting value by 113, then dividing this result by the corresponding USGA Slope Rating and rounding off to the nearest tenth.

The following information will help you determine your handicap.

Yardage Rating

"Yardage Rating" is the evaluation of the playing difficulty based on yardage only. It is the score a scratch player on his game is expected to make when playing a course of average difficulty.

USGA Course Rating

"Course Rating" is the evaluation of the playing difficulty of a course for scratch players. Course rating is expressed in strokes and decimal fractions of a stroke, and based on yardage and other obstacles to the extent that they affect the scoring ability of a scratch player.

Courses are rated by authorized golf associations, not by individual clubs.

USGA Slope Rating

"Slope Rating" reflects the relative playing difficulty of a course for players with handicaps above scratch. The lowest Slope Rating is 55 and the highest is 155. The average Slope Rating for men and women is 113.

When not everyone has a USGA handicap, here are three ideas to help handicap the unhandicapped:

SECOND BEST SCORE SYSTEM

The USGA has developed a simple estimator of a player's ability called the "Second Best Score System" or "Second Best Handicap" for short. Second Best Handicap is not a substitute for the USGA Handicap System, but it can produce acceptable results and is a reasonable system for handicapping those without handicaps.

To create a player's Second Best Handicap, the tournament committee simply asks each unhandicapped player to submit his or her last three best scores made on a regulation course (par 68 or more) in the last twelve months. They combine these scores with any previous scores the player has made in their tournament in the past two years.

The player's Second Best Handicap is the second best score he or she has given them minus 70 for men and 73 for women.

For example, if a male player submits scores of 92, 96, and 98, and he had a score of 90 in their tournament last year, his second best score would be the 92, and they would subtract 70.

There is a special qualification for beginners or players who can submit only one score. They subtract 74 from the score for a man and 77 for a woman's Second Best Handicap.

If necessary, 9-hole scores can be combined to produce an 18-hole scoring history.

If a player has never played, the Second Best Handicap is not appropriate. The committee should assign a maximum of 36 strokes for men and 40 for women. Some allow a maximum of 50 strokes, which generally gives three strokes on each hole except for par threes.

MODIFIED PEORIA SYSTEM

Another alternative is to use a hole-score selection system called the "Peoria System." Under this system, a player learns his or her handicap after the round is completed. The committee secretly selects a par-three hole, a par-five hole and four par-four holes from an 18-hole course. The par fours should be representative in length and difficulty with two chosen from the front nine and two from the back nine.

A modified Peoria handicap is then calculated by adding the player's strokes over par on the six selected holes and multiplying that number by 2.8. This will be the player's allowance, to be deducted from his or her gross score. The maximum hole score for allowance purposes is three over par on par threes and fours, and four over par on par fives.

Example: A player scores 98 for a round. She is 11 over par on the six selected holes. 11 × 2.8 = 30.8 = 31 allowance Her net score is, therefore, 98 − 31, or 67.

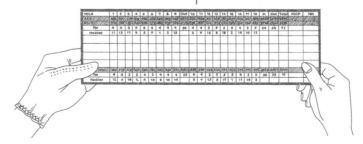

THE SCHEID SYSTEM

The Scheid System is a "worst-holes" system for large, unhandicapped events that is designed to give all golfers an equal chance, with a range of scores up to 151. The following table explains it.

SCORE	DEDUCT
72, 73	no holes and adjustment
74, 75, 76	½ worst hole and adjustment
77, 78, 79	1 worst hole and adjustment
80, 81, 82, 83	1½ worst holes and adjustment
84, 85, 86, 87	2 worst holes and adjustment
88, 89, 90, 91	2½ worst holes and adjustment
92, 93, 94, 95	3 worst holes and adjustment
96, 97, 98, 99	3½ worst holes and adjustment
100, 101, 102, 103, 104	4 worst holes and adjustment
105, 106, 107, 108, 109	4½ worst holes and adjustment
110, 111, 112, 113, 114	5 worst holes and adjustment
115, 116, 117, 118, 119, 120	5½ worst holes and adjustment
121, 122, 123, 124, 125, 126	6 worst holes and adjustment
127, 128, 129, 130, 131, 132	6½ worst holes and adjustment
133, 134, 135, 136, 137, 138	7 worst holes and adjustment
139, 140, 141, 142, 143, 144	7½ worst holes and adjustment
145, 146, 147, 148, 149, 150, 151	8 worst holes and adjustment

Adjustment to deduction
−3, −2 ,−1, 0, +1, +2, +3

A PRIVATE LESSON
FROM MARTY TRACHTENBERG

Marty Trachtenberg has been teaching golf for forty years. For many of those years he gave private instruction and taught classes at the Studio City Golf Course in Studio City, California. He now owns, operates, and teaches at the Alternative Golf Workshop Inc. in Santa Monica, California. Marty also gives personal instruction at the world-renown Bel-Air Country Club, as well as the Hillcrest Country Club. Trachtenberg also teaches in Hawaii, where pros from all over the globe seek his tutelage.

At the age of fourteen, Trachtenberg became a champion handball player in New York City, the toughest division in the country. After World War II he attended the University of New Mexico on the GI Bill, where he saw Babe Didrikson Zaharias making rounds on the college circuit. She challenged any man to drive a ball farther than she could. No one was able to. Zaharias intrigued Trachtenberg, and so he began his long journey toward perfecting the golf swing. Soon Trachtenberg found himself immersed in kinesiology (the study of the principles of mechanics and anatomy in relation to human movement) and how it related to the golf swing.

Trachtenberg admits that his views on golf may be controversial because he has broken away from standard golf teaching. "I'm not in conflict with pros or the PGA, what they do is wonderful for the game. I just offer an alternative." In fact many pros have found Marty's teachings a bright, guiding light for those who truly want to improve their game.

Q **One of the controversial things about your instruction is that you teach that the ball is the target, not the flagstick. Could you elaborate on that?**

A The animal species are broken up into separate genres—predators and preys. Prey usually have their eyes on the side of the their head, allowing them to watch for a predator. The predator usually has the eyes in front, which means that it strikes forward. When a predator powers up, its entire power goes from back to front or forward. Naturally, the human being is a predator. When humans shoot a rifle, they must be facing their target. When they throw a dart, or use a bow and arrows they must face the target. Millions of years of natural selection make our power go from back to front. In most natural sports, we wind up; we go back; and then we throw the ball forward. That's the way we're built. To generate our power and our balance we rotate around the spine. However, when we get into golf, we stand facing one way then pick a target that's on the side of us, which is the flag. We claim that that's the target, which means that we get back and front confused. To demonstrate this, what I do in my classes is I take a ball and I raise it above the student's head and I say 'Now let's say you're facing this ball and it is the moon. Where would the back of the moon be?' Of course, the student points to the rear of the ball. Then I take the ball and put it down at the student's feet, keeping it in the same relative position, except below him. 'Now where's the back?' I ask. And then all of a sudden the student says it's here on the side of the ball. And then I ask, 'Well, what happened? Why did the back change when it went from up here to down here?' We sort of become alchemists and change lead into gold. All of a sudden we make this transition and we call the back of the ball the right side of the ball.

Q So what we're actually doing is striking the right side of the ball.

A Exactly, we're striking the right side of the ball and making it go to the left. Since the flag is on our left, it can't be the target, because we must face our target. Take a back in football. When a back is running, he must square up to the line to get his full power. If he's running sideways, he's very vulnerable. That's because our power goes from back to front. The professional golfer, in a sense, understands this. When they describe the swing, they say make a backswing to hit the right side of the ball, so when the

golfer backswings, he's actually going to strike the right side of the ball, not the back. His mind doesn't understand what he should do. His mind is telling his body to do one thing, and his body doesn't understand how to make that kind of a move. So he has an enigma. So it must be driven into our minds that the ball is the target, otherwise we'll never hit the ball well.

Q You teach that the swing is round and that one hits down on the ball. It is not an up-and-down swing where one hits under the ball to lift it up. Do I have that right?

A Yes, because the golf swing is a vertical swing. When a golfer turns, the club goes up, and he should swing down. Instead, the average golfer's downswing comes under the ball and lifts it up. If you talk to a pro, he'll tell you he swings down on the ball. That's why they call it the backswing, and the downswing, you're coming down on the ball.

Q Does the putting stroke rely on any of these principles?

A To some degree. The interesting thing in putting is it's very important when a person putts that they swing the club like a pendulum. You bring the hands up and them let them swing back and bring the club down. The most important thing is, if you read, when the pros putt, the club must be accelerating when it comes down into the ball. Now, a lot of golfers take the putter back flat, then when they bring it through they have to push it to get acceleration, and that's not good. Whereas if you let the club come up with the hands and then down, it's a natural acceleration because of gravity. The hands bring the club down naturally and much more squarely. This needs to be exercised and developed. The stroke should come up like a pendulum and then down on top of the ball, just like is done with the actual swing.

Q Do you favor any kind of putter?

A The best putter probably is the simple blade. The other putters are deceptive because the eye contact on them takes the putter away incorrectly. So to me the blade is probably the most appropriate. The other kinds of putters are trying to compensate for your stroke. All heel-toe weighting is meaning you're not stroking well. So, no matter where you hit it you're going to get a piece of the face. Clubs are basically designed by engineers as compensations for bad swings. A pro will use the simplest club there is. He just wants it to be an attachment to his body swing.

Q Are there any swing philosophies from the pros that you like or have learned from?

A One of the key things that I teach in the swing is basically from Ben Hogan's book Five Lessons—Fundamentals. In the book, Hogan has an outline of a golfer hitting the ball. Inside of the outline is an illustration of a motor in the head, a motor in the body and torso, plus generators in his hips and legs. That really explains the golf swing. We first should get that image in our head, which is what I try to do when I teach. The motor is in the torso because that's the round part of the body that makes the turn. When we turn the torso (the rib cage) that will wind the shoulders and the arms back, and it'll also start to wind the hips and legs because that's their contact. And then when we come back, the hips and the legs take over, turn the torso, and bring the shoulders and arms in. So it's a very sequential action—it is not compartmentalized.

Q What are your feelings about grips?

A People get into these mechanical grips without really having a clue why the grip is that way. Basically, a good grip is set up so that it connects the hands through the arms, through the shoulders, to the body. Unfortunately, many golfers don't have this connection because they just do this grip in a mechanical way. Then they learn the swing in a compartmentalized way because that's the way it's taught. Teaching parts of it is, I believe, wrong. The swing is an entire entity.

Q Can you explain your philosophy about the swing?

A Here's a little of my philosophy, which is actually Hegelian philosophy. When

I study the swing, I study it as a dialectic, meaning that everything is an action. Two opposites are coming together and creating a completion. That's the way our body operates. Everything is in a dialectic. In the golf swing, when we see something on the outside, there's an opposite going on inside. That's what gives us our equilibrium. There has to be an opposite. You can't just tilt one way without having a thrust going the other way to keep your balance. The body is in a constant state of dialectic. What we see on the outside, something opposite is happening on the inside. The way the swing is taught today, it's as if we're some kind of an erector set. It's done in a mechanical way. Many teachers don't understand this unity of opposites within the body. That's the way I see the swing. When I make a swing and I start to go one way, I feel the torsion winding and holding me the other way, and that's what creates the torsion. If you just simply turned, you wouldn't get any wind.

Q **So, after you wind up, are you tightening up when you downswing and hit the ball?**

A Yes. If you saw pictures of Bobby Jones or even Chi Chi Rodriguez years ago, they would come down spinning so hard that they would actually go up on their toes like a ballet dancer. They're spinning; they're gripping. Look at Nicklaus or other pros when they're coming down. Look at their necks. Their sternal mastoids and their shoulders are holding the spine tight. You'll see these muscles bulging; their faces are grimacing while they're hitting. There's tremendous pressure there.

Q **What muscles, then, are we actually using?**

A Physiologically, there are two sets of muscles that the body works with. They're called aductors and abductors. Aductors tend to pull the muscles in toward the spine. Abductors go away from the spine. In golf or all athletics we use aductors. In the good golf swing, in every move we make, the body starts to tighten in and coil around the spine, and then when it comes down it tightens in around the spine again. That gives the body extreme balance and centrifugal force. Amateurs use their abductors when they swing. They pull their arms away from the spine, disconnecting, and that's why they get a weak swing. Pros, on the other hand, use their aductors because they're swinging their arms and shoulders down, tightening in and around the spine.

Q **What kind of golf ball do you like to hit?**

A I like a Balata ball or what's known as the three-piece ball. It has a center, rubber bands around it, and a cover. It's wound a certain way so you'll get more action from it. Two-piece balls, a Surlyn ball with a solid core and a tough plastic Surlyn cover, are basically for power hitters.

Q **Are there certain ways to hit, to use a club to get more spin out of the ball?**

A No. What people don't understand is, when you want to hit a ball and you want to get more power to it you don't hit with your left arm, you don't pull it out. You leave it together with the whole left side. It's all a one piece swing, meaning that the left side stays completely solid. If you watch a pro, take a look at the pictures, you'll see that his left arm is hooked into his body. It's level and even with his foot when he's coming down and hitting. When you're hitting a golf ball and you pull your left side down, it has to brace like a wall and then the right side will come through and hit. But if you don't brace that left side, it pulls the right side over and you never get a hit. Years ago they used to have a big discussion about whether the golf swing is a swing or a hit. They used to say Gene Littler was a swinger and Palmer was a hitter. I don't believe that's true. I think what it is, is

that the golf swing is a swing. The body swings the club around into what they call the hitting area, and then the left side stops and then the right side hits, and you'll find that the right hand will come over, or pronate. In other words, it turns over on the top of the ball. Your palm goes over, and that means that the wrists are uncocking.

Q **How did you get into golf?**

A I took up golf after my service, after the war. I was attending the University of New Mexico on the GI Bill, and Babe Didrikson Zaharias came around and did an exhibition one summer. She got up there and challenged any man to drive against her. Boy, she could hit that ball! At the time, I didn't know golf from anything. In the '30s golf was a country-club sport, and where I was from, nobody was into that.

Q **Did you challenge her?**

A I had never played golf before that. She just encouraged me to get into it. I started to hit the ball around after I saw her. When I was swinging I discovered that my natural actions and my body couldn't control the ball. I was a slicer because I was a righty, a dominant righty. That's when I began to study kinesiology so I could try to figure out why the body was doing what it was doing, why it was pivoting that way, etc. It consumed me.

Q Did golf bring you out to California?

A Yes. I came to California in 1962 just for golf because back east you were losing five to six months of golf a year. Playing early spring was brutal. I just had to get into a climate where I could play twelve months out of the year. I did a lot of playing back east, but I never really got as deeply into the swing as I did when I came to California. I started teaching in the middle of the '60s. Before that I went around on the tour a lot. At that time you were able to get close to the pros. I took a lot of Super 8 film of all the guys, Mike Soucheck and all those guys. I used to study them three hours a night, just to study the body and how it was working, and try to figure out what the muscles were doing and what the bones were doing to get into those positions. I used to see all those guys in the '50s and the '60s: Palmer, Thompson, Sarazen, Barber.

Babe Didrikson Zaharias was trained at Studio City where I taught for many years. She learned from one of my students there, Mickey Shouder. I taught and worked with Mickey from '69–'72. It's interesting how things come around.

Q Is there any course that you would like to play again that you haven't been to in a while?

A Pebble Beach is great. One day when I put my swing together the way I want it, I would like to play Pebble again. When I played it originally, I didn't play it that well. I haven't actually played in several years.

Q You haven't played a course?

A No. When I played I got down into the mid-'70s, but I felt I was just scrambling. I didn't have the swing where I wanted it, so I said I'm not going to play again until I put the swing in where I want it. And that's my objective.

Q Do you think you're close to playing again?

A I think I'm building it in now. You see,

every day I hit 500 balls. I used to hit 1,000, so I think maybe in another year I'll have what I think is the Jack Nicklaus or Arnold Palmer inner concept and then we'll see. I'll be about seventy-five, and I think I could play. Some people say to me, 'Oh, but you'll be older, do you really think you can play well?' The truth is I really don't feel older. I hit the ball much better now than I did when I was sixty-five. My doctors say my chemical composition is young, the muscles very strong, around twenty-nine years old.

Q What kind of exercises would you recommend?

A Well, for me I just hit balls. I feel you're building your muscle memory. Your muscles are being worked a certain way, and they're being patterned. So, if you're doing exercises that break that pattern, you're just going against it. So I won't do any exercises that contradict the pattern. When I hit balls, of course, I don't just get up there and burn, burn, burn. I'm working definite muscle reactions. And I know my muscles; I've been doing this for a long time.

Q What do you find is the most difficult part of the game?

A It's the swing. When these guys get up and they do a video on trick shots, and they hit the ball here and there, that's not hard. If you've got the swing, you can do

anything. As long as you know you can hit the ball, then you can manipulate it and do what you want. The big thing is to have the control of the body so you know you can hit the ball.

Q Could you elaborate on the four components of the game?

A The four components are the course, the golf club, the ball, and the golfer. Three of those components do not move. They are inert. The golf club doesn't move; the ball doesn't move; and the course doesn't move. The only thing that moves is you. You're swinging the club, making it hit the ball, and navigating the golf course. You must take responsibility for your swing. No one else swings for you. Therefore, the emphasis of those four components is on you. Everybody says, well, "This is a tough course." Not so. Every course has a fairway; every course has a green; and if you hit the ball straight down the fairway and onto the green, it's an easy course. But if you hit the ball into the trees or into the water, it's a tough course. My slogan is "Nobody plays bad golf; they just hit the ball lousy."

Q Is there a particular way to build a golf stance?

A Look at pros. They'll all be standing differently. And that's their stance; that's how they get their body into position.

Q **What do you consider the basics?**

A The basics are that you have to be balanced and coordinated. That's why they say, "Oh, this guy looks weird" or "That guy has a bad position," or Palmer's swing looks wild." Baloney. They're all making the same swing, and they all come into the ball. If you stop them at contact, you'll see they all look the same.

Q **What is a "playing lesson?"**

A It's a lesson on the course where you play a round with a student. After people take lessons from the range they want to go out there and play the course. There's a lot of diversions out there, and they get confused. They're looking at the flag; they're coming off the ball; etc., and you want to keep them on the swing. So when they miss a shot, I'll ask them why, why did you come off that? Why didn't you keep your eye on the right side of the ball? Why were you looking at the flag? Or when they make a certain move, they'll come up under the ball instead of coming down on the ball. I'm there for their chipping and their putting. It's important to reaffirm their lesson out on the course. In a playing lesson, the person will really try to do what you're saying. In the lesson given on the range, there's no flag—they're just following the body action.

Q **So you shoot eighteen holes with this individual?**

A Yes.

Q **Aren't people actually hitting better and farther today?**

A Companies develop all kinds of clubs for the amateur, big heads and all that stuff. Basically what companies are doing now are cutting the loft of the club. Years ago, 11.5 was a natural 1-wood (driver). Now they're hitting 9° and 7°, which means the ball will have less of a high trajectory and go longer. So people think they're hitting farther. That may be true, but it's only because the clubface is changing.

Q **What about shaft materials such as graphite?**

A Graphite is only good for an arm swinger because it's a snappy club. Of course, they put steel in it, so it's no big deal. Graphite, remember, was a fishing rod, a Diawa. It was a flippy thing. If a guy was hitting with just his arms and hands, he would get a little more snap to it. But if you're swinging with your body, you can't swing graphite because that club will bend, and you'll never get a square face on the ball.

Q So you would recommend an aluminum shaft?

A Oh, yeah. When Nicklaus used to swing years ago he used a triple X, a very stiff shaft like a telephone pole. He didn't want that much play in it. His body was doing the snapping. You've got to understand, the power you get out of the club, the distance you get from it, comes from speed and mass.

Q Is equipment changing the game at all?

A Equipment is really not changing the game that much. It's like when cars had chrome, automobile manufacturers used to change the chrome every year, and that's what golf club manufacturers are doing today. What's really changing the game is that the younger players really know that they have to hit big, so you find everybody going for power now. Whereas years ago the average drive when I was coming up, was 238 yards, today it's 278. You've got these kids coming up and they're pounding away. You're going to get one kid out of the bunch who's going to be accurate, and he's going to be the star. In fact, this phenomenon is making courses passé. Years ago, when a guy would drive 238 he had a good long shot to the green. Today, watch the pros. Their second shot is almost always a 9-iron or a wedge. They're breaking open the courses. For an amateur it's okay because he's not going to drive that far. But for a pro, when they play on these wide-open courses, it's apple pie for them. They're reaching every par five in two. They should start out with a 68 par instead of a 72. But you know it looks good when pros shoot 32 and under.

Q Can you explain more about the club's being an extension of the hands?

A Yes. When you take tennis lessons, you're shown how to hold the racket by making believe you're shaking hands with it. Well, basically that's the way you should be holding a club. It's a very natural function. If you're holding a hammer, you're going to hold it so that when you bring your hand up, then bring it back down, the peen is going to hit the nail. You wouldn't put an overlapping grip on a hammer. Unfortunately, many instructors get students into grips without any rhyme or reason. It works fine for the pro. His hands will always adjust to compensate to grip the club. Hands are very sensitive, perhaps the most sensitive parts of the body. Trying to lock students' hands into a grip and all that, that's murder. I never give my students a grip.

Q On the other end of the swing, how important is the follow-through?

A The follow-through is only an indication of how your body is coming into the ball. It has nothing to do with the swing. Most instructors say hold your hands this way, and follow through this way, then maybe your body will come through properly. The follow through and the hands are just the result of the swing. So, instead of starting from the beginning, they start from the end and back up onto it. That's coming into the swing backwards. I once took instruction from a guy way back in the '50s, and he was making me follow through a certain way, no matter how I swung. So, I would swing, hit the ball badly, and follow through great. I'd take a practice swing, and he'd say, 'That's a beautiful swing.' I'd say, 'Yeah, but I can't hit the ball!' I call that the television swing. When you see an advertisement on TV and you see a guy hit golf balls, it's usually not a pro—it's usually an actor who looks like he or she can play. I know because I used to train them.

Q **I'm not a professional golfer, but I play one on TV . . .**

A (Laughs) Exactly. The agencies used to send me these guys who looked the part, but they needed training to play the part. I would give them these beautiful swing lessons for two-hour sessions for two days in a row, and they would imitate them. So that's why I called it a television swing. They couldn't hit a ball, but they looked like they could.

Q **Where do you teach now?**

A I run the Alternative Golf Workshop in Santa Monica, California. I also teach clinics for professionals in Maui, Hawaii. One of the guys who is a pro now at the Wilshire Country Club here in Los Angeles comes into my class in Santa Monica and works with me. He's a PGA pro. I met him in Hawaii. I do clinics there because the pros want to get into the things I teach. They say, 'Look, we teach the standard stuff, and we never get anybody to play well.' A lot of the pros know that what they're teaching doesn't get results, but there's no other way to go. I had a good reaction over there; a lot of them over there really dug it. Pros are open. They know that there's really a need for some kind of an answer and it isn't there yet. The folks in Maui want me to go over there and set up a school, but I don't want to live in Hawaii, even though the course there is beautiful.

Q **What drives you to keep teaching after all these years?**

A Part of human nature is that we're driven to solve problems, and this golf is a problem. It can really be a downer. Think of it, it's hard to take rejection when you go out on a golf course and shoot 120. Out of that 120 you probably had a good shot, which means you're taking 119 rejections. That's a hell of a beating on your ego. That's what really disturbs me. The average golfer is not a beatnik. He's not a guy who's down on his luck. This guy is usually a success, perhaps even a captain of industry. He belongs to a country club. He knows his way around, and this game beats the hell out of him. Here he is, top of the world. He goes out onto the course, and it drives him into the ground. This is a problem I want to solve.

EXERCISES FOR GOLF

Swinging a golf club requires many movements. Besides using your arms, wrists, and back, your hamstring muscles (located at the back inside of your thighs) and your trunk are used to complete a golf swing. Even your neck, which is supposed to keep your head still while you're swinging, snaps up after you've hit the ball to see where it's going. If these muscles are not properly warmed up and stretched, your game will be affected severely and by the end of the round, you'll be hurting. When you feel flexible, your game flows more easily. You shoot farther and are more accurate. Flexibility also improves your chances of preventing injuries. Many a golfer has lamented that they could not return to the course because of an injury. A large part of their life that they enjoyed so much was sidelined until they healed. Don't let this happen to you.

This chapter addresses stretching and resistance exercises. Before embarking on any exercise program we recommend you consult a physician. All these simple stretches can be done in your office or home and do not require any specific weights or equipment. Weights can be used as well, but we suggest you consult a gym or personal trainer to work out a specific program for you.

Warm up with the stretches, perform the manual-resistance exercises, then warm down with the stretching. Stretching alone can be done on your off days if you desire. A full routine will take you about thirty minutes. Throw on some of your favorite music and enjoy. This is work, but it's also fun and your game will most certainly improve.

Keep in mind that one can stretch incorrectly too. When performing the following exercises, do not bounce. Bouncing at one time was considered proper, but, it has been proven to be detrimental. Next, stretching can and should be done often. Try to stretch at least once a day. Finally, if you encounter pain, stop. Stretch until you feel a little tension, hold it for thirty seconds, then stretch as far as possible without causing pain and hold it for another thirty seconds.

KEEPING FIT FOR GOLF

EXERCISE 1: THE FRONT SHOULDER

Standing with your back to the doorjamb and with your arm at your shoulder's height, grip the door jamb with your thumb pointing up. Turn away from your outstretched arm. You should feel this stretch in the front of your shoulder. After you finish, perform the exercise with the other shoulder.

EXERCISE 2: THE REAR SHOULDER

Hold the inside of the doorjamb with your thumb pointing down and your toes pointing in the direction of the doorjamb. Lean away from the jamb, keeping your body straight and inside shoulder close to your outstretched arm. You should be feeling this stretch in the rear of your shoulder. To perform this stretch correctly you need to keep a straight body position when leaning.

EXERCISE 3: THE SHOULDERS AND THE ARMS

Face a wall, standing about an arm's length away from it. If this proves to be too far, start out by being closer to the wall and eventually work your way to an arm's length away. Reach your hands as high as you can and place them on the wall, leaning forward. Arch your back and press your shoulders toward the wall while not allowing your arms to bend. You should feel this stretch in the back side of the upper arms. With your hands up against the wall, as you arch your back your fingers should be upward.

EXERCISE 4: FINGER/WRIST AREA

Placing the palm side of your fingers in the palm of your opposite hand, pull your fingers backward. The sensation in this stretch is felt in the inside of the forearms. Switch hands and perform the stretch again. Loosening up the wrists is paramount to a good swing. Although this is a simple exercise, don't overdo it.

EXERCISE 5: THE BACK OF THE LEGS

Lie on your back with your legs straight. Lift a knee to your waist. With your opposite hand, grab the knee and pull it across your body, letting your body roll and your shoulder lift a couple of inches off the floor. You'll feel the stretch in your rear and outer thigh. Experiment by pulling your knee higher. This stretches different parts of your body. You can also pull your knee in different positions to stretch still other parts of your muscles.

5.

EXERCISE 6: THE INSIDE MUSCLES OF THE LEGS

Place the bottoms of your feet together while sitting up, reaching out to your ankles. At the same time, place your forearms on your legs so that your elbows more or less rest on your knees. Pull your ankles toward yourself. Carefully apply some pressure to feel the stretch inside your thighs and in the groin area. It's easy to pull a muscle here, so go easy. To gain a greater stretch, pull your ankles closer to the groin or simply press your knees to the floor.

6.

EXERCISE 7: THE SIDE OF YOUR TORSO

Point your toes toward the inside of the doorjamb. With your outside arm and thumb pointing downward, take hold of the doorjamb and lean away from it. This will make your body arch to the outside. Your body should be aligned with the doorjamb, with your inside shoulder near the arm that's outstretched. Done properly, you'll feel this stretch on the side of your torso. Now reverse arms and stretch the other side. To keep your balance you may need to place your feet outside the doorjamb, but remember to keep your feet pointing at the doorjamb.

7.

8.

9.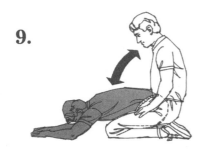

EXERCISE 8: THE STOMACH AREA

Lie on your stomach. Place your palms flat on the floor near your shoulders and push up until your arms are straight. Keep your hips close to the floor. Your back will arch, stretching your stomach muscles. Bend your arms and come back to the floor. Rest on your elbows if you find you cannot do the complete stretch from the floor. It is also a good idea to stretch your back before doing this exercise.

EXERCISE 9: THE LOWER-BACK AREA

With your knees on the floor, sit back on your heels. With your arms above you, lean forward and touch the floor in front of you. Do your best not to lift your hips. This can be a difficult stretch. Try this sitting in a chair.

TIMESAVING MANUAL-RESISTANCE EXERCISES

These exercises will help you the most when followed precisely. Slow, constant movement is the key to improving your physique. Any short cuts, such as applying more resistance to compensate for posture or procedure, will only hinder your ability to improve your strength. Done properly, these exercises will help you become fit in no time. These workouts are designed to improve your strength and stamina by focusing on specific muscle groups. This is accomplished by utilizing gravity and your body.

Perform ten repetitions, or reps, of each exercise, or five reps, take a brief break, then do five more to make up one set. When starting out, one set of each exercise will do. As you get stronger you can perform up to four sets. More sets than that really won't help much, so don't knock yourself out. In fact, chances are, more than four sets of each rep will start the mind wandering, and you'll probably lose track of where you were. Each rep should be carried out to a slow, comfortable count of three. Performing these reps three times a week is good. Twice a week is okay, but four times a week is optimal.

EXERCISE 1: HORIZONTAL PALM PRESS

With your elbows at shoulder height, press your palms together (your thumbs are pointed to your chin). While keeping the lower part of your torso still, push a little harder with one hand while still resisting with your other. When you reach the point just past the opposite shoulder of the hand pushing (your right hand pushes just past your left shoulder), increase the resistance from the less-resistant hand and push back to the other shoulder, reversing the first movement. This is considered one rep. Perform nine more to complete a set. For the exercise to be effective, it is essential to keep your lower torso as still as possible.

EXERCISE 2: THE FINGER CLASP

Clasp your fingers together in front of you at shoulder length, with one thumb up and one thumb down. Pull one hand more than the other across your body so that the opposite hand just passes the opposite shoulder, allowing your lower torso to slightly twist. Now reverse the resistance and pull the less-resistant hand to your other shoulder. Allowing your lower torso to slightly turn gives you the true full range of motion to make the exercise effective.

1.

2.

3.

EXERCISE 3: VERTICAL PALM PRESS

Place your palms together at chest level. Thumbs should be pointing outward. Resisting with the bottom hand, press downward with your top hand until you reach your waist. Bring your hands back up to chest level without resistance. Now change your hands so that the bottom one is on top and vice versa. Press down again with resistance to your waist and allow your hands to come back to chest level without resistance. Remember, each resistant motion is to a count of three. This exercise works best when the palms are as close as possible to the chest.

4.

EXERCISE 4: ROLLOVERS

Place your palms together at waist level, interlocking your thumbs while keeping your elbows at a 90° angle. With your top hand, push to one side by straightening out your elbow. Now take the hand that's under and slowly turn it over and push to the opposite side of your body, straightening the elbow out. Switch hands and proceed back to the other side. This movement simulates club takeaway and follow-through, so keep that picture in mind when performing this exercise.

5.

EXERCISE 5: SINGLE-LEG RAISE

Lie on your side with your legs slightly bent. With your toes pointing forward, raise your top leg and then slowly lower it. Perform this exercise ten times, then switch sides. It's important to keep your toes pointing forward to achieve the proper results from this exercise.

6.

EXERCISE 6: DOUBLE-LEG RAISE

Lie on your side while slightly bending your legs. With your toes pointing forward, raise your top leg and then bring up your other leg to meet it. Keep your arms folded in front of you. Slowly let your bottom leg return to the floor. Do ten reps, switch sides, then perform ten more. Keep your toes pointing forward while performing this exercise.

EXERCISE 7: ON YOUR SIDE

Lie on your side with your arms folded in front of you and your legs slightly bent. Lift your shoulders from the floor and slowly let them back down.

The muscles affected in this exercise are an integral part of the golf swing. If this exercise is too difficult, start by allowing your hand to press your body up from the floor.

EXERCISE 8: ABDOMINAL CRUNCHES

Lie on your back with your knees bent and pointed upward. Crossing your arms over your trunk, tuck your chin to your chest and lift your shoulder blades off the floor. Slowly lower your shoulder blades back to the floor. One can perform this exercise with different arm positions to affect different parts of the abdominals. Try putting your hands straight out behind your head and lifting them past your knees, or even placing your arms through your knees. The higher you lift your shoulder blades from the ground the stronger your abdominals become. Keep your lower back planted to the floor.

ADDITIONAL EXERCISES

HANDY WRIST EXERCISE

Hold a small, soft ball in the palm of your hand, squeeze it, and then bend (or cup) your wrist toward you. When you feel the pressure build in the forearm, stop. Let your wrist return, then perform the exercise again. Start with twenty-second intervals and increase the time gradually. Repeating this drill often will add strength to your wrists.

7.

8.

BRACE YOURSELF

Copper bracelets worn by many golfers are not a fashion statement, but are used to relieve pain in legs, backs, and fingers. How do they work? Copper acts as a natural anti-inflammatory and seems to help the whole body, not just the area where it's being worn.

Another popular bracelet worn on the tour is a six-metal alloy made by a company called Grupo Rayma of Spain. Rayma says the spheres on both ends of their bracelets conduct a type of electric current that creates more negative ions, restoring balance in the body and relieving pain. As far as the medical community is concerned, there is no basis of fact in this idea, and the manufacturers of these bracelets do not make any medical claims. Manufacturers say the proof is in the pudding.

And what pros are in the pudding? Well, the copper boys are Tom Kite, Vijay Singh, Justin Leonard, Vincente Fernandez, and Tim Herron to name a few. Tom Wargo and Fuzzy Zoeller prefer the metal-alloy breed, a bracelet that is gaining popularity. Beware, though, this jewelry is not a cure for the yips.

TAKE A WALK

Walking on the course keeps you warmed up. Hitting a shot, getting into a cart, sitting down, starting the cart up, driving to the golf ball, shutting the cart off, selecting more than one club, getting up, and walking over to your ball is both sedentary and distracting. Improve your score on the course. Walk it. It keeps you stretched, loose, and relaxed. It allows your mind to wander a bit too. It's great therapy and eases stress.

PREVENTING GOLF INJURIES

Believe it or not, injuries rather than old age end athletic careers. Once a body is injured, it heals itself by building up scar tissue. Scar tissue is tough and not very flexible. The good tissue under the scar tissue is taxed by unusual stress and is more susceptible to injury. As injuries increase over the same area, one gradually loses the ability to use that muscle. The best way to handle this problem is to prevent injuries from occurring in the first place. Approximately

70 percent of amateur golfers incur injuries to the back, elbow, wrists, knees, and shoulders during their golfing years. Why? According to sports-training professionals, it is due to lack of conditioning. Another contributing factor is the use of poor mechanics during the golf swing.

ON-COURSE DIET

Avoid foods high in sugar like candy bars and sodas. These foods tend to give you a quick high and then a crash. Find natural sugars in fruits and juices. Beer especially doesn't help your game when you're out on the links. The alcohol in it dries out the body and hampers your ability to play.

Between the 9th and 10th holes the body tends to fatigue. This is a good time to eat. Most golfers eat lunch at that point. If you want to keep on playing, that's fine, but do take a moment to ingest something. It will keep your blood sugar up and help your game.

GOLFERS AND HEART DISEASE

It has been significantly demonstrated that walking, even at a casual pace, reduces the risk of heart disease. It also helps reduce stress, a major contributor to heart disease. Some may contend that playing golf might increase one's anxiety if one plays poorly, but overall, walking the course is great for your heart. Walking and playing the links is an aerobic activity, and aerobic activity reduces bad (LDL) cholesterol and increases your HDL, a good cholesterol that scavenges the bad cholesterol. Walking also improves your muscle mass, burns off fat, and in the case of post-menopausal women, increases bone density.

Walking eighteen holes is equivalent to walking at least three miles. Of course, if you don't hit the ball straight all the time, you'll walk even more. You can use your poor shots as an excuse, claiming that you hit them on purpose to get more exercise.

MENTAL CROSSTRAINING

Professionals and amateurs agree that golf is a physical activity dominated by mental strategies. Unlike fast-paced sports where reflex, reaction, and quickness are often paramount to success, golf presents you with what often seems like an eternity between shots to think, rethink, and on occasion overthink your game. While other sports require a strategy versus an opponent, golf is a strategy against a course using one's own abilities.

THE MODERN MENTAL APPROACH: PRACTICE AND VISUALIZATION

The mental approach to the game has become the trademark of the new generation of golfers. Golfers are constantly trying to outthink, or at least keep pace with course designers who for years have been strategically laying out courses that test all aspects of a player's game.

To keep your mental game sharp, you need to practice not just your swing but visualizing your shot going where you want it to

go. Visualization is a helpful technique in setting up and readying yourself for the next shot. It is a mental process whereby you visually take in what is around you and mentally create the image of your shot going from where you are standing (and about to hit the ball) to the destination you would like to see it land. Picture the shot leaving the ground and watch it travel as though you were watching a video tape of your upcoming shot.

The best way to make practice work for your game is to make the practice area as similar to the course as you can. If you focus on each shot from that bucket of 100 balls as your first and only drive for the hole, you will take more time and concern over making that shot count. Conversely, if you've practiced with the same mental approach, you can easily step up to that first tee, or any tee, and tell yourself it's the same as the practice range. Some golfers even visualize the driving range around their ball as they tee off.

COURSE MANAGEMENT

Course management is a way of planning your trip around a course. It refers to thinking your game through in much the same way a football coach maps out a strategy before the weekend match. Naturally, just as a coach will become more familiar with an opponent after a few meetings, the more you play a particular course, the more familiar you will become with the various ways to play that course. But, it's to your advantage to familiarize yourself with the strengths and shortcomings of your own game. Silly as that may sound, many golfers are still unaware of their own strengths and weaknesses, or unwilling to admit their shortcomings.

One of the keys to course management is knowing how far away you are from the pin. Markers notwithstanding, your particular angle to the pin matters, as do wind and obstacles. If you know how far away you are, know which club is best for your game, and determine the lie accurately, you'll be able to spend a few extra seconds lining up the clubface and mentally watching the ball go where you want it to land.

SETTING UP YOUR ROUTINE

To make the thought process and physical activity of hitting the ball merge together most effectively, it is to your advantage to try to set up a routine. A smooth routine will enable you to relax and take away a lot of anxiety.

Watch the pros and see how they go through the motions with ease, not pressure. You can follow a similar routine for each and every shot.

First, do not rush up to the ball, especially if you've just zoomed over via electric cart. If that's the case, walk away from the ball and back; make sure to slow yourself down. Electric carts can speed up the round, but they also speed up your game and a hurried game is often not a well played one.

Stand behind the ball, judge the distance, look at the lie, and select a club. Pick a target a few feet in front of the ball, then select a desired target down the fairway. You might even imagine a line or clothesline connecting the two targets. Take a deep breath, take a practice swing or two, and imagine the ball going where you want it to go. Line up the clubface properly. Be aware of your body, knees, shoulders, and arms, as well as your hands on the club. Once everything feels comfortable, stop thinking and swing. The more you do a routine, the less you will have to think about it.

IT'S STILL A GAME, HONEST IT IS!

One of the most important things to keep in mind while putting together a routine and practicing your physical and mental approach to the game, is to remember that no matter how seriously you take it, golf is a game. When you have a bad day, enjoy the scenery; when you have a great hole, enjoy it, savor it. Golf is a game you can play for many years, but you may never master it. That's why you'll tell the tale of that one great round, or that ace, or another great moment on the course, time and time again.

"Golf is a game played within the space of six inches. Those are the six inches between your ears."

—Bobby Jones

Even the pros have their off days. That's why it's important to maintain a proper perspective, even while wrapping an unforgiving 9-iron around a tree. Golf can take you away from the real world. So why give yourself more stress and aggravation on the course?

Peter Jacobsen, after two poor rounds at the U.S. Open, commented that he was simply not going to let the game get to him, that he was going out to "Have some fun." So he proceeded into the next round, relaxed, feeling loose, and without concern for his scorecard fate. He proceeded to birdie five of the first six holes and shoot a course record of 64.

It's not easy to take the game with a grain of salt, especially when it looks so easy. It isn't ever going to be easy—it hasn't been for centuries, so just try to enjoy yourself.

TO THINK OR NOT TO THINK? THAT IS THE QUESTION.

It's important to try to focus on each shot. Don't focus on the last three shots, or foresee the upcoming hole. Just as every pitcher makes each pitch count and every pass by a quarterback is consequential, so is your every shot. The more significant each shot is, the less of them you'll have to make.

You can overanalyze, think out every movement carefully, and be successful; or just step up to the ball and hit it. But, since golf requires so many different skills and abilities, your best chance of being consistently successful is to find a comfortable balance between the two approaches. First determine in which direction you lean: analytical or impulsive. If you can ascertain which side your personality leans toward, you can compensate on the course.

Are you the golfer who dares take the short cut through the trees, or the one who takes an extra shot and plays it safely around the dog leg? The daring, low-percentage shot can gain you a birdie or a ten, while the safe way yields a par or a bogey. The good course manager knows when to take the risk and when to play it safe. Factor in the way you've been hitting, the weather—especially the wind—and how much you have wagered on the hole. Sometimes your decision will be made for you by watching your partner's ball smash into a mighty oak and careen down a 200-foot ravine.

On the other hand, there are times you might want to try a new adventure. If you play the same course often, try playing it in different ways and see which works best for you. On an unfamiliar course you are probably best playing the safe route.

DECISIONS

Your mission in golf is to make decisions that you feel comfortable with in terms of lining up the shot, judging the distance, deciding where your target is, and so on. You need to make these decisions rather quickly, then let the physical side take over. Let reflective, analytical thinking take you only so far, then switch gears and swing. There's a point at which some golfers actually tell themselves, "Okay, stop thinking so much and hit it."

HAZARDS

Don't let hazards intimidate you. If you can't get around or over the hazard, sneak up on it. Sometimes playing it safe is better than playing it sandy.

Teeing the ball up on the left to avoid a hazard on the right is a great idea, and vice versa. However, if you know that you slice or hook more often than you hit the ball straight, take that into account. As for bunker shots, take some time to determine the depth of trouble you're in. Consider the lie of the ball, the amount of sand between the ball and the lip of the bunker, and the amount of green between the ball and the hole. If the ball is sitting up, you have a much easier situation than if the ball is buried so deep that in the process of hitting it you may strike oil. Sometimes you can plan your escape, while other times the best thing to do is just get out, no matter how or where.

THE RAIN, THE WIND, AND OTHER THINGS

Weather is a factor in golf, as are well-watered fairways and greens. The mental approach also means taking into consideration every step you take that produces a sloshing sound. Wet grass will slow up any roll you might have anticipated. Keep the conditions in mind as you play, and don't let them frustrate you since they are out of your control. One of the biggest mental hazards of golf is the idea that you can control everything on the course. You cannot. Therefore it's important to let that anxiety-provoking idea leave you from the onset. If you are playing on a damp or windy day, know from the moment you point your car toward the course, that this might not be your best round.

The mental approach for playing in the wind says to swing smoothly and in balance and don't try to overpower the wind. You can't outswing it, so as the old saying goes, when it's breezy, swing easy.

THE APPROACH

The approach we talk about here is not the approach to your shot, but to the course. Since your tee-off time does not always allow for a leisurely approach to the course, you have to mentally develop a way of taking yourself from the outside world onto the golf course. Once you see the majestic scenery of the fifth or sixth hole, the gentle brook, or the lake in which you've deposited a ton of balls, or you hear the birds chirping while you wait to tee off, the course itself will take you away from the real world. Golf can do that simply by the sheer beauty of the environment in which the game is played. But how can you more deliberately break from the real world and enter the world of golf?

Practical solutions include doing something relaxing just before going to the course or even in the car while driving to the course. For example, you may put on some relaxing music. Define what relaxes you and use a few minutes to focus on that particular area. Prior to relaxing you might clear your head by using a pad of paper and a pen, or a portable voice recorder to take down all the pertinent information that you are grappling with in other areas of your life. Note the office "TO DO" list or other plans, errands, or work-related activities and let the paper or tape recorder hold on to them so you can clear your mind and focus on relaxing. Some golfers like to find a few minutes before going on the course to simply close their eyes and picture the course they are playing.

Relaxation gives you an acceptable transition into the golf mindset. Once you are there you can allow yourself to get psyched up and excited about your day on the course. A little apprehension about stepping up to the first tee is only normal. Even the pros have some butterflies in their stomach. Different players will reach different levels of excitement. Some players can play at their best when they are revved up, while others must be in a more tranquil state of mind.

It's also important that your expectations be reasonable. If you've just watched a PGA tournament on television on Saturday and you, an 18-handicap golfer, expect to go out and hit like the pros, you're setting yourself up for a major letdown. Know your skill level. If you play once a week, you won't be as proficient as the golfer who plays three or four times a week. If, unfortunately, you can't get out to the course more often because of other responsibilities, then

accept that you'll be as good as you can be for an occasional golfer.

The same holds true for various clubs. If you've convinced yourself that you can't hit with a 3-wood, then you won't. If you tell yourself that just the way you became proficient with a 5- or a 7-iron, you will master the 3-wood, then you can learn to hit with it.

Also expect that much of what you do in a day on the course won't be to your liking. That's what makes the game so challenging and so tough. If the average golfer has a few good shots in a day, then he or she should focus on those, recount them fondly, and forget the rest. Conversely, pros will focus on their three or four bad shots in a day, because they are in a very tight competition and those few shots will make or break their chances of winning.

If you are in any type of competition, it should be one that is not over your head. Assess your handicap, which will help balance out the field, and play within your game.

The bottom line is to set up realistic expectations and not to create fears and myths about your game. If you believe it, you will make it a self-fulfilling prophecy. Be honest with yourself about your game, and you'll enjoy the game more and will probably improve because you'll know what level you are at and what level you are moving toward.

This is not to say that the average golfer should not venture onto a course that challenges low handicappers. You want to feel what it's like to play on the tougher courses.

CONCENTRATION

A downfall of many golfers is their inability to concentrate.

It's important to practice with distractions. They are part of the game and not the exception. The person who can study for an exam with the radio on is used to having the distraction and has learned to tune it out. The golfer who becomes used to sounds and various distractions will be able to concentrate through them.

Concentrating is a matter of mind control and focus. If the scenery or other distractions are allowed to take away that focus, you will not be able to concentrate on your game. It's a matter of zeroing in on what you are doing and taking yourself away from everything else when necessary. It does not, however, mean playing in a trance. Concentration works best when it is applied at the right times.

STRESS MANAGEMENT

We've all seen someone throw a club; sometimes we've been the club tosser ourselves. So what does one do to control anger on the course? Roll with the course, don't fight with it. If you get frustrated easily, golf will drive you crazy. It's hard to maintain your composure on a day when every hole becomes a new and creative nightmare. If you can keep your cool and go with the flow, you'll be better off. That's easier said than done. There are occasions where you simply have to let it out, but try to keep them to a minimum. You'll play better if you approach the first shot after a bad one as the beginning of the rest of your game. You might even draw a line on the scorecard and tell yourself the day begins there. Give yourself a fresh start as many times as necessary, but keep the faith.

There are several manners in which to defuse anger while on the course. Walking off anger, trying to feel it leaving your body through your feet or your head may work. Humor is often a great way of diffusing anger. Joke about the shot, the game, the course, the cart, or the caddie, but filter your frustration through something funny.

If you need a place to vent anger, wash the ball in the ball washer with added vigor or carry an old rolled-up pair of socks or some similar benign, harmless object to pound or squeeze. The important thing is to diffuse your anger before your next shot, or it will take over your game. As anger builds, so does your score.

BREATHING AND RELAXATION

It may sound odd, but it's important to remember to breathe before your shots. Too often, tension and anxiety result in short breaths or rapid breathing. A deep, cleansing breath is important for relaxation, for setting your sights on the desired goal, and for clearing the mind from other passing thoughts. It will also break your flow of bad breathing that will lead to bad shots. Taking in air will invigorate and wake you up.

Full relaxation exercises may not work well on the golf course, as there aren't too many places to lie down without someone running a cart over you. While watching others hit, you may try relaxing parts of the body that affect your game. Try tensing up and then relaxing the muscles in your arms and legs. Loosen up your neck and shoulder muscles and then relax your mind as well. One of the nicest aspects of golf is that the marvelous scenery that surrounds most courses can give you a nice diversion and take your mind away from everything else, even the pressures you are putting on yourself regarding your game.

Another relaxation technique is to picture something else on the course. Visualize something soothing, something that makes you smile. A brief daydream, particularly a tranquil or funny one, can relax you.

JITTERS AND INTIMIDATION

Water jitters, first-hole jitters: golfers commonly are intimidated and develop performance anxiety in these areas. Water and other hazards are a challenge that one needs to surmount to conquer the hole. You cannot hit a bad shot and get away with its rolling 150 yards to the green when a lake is in the way. And, whereas you may not have hit such a ground ball in years, the lake makes you think about it, just as standing on a fifty-sixth floor terrace makes you think about how high up you really are. And that is what hazards, bunkers, tree-lined fairways, and breaks in the green are all about. They make you use your skills, but more importantly, they make you think about the potential consequences.

The trick, and it's not easy, is to mentally remind yourself of the physical activity you have done so many times before. If you know you can hit the ball straight 200 yards, then the woods on either side of you should not be a factor. If you know you can comfortably hit a 9-iron and reach the green, then the water that sits between you and that green should not be a factor. The trick is to block out what interferes with your game. The anxiety is only valid if it is something that is not within your range as a golfer. If you cannot overcome the lake, then you must devise a strategy to sneak up on it and clear it on the second shot, or find a way through the rough around it.

First-hole jitters are a special, very common concern. The butterflies are in your stomach because you are just starting out. It is the first swing of the day, and you have people watching you. It's important that you take the first swings of the day on the practice tee and consider the first tee shot as your follow-up swing. Focus on the fact that you have already comfortably swung the club. As for the gallery, you

DR. STERN, GOLF THERAPIST

Dr. Stern has made a sixty minute audio tape called _Cerebral Golf_, and has worked with numerous golfers, often taking three to six weeks to alleviate their mental golf-related problems. She's not only helping people, but says she really loves the game and finds the mental aspects fascinating.

"My approach is a psychological practical approach in terms of skill, such as overcoming performance anxiety in a certain area, like on the first tee," explains Dr. Frances Meritt Stern of the Institute for Behavioral Awareness in Springfield, New Jersey. "A lot of people are thinking disaster on the first tee. They think about people watching, that they have to do well, about starting off well, and that this hole is such a misery. Many people have difficulty on the first hole."

Dr. Stern refocuses them, working to stop the current thought process and replace such thoughts with neutral thoughts and even non-golf thoughts. She wants the golfer to keep in mind that if he or she can physically hit the ball five times the same way, physiologically the same person can hit it 5,000 times. Therefore the first tee shot should be no different than the other 4,999 shots. "I work with people who are fairly good players seeking a competitive edge. They want to get

better, but their psychological state, anxiety, and tension is getting in the way of what they can physically accomplish."

Besides first-tee anxiety, Dr. Stern, who quite often walks the course with her patients, notes putting as a point of tension and mental fatigue. "When it comes to putting, it's common to think the hole is very convoluted when it's not. People tend to look for greens to be more difficult than they are. They over-think the hole, so I tell them what the pro told me when I was learning to play. He said that 'everything is a straight line in a sense.' I ask them to really look at the lay of the land, try to understand where the straight line might be, and get them to practice putting by thinking it through, closing their eyes, and putting. More times than not, once they've seen it and truly evaluated what the putt really is, they tend not to over- or undershoot."

Dr. Stern believes that if you get a good feel for putting and don't crowd your mind with "the garbage," you'll improve. "Start with the idea that everything is a straight line, or at least 80 percent of the time it is," she adds. As for overshooting, says Stern, "It's two extra strokes, one because you're pissed and two to correct it."

know you'll do just fine on the second tee, where it's just you and your cohorts. So think of the first tee as the second tee, and that no one is around. Even top pros have first-hole jitters.

BUT WHAT WILL OTHERS THINK?

Beyond the first tee, there are concerns about what other people will think and say about you. Golf very much encompasses a sense of pride and demonstrates one's abilities. It is a test of one's manhood and womanhood. More often than not, the other golfers around you are far more focused on their own games than they are on yours. Just as you aren't really thinking about how well they are doing, in a friendly outing, they aren't focused that intensely on how you are doing. And if they are, because you are in a friendly competition, in most cases, once it's over, they'll be focused on their own great shots of the day and not your bad ones.

Daily-fee golf, with its new-found popularity, also creates a new form of intimidation: playing in a foursome with strangers. It's important that you establish from the outset that you are a casual golfer, not very good . . . unless, of course, you are a scratch golfer. Downplay

your abilities, but approach the situation so that you have nothing to prove. Chances are, the other golfers are not much better or worse than you are. If they are better, compliment their game. Ask advice if they are friendly. If they do not play as well as you, do not volunteer advice; you were once at that level too.

EXCUSES, EXCUSES, EXCUSES

The United States has around 15,000 golf courses. There are probably an equal number of popular excuses heard on courses coast to coast. Excuses are a part of life. They may serve to alleviate the immediate situation, but when you begin to use excuses as an out for everything that goes wrong and you begin blaming things such as the weather conditions, which are out of your control, you are only setting yourself up for more aggravation.

Don't become a golfer who finds an excuse for everything that happens on the course. Let some of what happens simply happen, for better or worse. It's a tough game, and nobody said you have to be the one to conquer it.

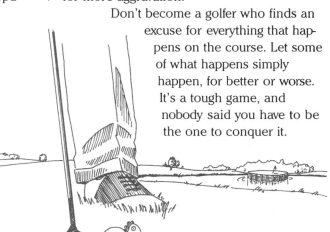

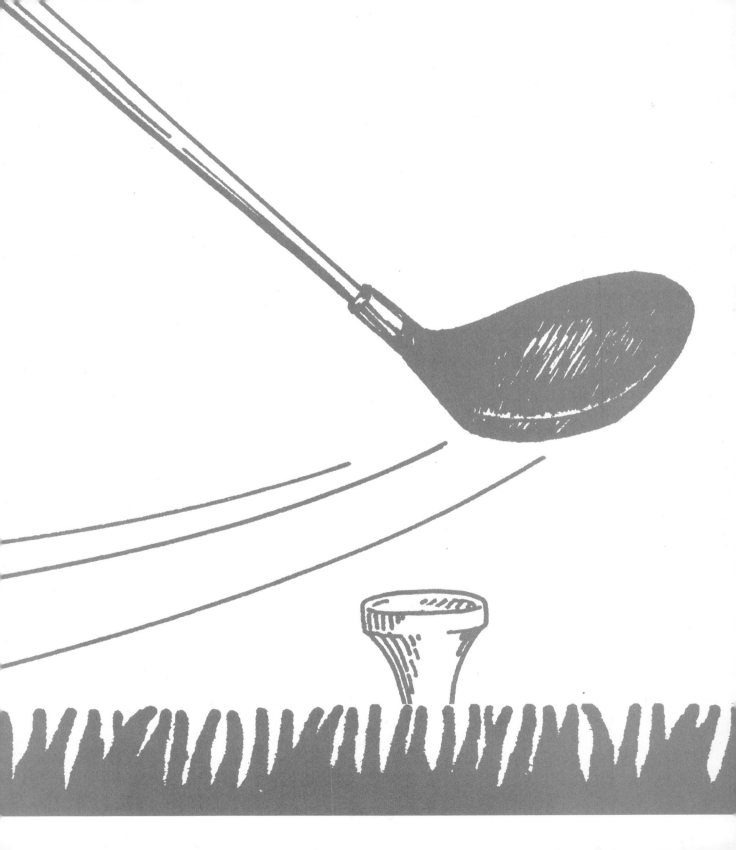

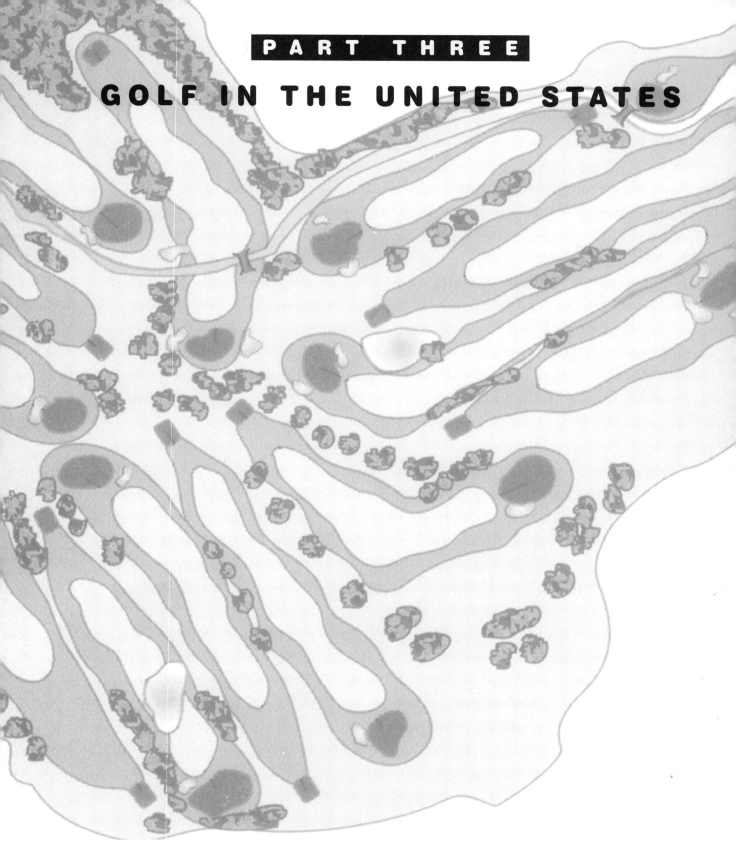

PART THREE
GOLF IN THE UNITED STATES

THE FINEST GOLF RESORTS IN AMERICA

The sign reads: A VERY VERY FINE GOLF RESORT

Some of the top resorts in the United States, are prominently known for golf.

This extensive course section lists and posts comments on most of the resort courses listed. Nonetheless, these are some of the top resorts in the country, featuring fine food, entertainment, health spas, tennis, and a host of other amenities designed to take your mind off your main concern: GOLF!

Resorts run the gamut from state-of-the-art modern highrise complexes to quaint old-fashioned homesteads or plantation houses on sprawling acres. One thing golf resorts have in common is that they are surrounded by vast amounts of land . . . at least enough acreage for one golf course and in many cases two or more.

Golf resorts often have practice tees, putting greens, and marvelous clubhouse facilities. Guests are given preference in regard to tee times as well as greens fees and equipment rentals. Golf pros, sometimes PGA pros, are often on hand to give lessons and provide important tips to improve your game.

Some resorts offer golf packages (in areas of dense course population) whereby guests can stay at one hotel and enjoy the other courses in the vicinity. In areas such as Myrtle Beach, one may want to explore other resort courses and should inquire about deals and rates offered.

Below are twenty-five of the top-rated golf resorts in the United States offering the game and much more. There are many others to choose from, especially in highly popular, year round travel destinations such as Hawaii, Florida, and Arizona, with similar amenities to those listed below. They all offer activities and fine service, but most of the finest resorts also have a character and ambiance all their own. There are also many extravagant resorts throughout the world that feature top-rated courses. Some are built by United States–based hotel conglomerates, while others are part and parcel of the countries in which they were built. More resorts are listed in the international section.

25 OF THE BEST GOLF RESORTS IN THE UNITED STATES

The Arizona Biltmore in Phoenix

The Arizona Biltmore in Phoenix is a classic old-style resort that has been completely renovated since its 1929 opening. Featured at this award-winning property are several top-rated restaurants, various health and sports facilities and, of course, golf.

The Lodge at Ventana Canyon in Tucson

The Tom Fazio–designed course is very scenic. The Lodge at Ventana Canyon in Tucson is a sports resort in the mountains. The views are breathtaking, and there are many athletic activities to indulge in.

Scottsdale Princess in Scottsdale, Arizona

The Scottsdale Princess in Scottsdale, Arizona, is home to the Phoenix Open (a PGA event). This spectacular 600-room resort sits on 450 acres, has two courses for golf, and has spectacular meals. Plus there are three heated pools, a health club, and a spa!

The Lodge at Pebble Beach, California

The Lodge at Pebble Beach, California, is one of the top-rated resorts in the world. It offers a host of amenities and superb service. Sitting on the Monterey Peninsula, the views are amazing. The golf is first rate, and the food ranks right up there too.

La Quinta Resort and Club, California

The La Quinta Resort and Club in La Quinta is one of the best resorts in the state and in the country. This marvelous mountain retreat has been around since the 1920s.

The Broadmoor in Colorado Springs, Colorado

The Broadmoor in Colorado Springs, Colorado, has been accommodating guests for more than eighty years in some 700+ rooms in grand style. The Broadmoor offers everything from skeet shooting to hot air ballooning, plus a theater, shopping, and nine restaurants. This is a landmark hotel resort with three top courses.

The Peaks at Telluride, Colorado

The Peaks at Telluride, also in Colorado, is a relatively new golf resort in a fabulous mountain setting, offering the latest in amenities, including three pools, a European

health spa, fabulous food, and of course, golf!

Boca Raton Resort and Club, Boca Raton, Florida

The Boca Raton Resort and Club, Boca Raton, Florida, has a hefty 963 rooms, five pools, shopping, fabulous beachfront views, and challenging golf. The resort, some seventy years old, is as spectacular as ever.

The Doral Golf Resort and Spa in Miami, Florida

The Doral Golf Resort and Spa in Miami, Florida, has 699 rooms including 106 suites, plus a spectacular health spa, tennis, entertainment, and great dining. What more do you need—five golf courses and the warm weather of Miami!

Sawgrass Marriott at Ponte Vedra Beach, Florida

Sawgrass Marriott at Ponte Vedra Beach, Florida, is one among a number of spectacular Marriott properties throughout the country. Sawgrass has everything, featuring numerous villas along miles of beach, with lakes galore and all sorts of activities including five golf courses!

Kapalua Bay Hotel and Villas in Maui, Hawaii

Kapalua Bay Hotel and Villas in Maui, Hawaii, is one of many resorts in Hawaii—all of which feature natural beauty, spectacular beaches, native ambiance, sports and health facilities, fine food, and great golf. Kapalua is one of the finest, featuring three golf courses, along with three private beaches and three oceanview restaurants.

The Hyatt Regency in Kauai, Hawaii

The Hyatt Regency in Kauai, Hawaii, is one of several Hyatt properties. This one exemplifies Hawaii, with 600 rooms on the beach with ocean views. There are five places to dine and to cool off, and five acres of watersport activities. Plus the golf is first rate.

The Coeur d'Alene Resort in Coeur d'Alene, Idaho

The Coeur d'Alene Resort in Coeur d'Alene, Idaho, is a 358-room $60 million first-class resort with a host of watersport activities ranging from boating to skiing, plus, of course, golf on a picturesque course. The resort is considered among the best in the Midwest.

Eagle Ridge Inn and Resort at Galena, Illinois

The Eagle Ridge Inn and Resort at Galena, Illinois, is nearly 7,000 acres.

Accommodations include several four-bedroom homes. All sorts of activities are offered, including an equestrian course.

Grand Traverse Resort in Acme, Michigan

Grand Traverse Resort in Acme, Michigan is one of several marvelous Michigan resorts featuring skiing in the winter and golf in the summer. The range here is from plenty of hunting to plenty of shopping to water skiing and two golf courses.

Izatys Golf and Yacht Club in Onamia, Minnesota

The Izatys Golf and Yacht Club in Onamia, Minnesota, is a luxury resort offering a range of activities from snowmobiling and ice fishing in winter, to boating from their 120-slip marina and golfing on their Pete Dye course in warmer months.

The Balsams Grand Resort in Dixville Notch, New Hampshire

The Balsams Grand Resort in Dixville Notch, New Hampshire, is an old-fashioned luxury resort. Built in 1866, this is classic New England, with great food, and the beautiful scenery of all four seasons.

Marriott's Seaview Country Club Resort at Abescon, New Jersey

Marriott's Seaview Country Club Resort at Abescon, New Jersey provides a highly rated resort experience just outside of the frantic pace of Atlantic City. From fine dining, to the health and fitness center, to tennis and golf, this is a first-rate resort.

Pinehurst Resort in Pinehurst, North Carolina

Pinehurst Resort in Pinehurst, North Carolina is a 500-room luxury resort that offers everything from exquisite dining to a sports lake, gun club, and concierge services. Offering old southern charm and accommodations ranging from hotel suites to villas, Pinehurst is heaven for golfers. Besides the legendary courses, there's even a golf school.

The Grove Park Inn Resort in Asheville, North Carolina

The Grove Park Inn Resort in Asheville, North Carolina, is one of the South's oldest and most famous grand resorts. The spacious facility offers massive fireplaces, Old World Charm, and exceptional hospitality. Many of the 510 rooms overlook the golf course.

Kiawah Island Resort on Kiawah Island in South Carolina

Kiawah Island Resort on Kiawah Island in South Carolina offers 300 villas in which to relax after a day on one of the four courses and an evening of exquisite dining. Besides the birdies you hope to see on the course, there is a wide array of wildlife around the island, from bald eagles to dolphins.

The Resorts at Hilton Head, South Carolina

Equally spectacular in their own right are the Hyatt Regency Hilton Head, with 72 holes of golf; a three-mile private beach; Palmetto Dunes Resort, with five courses designed by top designers and featuring 500 villas; and the Sea Pines Resort, with three courses, deep-sea fishing, seven restaurants, and 400 villas. The Hilton Head resorts, and there are a few others, have marinas, and fabulous beaches and are top rated.

Barton Creek Conference Resort in Austin, Texas

The Barton Creek Conference Resort in Austin, Texas, is a 147-room layout that is well known throughout the state for its championship courses. In the suburbs of Austin, Barton Creek offers a rare European health spa in the middle of Texas and seven distinct restaurants.

The Hyatt Regency Hill Country Resort in San Antonio, Texas

The Hyatt Regency Hill Country Resort in San Antonio, Texas, sits on 200 acres, and features an Arthur Hill golf course, first-rate service and amenities, and a 950-foot rafting river. The 500-room property is one of the state's finest resorts.

The Equinox Hotel & Resort in Manchester Village, Vermont

The Equinox Hotel & Resort in Manchester Village, Vermont, sits among the mountains and provides classic New England grandeur along with the latest in health-spa and fitness facilities. Nearby the 163-room landmark sits the 18-hole Gleneagles course.

50 STATES OF
GOLF COURSES

he United States has nearly 15,000 golf courses. From hundred-year-old classics to the more recent state-of-the-art courses, the United States has every type of course imaginable. Courses are designed through forests, around lakes, on marsh lands, in deserts, and even on inactive volcanoes. Courses are even built on landfills. With the environmental concerns growing, courses are also being built to preserve wildlife and provide green belts. There are those with gimmicks such as re-creations of classic holes, mountainous courses, woodsy New England favorites, wide open Midwestern layouts, and old links-style gems. Target golf courses are popular, as are the desert courses in Arizona and parts of California. If variety is the spice of life, it's also the signature of golf courses throughout the United States.

From championship-caliber to the basic simple layout for the Sunday golfer, the courses run the gamut in style, design, and price. In Florida or Pebble Beach you can pay $250 to play, while in the Midwest there are courses to be played for $8 to $10. That's the beauty of golf and its many courses, variety!

Courses today also offer golfers a look at every kind of background scenery imaginable, from quarries to majestic mountain ranges to breathtaking waterfalls. Wherever there's a lake, a stream, or an ocean, you can be sure a nearby course has some player agitated because he or she has just landed a ball in it. Some of the most picturesque spots in America are found on the golf courses.

The extensive list below features many highly rated courses culled from journalists, top players, magazines, casual golfers, architects, and other sources. It is designed to point you in the direction of a fairway in every section of the country.

Some of these courses require you to stay in a hotel, while others mean joining a club, or at least being the guest of someone who belongs. To play on others, you need only sign up and set your sights on the first flag. There is an emphasis on public and daily-fee courses. Daily-fee courses are public courses, as are municipal city courses and those in state parks. Other semi-private courses allow you to play during the week or at other designated times.

From Albany to Zanesville, we tried to pull together a smattering of courses within a reasonable distance of anywhere in America. And in case you're wondering, Florida beats California as the state with the most golf courses. Together, their courses combine for close to 2,000. Alaska, meanwhile, has the fewest courses, followed by Delaware.

Greens fees, membership fees, and other regulations regarding play vary greatly, so it's advised that you call the course for its golfing specifics. Prices may also vary.

Country-club courses are not always easy to get on, but don't be discouraged. The most determined golfers have found a way to play the courses on their wish list. Rumor has it that one golfer even married the club owner's daughter just to have a chance to play the club's course.

EVERYTHING GOLF'S BIG COURSE LIST

ALABAMA

▷ Eagle Point Golf Club, Birmingham, Alabama
Stay alert: the first four holes are very close together. Highly rated short course, popular with older golfers. Fabulous mountain view and only $19–$20 to play.

▷ Oxmoor Valley Golf Course, Birmingham, Alabama
Oxmoor offers three courses, including a tough Valley Course, Ridge Course, and short course. Short, tough par-three course, and two 7,000+ yarders feature some good target golf.

Still Waters Resort, Dadeville, Alabama

▷ Rock Creek Golf Club, Fairhope, Alabama
Still pretty new (1993), this course has hills, woods, and a host of bunkers to contend with. It's well planned and only fifteen minutes from Mobile.

Cotton Creek Club, Gulf Shores, Alabama
Well-manicured, this is an Arnold Palmer–designed course. Great layout. Twenty-seven holes are available since 1987 opening. Worth the price: $36–$48.

▷ Gulf State Park Golf Course, Gulf Shores, Alabama
Good course for all golfers, but watch the gators. Very popular state-park course, so plan ahead.

Kiva Dunes Golf Club, Gulf Shores, Alabama

▷ Lake Guntersville Golf Course, Guntersville, Alabama
Great well-kept state-park course, complete with water and lots of wildlife. Only $14. Bring a camera for some great scenic photos and be careful reading the greens.

▷ Grand National Golf Club, Opelika, Alabama
Grand National features three excellent courses: the challenging Lakes Course, the scenic and very demanding Links Course, and the highly rated but more reasonable short par-three course. About an hour from Montgomery, and it runs $20–$32.

Goose Pond Colony Golf Course, Scottsboro, Alabama
Very scenic course in northern part of the state. Plenty of water and plenty of geese.

ALASKA

Anchorage Golf Course, Anchorage, Alaska
This is one of the best in a state that has less than twenty. A good tree-lined, tight course with four water holes.

▷ Eagleglen Golf Club, Anchorage, Alaska

Chena Bend Golf Club, Fairbanks, Alaska

▷ North Star Golf Course, Fairbanks, Alaska

▷ Palmer Municipal Golf Course, Palmer, Alaska

▷ **PUBLIC COURSES**

▷ Moose Run Golf Course, Richardson, Alaska

Built by the Army Corps in the '50s, this course sees over 40,000 rounds played annually, many in May when the days are twenty-one hours long. Ever play at 10 P.M. outdoors?

ARIZONA

The Boulders Club, Carefree, Arizona
Top-rated desert course about forty minutes from Phoenix.

Desert Forest Golf Club, Carefree, Arizona
Another top-rated desert course.

Forest Highland Golf Course, Flagstaff, Arizona

▷ Sedona Golf Resort, Flagstaff, Arizona
This is one of the most beautiful courses in the world. It features long, difficult par fours and a kidney-shaped green. About two hours from Phoenix.

Sun Ridge Canyon Golf Course, Fountain Hills, Arizona
Less well known, good course. It's nice to hear water in the name.

▷ Superstition Springs Golf Club, Mesa, Arizona
Don't let the thirteenth spook you at the Superstition course. Course is well planned, and water comes into play on half of the holes. Features challenging par threes. About thirty minutes from Phoenix.

Los Cebelleros Golf Club, Phoenix, Arizona
One of the top seventy-five resort courses according to Golf Digest *magazine. Features lush Bermuda fairways. A favorite among golfers in the area. The 598-yard par 5 thirteenth should challenge you.*

▷ Maryvale Golf Course, Phoenix, Arizona

▷ Stonecreek Golf Course, Phoenix, Arizona

▷ Asu Karsten Golf Course, Scottsdale, Arizona
Pete Dye–designed course welcomes Ping clubs, as it's named after the founder of Ping. Challenging course in the scenic valley.

Desert Highlands Golf Club, Scottsdale, Arizona
Yet another top-rated desert course.

▷ Tournament Players Club of Scottsdale, Scottsdale, Arizona
Built in 1987, TPC has two 18-hole layouts, with the Stadium Course ranked very highly. Picturesque scenery and plenty of room for friends and relatives to watch your game from stadium-seating facilities. Desert Course is a good, shorter course.

▷ Troon North Golf Club, Scottsdale, Arizona
Two picturesque, very highly rated courses near base of Pinnacle Peak Mountain. Lots of cactus. Senoran Desert just a slice away . . . talk about a sand trap! The Mountain Course gives golfers a wide range of options.

La Paloma Country Club, Tucson, Arizona
Twenty-seven-hole Jack Nicklaus–designed course(s) with a beautiful mountain view. Long par fours on this desert course.

Ventana Golf & Racquet Club, Tucson, Arizona

▷ Tournament Players Club at Starpass, Tucson, Arizona
Fast bent-grass greens, desert sand, horseshoe-shaped fifteenth green, junior Olympic swimming pool with spa. What else do you need?

ARKANSAS

▷ Degray State Park Golf Course, Bismark, Arkansas
Lots of hills, nice scenery. Starts more open then becomes tighter as you play. Inexpensive too!

Mountain Range Golf Course, Fairfield Bay, Arkansas
Front nine open with rolling fairways; back nine tight with lots of southern trees, dogwoods. Over seventy bunkers on the course.

▷ Ben Geren Regional Park Golf Course, Fort Smith, Arkansas
Popular, wide-open course with some water. One of the better public courses in the state

The Red Apple Inn and Country Club, Heber Springs, Arkansas

Hot Springs Country Club, Hot Springs, Arkansas
Two classic old courses, both enjoyable, just over an hour from Little Rock.

Pleasant Valley Country Club, Little Rock, Arkansas

▷ Burns Park Golf Club, North Little Rock, Arkansas

▷ Prairie Creek Country Club, Rogers, Arkansas

The Course at River Oaks, Searcy, Arkansas
Lakes, streams, bent-grass greens, scenery, and nearby trout fishing.

Dawn Hill Golf Club, Siloam Springs, Arkansas

Texarkana Country Club, Texarkana, Arkansas

CALIFORNIA

Bodega Harbour Golf Links, Bodega Bay, California
Concentrate or you'll forget your game and get lost in the magnificent ocean view. Front nine has been known to really test skills; back nine gives you a little reprieve. Tricky, interesting layout and one of the top-ranked courses in the northern part of the state.

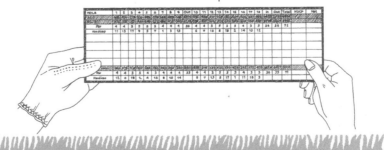

Carmel Valley Ranch, Carmel, California

Aviara Golf Club, Carlsbad, California
Very highly rated Palmer/Seay Southern California course. Five tee-off options, large greens, great scenery, and half an hour from San Diego.

Lawrence Welk's Desert Oasis Country Club, Cathedral City, California
Two courses: one nine, one eighteen. Lots of water, probably from the champagne bubbles. Not far from Palm Springs; not overly expensive either.

▷ Coronado Golf Course, Coronado, California
Inexpensive, forty-year-golf-old course. Flat, fun, and a chip shot from San Diego.

▷ Desert Dunes Golf Course, Desert Hot Springs, California
Excellent Robert Trent Junior links-style desert course. Fun, but "Everyone knows it's Windy."

Fall River Valley Golf and Country Club, Fall River Mills, California
Highly rated by Golf Digest, *this little-known northern-California course is 7,300+ yard long, featuring a 666-yard "devilish" par-five third. Great scenic course as well.*

▷ Day Creek Ranch Golf Course, Galt, California
Less than a half hour from Sacramento, this very popular public course is well kept and demands accuracy.

▷ Sandpiper Golf Course, Goleta, California

▷ Castle Oaks Golf Club, Ione, California
Water, a double fairway, five sets of tees—this course pulls out all the stops. New course, becoming better known, not far from Sacramento . . . check it out.

▷ Torrey Pines Golf Courses, La Jolla, California

PGA West Resort, La Quinta, California
Both the Jack Nicklaus Resort Course and PGA West challenge all your golfing skills.

The Quarry, La Quinta, California
Not much water here, but along with PGA West, one of the highest-ranked desert courses in the state by The Golfer *magazine.*

La Purisima Golf Course, Lompoc, California
Very tough, very windy, not very expensive. Practice first.

Silverado Country Club and Resort, Napa, California
Thirty-six-hole complex is a challenging course at all competitive levels. The North Course is hillier, but the South Course has more long par fives.

▷ Chardonnay Golf Club, Napa, California
This public-access course is deep in the heart of Napa wine country, so if your game isn't going well, just sample the local "flavor" and you'll have a good time no matter what you shoot.

Black Lake Golf Club, Nipoma, California

Ojai Valley Inn, Ojai, California
Tough course, not far from L.A. Going strong since 1923, this short course is a most entertaining challenge for all-level golfers. Well-kept and well maintained.

Cypress Point Club, Pebble Beach, California

The Links at Spanish Bay, Pebble Beach, California
Honest to goodness links course complete with wind, dunes, and ocean views. Very highly rated (see chapter on resorts).

Pebble Beach Golf Links, Pebble Beach, California
One of the top-rated courses in the world: golfer's heaven! Expensive but worth playing at least once before you die. Bring a camera.

Spyglass Hill Golf Course, Pebble Beach, California
Another Pebble Beach classic. Every hole is a unique experience. Not easy, not cheap, but well worth it!

▷ Missions Hills North Golf Course, Rancho Mirage, California

Carmel Mountain Ranch Country Club, San Diego, California
Challenging course. Read the greens carefully and don't hit out of bounds or you're liable to land in someone's living room. Plenty of hills and lots of fun.

San Francisco Country Club, San Francisco, California

▷ Pasatiempo Golf Club, Santa Cruz, California
One of the highest-ranked public courses in a state with over 800 golf courses. This tree-lined old-style course built in 1929 is a delight.

▷ Bennett Valley Golf Course, Santa Rosa, California
Less than an hour from San Fran, less than $20, and less than 7,000 yards, but popular and a solid-fun outing for the typical golfer.

Sonoma Golf Club, Sonoma, California
Given a facelift in 1992 by Japanese investors, this seventy-year-old course offers excellent conditions amid a sweeping view of the mountains.

Horse Thief Country Club, Tehachapi, California
Don't park your horse there! Little-known southern California course; fun, challenging, and full of surprises. High elevation will have you hitting Colorado Rockies drives.

COLORADO

▷ Aspen Municipal Golf Course, Aspen, Colorado

▷ Lake Valley Golf Club, Boulder, Colorado

▷ Breckinridge Golf Course, Breckinridge, Colorado
Some eighty-six miles from Denver, this one sits in John Denver's Rocky Mountains and winds through the mountains as well as valleys, streams, and forests. It is ranked among the best in the state. At 9,300 feet you too can tee off like the Colorado Rockies on this Jack Nicklaus course.

Castle Pines Golf Club, Castle Rock, Colorado

▷ Plum Creek Golf Course, Castle Rock, Colorado

▷ Cole Creek Golf Course, Louisville, Colorado
Fun, inexpensive course even lets you bring the kids. The creek is part of the course on a few holes, otherwise it's not too much trouble. Relaxing.

▷ Arrow Golf Club, Littleton, Colorado
Only twenty-five miles from Denver, this course features spectacular red rock and wildflowers. Keep an eye on your ball, as it may be lunch for elk, deer, falcon, or other wildlife. An experience you'll long remember.

▷ The Golf Course at Highland Hills, Westminster, Colorado
Eighteen-hole regulation course and two nine-hole courses. Hosted the 1990 Women's Public Links Championship. Good layout, rolling fairways, and lots of water in the lakes and creeks. Lots of tournaments play here.

▷ Pole Creek Golf Course, Winter Park, Colorado
Seventy miles from Denver. Lots of wildlife, forests, and well-placed bunkers, and if you show up at the wrong time of year, lots of skiers (popular ski location too).

▷ Rifle Creek Golf Course, Rifle, Colorado
Hills, canyons, various other rock formations, challenging, scenic, inexpensive—what more do you want?

Eisenhower Golf Club, USAF Academy, Colorado

▷ Vail Golf Course, Vail, Colorado

CONNECTICUT

Brooklawn Country Club, Bridgeport, Connecticut

▷ Richter Park Golf Club, Danbury, Connecticut
Best for low to mid handicap players. Tough to play, tough to get tee-off times, and tough if you don't like water—sixteen of eighteen are water holes.

Wee Burn Country Club, Darien, Connecticut

Goodwin Park Golf Club, Hartford, Connecticut

▷ Whitney Farms Golf Course, Monroe, Connecticut
Tight fairways, plenty of water, and tough greens. Interesting; you can't rest on any hole.

Yale Golf Course, New Haven, Connecticut
Highly rated, challenging collegiate course. Need brains to play here.

▷ Norwich Golf Course, Norwich, Connecticut

▷ Portland Golf Course, Portland, Connecticut
Not very long, but tough and challenging and inexpensive, around $25. Greens can be tricky, so study and pray.

▷ Richfield Golf Course, Richfield, Connecticut

▷ Sterling Farms Golf Course, Stamford, Connecticut

Crestbrook Park Golf Course, Watertown, Connecticut
One of the most challenging courses in the state. Also one of the least expensive, at $12–22.

▷ Simsbury Farms Golf Club, West Simsbury Farms, Connecticut
Beautiful, hilly municipal course winds its way through an apple orchard. Best for those with mid to low handicaps.

▷ Crestbrook Park Golf Course, Watertown, Connecticut

Willimantic Country Club, Windham, Connecticut

DELAWARE

▷ Garrison Lakes Golf Course, Garrison Lakes, Delaware
Just over an hour from Philly, it sits in what used to be prime farm land, so watch your step. Par fives can seem short, while some of the par fours can seem tough. One of the best in the state.

Wilmington Country Club, Greenville, Delaware

Rehoboth Beach Country Club, Rehoboth, Delaware

Del Castle Golf Course, Wilmington, Delaware

DuPont Country Club, Wilmington, Delaware

▷ Ed "Porky" Oliver Golf Club, Wilmington, Delaware
This popular course is not too tough. Good for beginners.

▷ Three Little Bakers Country Club, Wilmington, Delaware
Streams and hills are featured on this well-groomed, creatively planned public course. One of the best courses in a state without a lot to choose from. Great name too!

FLORIDA

▷ World Woods Golf Club, Brooksville, Florida
Two first-class courses rated among the best in a state with over 1,000 courses!

Cocoa Beach Golf Course, Cocoa Beach, Florida
Three interesting courses featuring the three "w's," wind, water, and wide-open spaces. Less than an hour from Mickey and the gang.

▷ The Biltmore Golf Course, Coral Gables, Florida

Deer Creek, Deerfield Beach, Florida

Delray Beach Golf Club, Delray Beach, Florida
Flat, well-laid-out course. Good for the many seniors in the area.

Cimarrone Golf Club, Jacksonville, Florida
If you like water, you'll find it here on every hole. Challenging public/semi-private course. Well-kept.

▷ The Golf Club at Jacksonville, Jacksonville, Florida
Only $20–35 to play this tough public course complete with water, marshlands, and airplanes overhead. Well-run and well-kept.

Jupiter Hills Golf Club, Jupiter Hills, Florida

Black Diamond Ranch Golf and Country Club, Lecanto, Florida

Marco Island Marriott Resort and Golf Club, Marco Island, Florida
Great if you like long stretches of white sand and fabulous water views while you play a championship course. This is a nice resort at which to park your golf bag.

▷ Baytree National Golf Links, Melbourne, Florida
Lots of decisions, as this Gary Player–designed course has five sets of ball markers on every hole. Good for players at all levels.

Doral Park Golf and Country Club, Miami, Florida
Narrow fairways, lots of water and long holes. Rest up and hit straight or else.

Doral Resort & Spa, Miami, Florida
Terrific accommodations and first-rate golf shop, but bring your checkbook. Greens fees are $200.

Don Shula's Golf Club, Miami Lakes, Florida
Nice course—not too tough, but interesting. More importantly, maybe you'll meet Don there.

The Golf Club at Marco, Naples, Florida

Seminole Golf Course, North Palm Beach, Florida
Home to many tournaments, this top-ranked private club course is not one you'll likely get to play, but it is great for watching some of the best.

▷ Golden Ocala Golf Course, Ocala, Florida
The closest you may ever get to playing St. Andrews or Augusta. Features replica holes of some of the classics. Fun.

Bay Hill Golf Club, Orlando, Florida
Challenging for the golfer and his or her wallet, checking in as one of the nation's most expensive at $225. It is, of course, a pro course from Arnold Palmer.

Grand Cypress Resort, Orlando, Florida
Four courses in all, including the highly rated and wide-open "New Course." Fun and near Disney. Plenty of water, some wind, and lots of challenges.

Walt Disney World Resort Golf Courses, Orlando, Florida
Five courses make up Disney's own golf complex. Slip away from the Magic Kingdom long enough to play one of these magic courses.

PGA National Resort and Spa, Palm Beach Gardens, Florida
Five top courses, varying in difficulty and topped by the Championship Course. Worth the experience if you get the opportunity.

Cypress Knoll Golf Club, Palm Coast, Florida
Bring lots of balls. Tight layout, plus water, marshes, and probably alligators. Challenging— never a dull moment.

Innisbrook Hilton Resort, Palm Harbor, Florida
Three super and scenic courses just a half hour from Tampa. One long, one in between, and one shorter course.

Crystal Lake Country Club, Pompano Beach, Florida
Marvelous Rees Jones course redesigned from the Crystal Lago Course in 1981. Challenging and beautiful.

Tournament Players Club at Sawgrass, Ponte Verde, Florida
The Stadium Course, a Pete Dye masterpiece, is rated one of the finest in the world. The Valley Course is no slouch and easier to get on. Play them both at least once.

▷ Tatum Ridge Golf Links, Sarasota, Florida

▷ University Park Country Club, University Park, Florida

Atlantic Country Club, West Palm Beach, Florida

Emerald Dunes Golf Club, West Palm Beach, Florida

GEORGIA

University of Georgia Golf Club, Athens, Georgia
Good value for less than $20. Long, wooded course will have you hitting them far and straight, or looking for them.

▷ Browns Mills Golf Course, Atlanta, Georgia

Peachtree Golf Club, Atlanta, Georgia

Augusta National Golf Club, Augusta, Georgia
One of the premier tournament courses in the country. You won't get to play here, but it's nice to stop by and say you were here.

Lake Creek Golf Club, Bishop, Georgia

Fields Ferry Golf Club, Calhoun, Georgia
Less than $15 to play this countrified course. Only an hour from Atlanta.

▷ Bob North Golf Course, Cohutta, Georgia

▷ Georgia Veteran State Park Golf Course, Cordele, Georgia
Great for the weekend golfer. A challenging, well-designed course, but not too tough. Well-priced at $15–20 depending on when you play.

▷ Bull Creek Golf Club, Columbus, Georgia

Atlanta Athletic Club, Duluth, Georgia

Chicopee Woods Golf Course, Gainesville, Georgia
Hilly, contoured greens; fun course. Less than an hour from Atlanta.

Port Armor Country Club, Greensboro, Georgia

▷The Boulders Course, Lake Achworth, Georgia
Tough course with plenty of water in a picturesque setting.

Lake Lanier Island's Hilton Resort, Lake Lanier, Georgia

Atlanta Country Club, Marietta, Georgia

Wallace Adams Golf Course, McRae, Georgia
State-park course in excellent condition and only $15–20!

Osprey Cove Golf Club, St. Mary's, Georgia
Outstanding scenic course with plenty of water, sand, bunkers, and even a few gators. Nice, out-of-the-way, relaxing place to play.

Hampton Club Golf Course, Hampton Club, St. Simon's Island, Georgia
Around $75 to play, less if you stay at the King of Prince Beach & Golf Resort, and well worth it. Water holes, marshes, alligators, great scenery, and challenging holes. What more could you want? It's fun.

Ocean Forest Golf Club, Sea Island, Georgia
Fabulous Rees Jones design that will play host to the 2001 Walker Cup Matches.

Foxfire Golf Club, Vidalis, Georgia
Course is just five years old and gaining in popularity. Bring plenty of balls; 13 of 18 holes have water.

HAWAII

▷Hilton Municipal Golf Course, Hilo, Hawaii

The Prince Golf Club, Kauai, Hawaii
Rolling land, ravines, mango trees, streams, and an ocean view take you away from the rest of the world on this Robert Trent Jones Jr. masterpiece. Wind, water, and everything Hawaii has to offer will make this an experience!

Kauai Lagoons Golf and Racquet Club, Kauai, Hawaii

Kiele Lagoons Resort, Kauai, Hawaii
Two Jack Nicklaus courses sit on 800 acres among the world's most beautiful terrain. Played host to the 1991 PGA Grand Slam of Golf. Need we say more?

Kiahuna Resort, Kauai, Hawaii
Water hazards, ancient Hawaiian burial sites, and lava-rock walls are part of your experience on this Robert Trent Jones Jr. course.

Princeville Makai Golf Course, Kauai, Hawaii

▷Wailua Municipal Golf Course, Kauai, Hawaii
This public course is possibly the best in the state. A 6,981-yard layout that hosted the 50th annual USGA Amateur Public Links Championship, Wailua Municipal is a well-kept, challenging course.

The Experience at Koele, Lanai, Hawaii
An experience indeed, the course starts off at 2,500 feet in the air, and you dip in and out of tropical canyons and spectacular scenery. Best on the island of Lanai. Watch the winds!

The Challenge at Manele, Lanai, Hawaii
Oceans views on all 18 holes, so if you're playing poorly, take some photos. Jack Nicklaus designed this challenging, dramatic course.

Kapalau Golf Club, Maui, Hawaii
Three courses in a majestic setting. Hills, blind shots, narrow fairways . . . something for everyone. Very highly rated, challenging championship courses.

▷ Pukalani Country Club, Maui, Hawaii

Koolau Golf Course, Oahu, Hawaii
Long, challenging, highly rated tough course that plays over ravines. Scenic, but it's Hawaii, so what course isn't?

Turtle Bay Golf and Tennis Resort, Oahu, Hawaii

▷ Olamana Golf Links, Waimanalo, Hawaii

IDAHO

▷ Blackfoot Municipal Golf Course, Blackfoot, Idaho

Crane Creek Country Club, Boise, Idaho

Hillcrest Country Club, Boise, Idaho

▷ Quail Hollow Club, Boise, Idaho
Hilly course with some dramatic elevated tees and bent-grass tees and fairways. Target golf on front nine; lots of water on 11 of 18 holes. Highly rated.

▷ Purple Sage Golf Course, Caldwell, Idaho

Coeur D'Alene Resort Golf Course, Coeur D'Alene, Idaho
One of the most popular courses in the state because of the famed floating green. Open, links-style course is very enjoyable. The $60 million resort is the pride of the state.

Avondale Golf Club, Hayden Lake, Idaho
Trees, hills, wind, tight fairways—everything you need in a nice, quiet atmosphere . . . and only $20.

▷ Pinecrest Municipal Golf Course, Idaho Falls, Idaho
This sixty-year-old, well-maintained course has plenty to offer. At $10–12 how can you go wrong?

▷ Bryden Canyon Public Golf Club, Lewiston, Idaho

Elkhorn Resort, Sun Valley, Idaho
Robert Trent Jones Sr. and Jr. designed this challenging course. The front nine is hilly, and the back nine flatter; contains eighty-five bunkers.

Sun Valley Golf Course, Sun Valley, Idaho
Challenging par threes and tough par fives are the hallmark of the course at this famous year-round resort. Home to a Golf Digest *instructional school.*

ILLINOIS

▷ Highland Park Golf Course, Bloomington, Illinois

▷ Prairie Vista Golf Course, Bloomington, Illinois

▷ Fox Run Golf, Elk Grove, Illinois
Well-kept and challenging, this public course offers a discount if you start after 3 P.M.

Eagle Creek Resort Golf Course, Findlay, Illinois
Bent grass from tee to greens at the end of tree-lined fairways. You must be accurate.

▷ Glenwoodie Golf Course, Glenwood, Illinois
Very large greens highlight this championship seventy-year-old, not too long, scenic course.

▷ Highland Woods Golf Course, Hoffman Estates, Illinois
Top-notch championship course in the suburbs, with water, lots of hills, and all the usual fun stuff. Not too pricey either.

▷ Pinecrest Golf and Country Club, Huntley, Illinois

▷ Cog Hill Golf Club, Lemont, Illinois
Don't miss these if you're in the Chicago area. All have their own challenges, but #4 is a pro-caliber course; long, hilly, with a great layout.

Ruffled Feathers Golf Course, Lemont, Illinois
This well-planned course tests all aspects of your game. When you're done you'll feel like you've worked hard but enjoyed it. Have fun and don't let this tough one ruffle your feathers.

▷ Kemper Lakes Golf Course, Long Grove, Illinois
Lots of sand, bunkers, trees, water, and challenges. If the PGA can play here, so can you for $100. Long and intimidating, but worth experiencing at least once.

Medinah Country Club, Medinah, Illinois

▷ Gibson Woods Golf Club, Monmouth, Illinois
Trees, trees, trees, and more trees. Inexpensive course, which is good because you'll spend a few bucks on balls if you don't hit straight. Challenging and not too long, but scary.

▷ Old Orchard Country Club, Mt. Prospect, Illinois

▷ George W. Dunne National Golf Course, Oak Forest, Illinois
Long, highly rated fifteen-year-old course about a half hour from Chicago. Lots of bunkers, sand traps, and people on this popular course.

Silver Lake Country Club Golf Course(s), Orland Park, Illinois
Three courses in all, one of which has played host to the National Public Links Tournament.

Westgate Valley Country Club, Palos Heights, Illinois
Billed in an Illinois travel guide as "A course where friendly people play."

▷ Lick Creek Golf Course, Pekin, Illinois
Carved out of woodlands, this challenging course offers rolling terrain with large sand bunkers. Be careful: if you don't hit it straight, you'll get licked.

▷ Aldeen Golf Course, Rockford, Illinois
Four sets of tees, lots of interesting holes, and plenty of bunkers on this more than 7,000-yard course within two hours of the Windy City. Nice excursion for Chicagoans.

▷ The Legends Golf Club, Roscoe, Illinois

▷ Rail Golf Club, Springfield, Illinois
*LPGAers play here and make it look easier
than it is. This fun, tricky, wide-open course has
tough greens.*

▷ Bonnie Brook Golf Club, Waukegan,
Illinois
*This seventy-year-old course is still priced to
please in the $15–25 range, and well worth it.
Clever, tricky course will test your skills.*

INDIANA

Pointe Golf and Tennis Resort, Bloomington,
Indiana

Bear Slide Golf Club, Cicero, Indiana

▷ Otter Creek Golf Club, Columbus, Indiana
*One of best-in-state, this Robert Trent Jones Jr.
course offers a nice view of the Indiana countryside. Par 3, 18th hole, Alcatraz, plays off a
cliff. Worth checking out if you're in Indiana.*

Pheasant Valley Golf Course, Crown Point,
Indiana

▷ Eagle Creek Golf Course, Eagle Creek,
Indiana
*Part of 500-acre golf complex. Clubhouse is part
of farmhouse. Target golf required at this highly
rated public course.*

Autumn Ridge Golf Club, Fort Wayne,
Indiana

▷ Brookwood Golf Course, Fort Wayne,
Indiana
*At $15 you won't mind the airplanes overhead
while playing a challenging, sandy course from
1925.*

Sycamore Hills Golf Course, Fort Wayne,
Indiana

▷ The Legends of Indiana Golf Course,
Franklin, Indiana
*Well-kept championship Jim Favio course with
impressive name. Lots of sand to boot.*

▷ Brickyard Crossing Golf Club, Indianapolis,
Indiana
*This Pete Dye masterpiece takes you around
and inside the Indy 500 track. The four holes
offer lush fairways and undulating greens; entertaining and extremely challenging. It's one you'll
tell your friends about.*

▷ Sultan's Run Golf Course, Japser, Indiana
*This beautiful 1992 course is a world-class
facility. The 18th hole has a fabulous waterfall
backdrop. Worth the $32–36 for the 18th alone.*

▷ Green Acres Golf Club, Kokomo, Indiana
*"Green Acres is the place to be," especially if
you like long par fives and lots of woods.
Eighth hole has men's and women's greens—
separate but challenging, and unique.*

▷ Golf Club of Indiana, Lebanon, Indiana
*Tough par fours and fives on this challenging
sandy public course. Bent-grass green, open
course with water hazards on fifteen of eighteen
holes. Wow!*

Valley View Golf Course, Middletown, Indiana

Covered Bridge Golf Club, Sellerburg, Indiana

▶ Blackthorn Golf Club, South Bend, Indiana
A new course that is maturing quickly, this challenging layout features a practice hole—a good idea for getting over those first-hole jitters.

South Bend Country Club, South Bend, Indiana

▶ Rock Hollow Golf Club, West Peru, Indiana
Tough, well-designed, tight new course; well worth the $20–25 price.

Wolf Run Golf Club, Zionsville, Indiana

▶ Zollner Golf Course at Tri-State University, Angola, Indiana
Inexpensive, well-designed course sits less than an hour from Fort Wayne. Entertaining and scenic, hilly course will allow you to start with Autumn Ridge in Fort Wayne and play Indiana golf courses from A to Z.

IOWA

▶ Amana Colonies Golf Club, Amana, Iowa
Woods all around, so hit it straight! Hills too. Not for the hackers.

▶ Veenker Memorial Golf Course, Ames, Iowa
Going on forty years old, this course has it all: woods, hills, water, elevation changes, and tough greens.

Crow Valley Golf Course, Bettendorf, Iowa

▶ Palmer Hills Municipal Golf Course, Bettendorf, Iowa

▶ Ellis Park Municipal Golf Course, Cedar Rapids, Iowa
Old course that seems like two courses in one. Front nine is wide open; on the back nine they ran out of room and built a tough, tight nine.

Des Moines Golf and Country Club, Des Moines, Iowa

▶ Jester Park Golf Club, Des Moines, Iowa
Located on the outskirts of Des Moines, this twenty-seven-year-old course tests your skills. Only $10–15, and has a nice little par-three nine holer to start or end your day with.

▶ Waveland Golf Course, Des Moines, Iowa

▶ Willow Creek Golf Course, West Des Moines, Iowa

▶ Beaver Run Golf Course, Grimes, Iowa

▶ Bos Landen Golf Club, Pella, Iowa
Woods, woods, and more woods—and you'll need irons to get through them on this tightly plotted course. One of the newest courses and toughest in the state. Less than an hour from Des Moines and worth the trip.

Davenport Country Club, Pleasant Valley, Iowa

KANSAS

▷ Sunflower Hills Golf Course, Bonner Springs, Kansas

▷ Hidden Lakes Golf Course, Derby, Kansas
A sand wedge from Wichita, this one is a lake lover's delight.

▷ Dubs Dread Golf Course, Kansas City, Kansas
Any course with the word "dread" in the title can't be too easy. Hit it long and hit it straight on this more than thirty-year-old course.

▷ Painted Hills Golf Course, Kansas City, Kansas

▷ Jayhawk Golf Course, Lawrence, Kansas

▷ Turkey Creek Golf Course, McPherson, Kansas

▷ Deer Creek Golf Course, Overland Park, Kansas
Eight-year-old Robert Trent Jones Jr. course is one of the finest in the Kansas City area. Sand, water, woods, creeks, and length give you all the golf experiences you need from one course.

▷ St. Andrews Golf Club, Overland Park, Kansas

▷ Salina Municipal Golf Course, Salina, Kansas

▷ Tomahawk Hills Golf Course, Shawnee, Kansas

▷ Western Hills Golf Course, Topeka, Kansas

▷ Braeburn Golf Club, Wichita, Kansas
Big trees and small greens make for some interesting golf on this old course that sits on the campus of Wichita State University.

▷ Echo Hills Golf Course, Wichita, Kansas

▷ MacDonald Park Golf Course, Wichita, Kansas

▷ Quail Ridge Golf Club, Wichita, Kansas
An inexpensive, fairly new course within an hour of Wichita, this top-rated public links-style course is steadily becoming more and more popular.

KENTUCKY

▷ A.J. Jolly Golf Course, Alexandria, Kentucky
"Jolly" public $15 course that plays around a 250-acre lake.

▷ My Old Kentucky Home State Park Golf Course, Bardstown, Kentucky
With a name like that, how can you not want to play it? Wide-open fairways on the front nine, tree-lined fairways on the back nine.

▷ General Butler State Resort Park Golf Course, Carrollton, Kentucky

▷ Fox Run Golf Course, Covington/Ft. Mitchell, Kentucky
Arthur Hills–designed course, rated as one of the toughest in the state.

▷ Old Bridge Golf Club, Danville, Kentucky
The first hole features an island green. You'll talk about it the rest of the day!

▷ Lincoln Trail Country Club, Ft. Knox, Kentucky

▷ Juniper Hills Golf Course, Frankfort, Kentucky

▷ The Links at Duckers Lake, Frankfort, Kentucky

▷ Bright Leaf Golf Course, Harrodsburg, Kentucky
Actually several courses, two nines and one 18 with plenty of water holes.

▷ Cole Park Golf Course, Hopkinsville, Kentucky

▷ Campbell House Golf Course, Lexington, Kentucky
Scenic course dating back to 1929. Still fun after all these years.

▷ Kearney Hills Golf Links, Lexington, Kentucky
Water, wide-open fairways, plenty of sand and water, and tricky greens mark this one. Home to a PGA Senior Tour event.

▷ Iroquois Golf Course, Louisville, Kentucky
Hills, creeks, and a challenging terrain are all part of this tight, tree-lined course. A popular course, but worth waiting for, especially at less than $10.

Persimmon Ridge Golf Club, Louisville, Kentucky

▷ Shawnee Golf Course, Louisville, Kentucky
Wide-open, flat, basic golf on this relaxing sixty-five-year-old course sitting right along the Ohio River.

Charles Vettiner Golf Course, Louisville, Kentucky
This is a championship-caliber course with fifty white-sand bunkers, making it a day at the beach for some.

▷ Lansing Pointe Golf Club, Union, Kentucky

LOUISIANA

Country Club of Louisiana, Baton Rouge, Louisiana

Oakbourne Country Club, Lafayette, Louisiana

▷ Bayou Oaks Golf Courses, New Orleans, Louisiana
Four sixty-year-old courses, all less than $15, from Little Course to Championship Course.

English Turn Golf and Country Club, New Orleans, Louisiana

The Bluffs on Thompson Creek, St. Francisville, Louisiana
This Arnold Palmer–designed course is fair but fun, featuring tough greens and great scenery. About a half hour from Baton Rouge.

▷ Huntington Park Golf Course, Shreveport, Louisiana
At nearly 7,300 yards, you better bring your muscle. Hills help or hinder depending on which way they're sloping. Popular and enjoyable.

▷ Oak Harbor Golf Club, Slidell, Louisiana
Hit it straight or hear it splash. Lots of water on this fairly new links-style course about a half hour from New Orleans.

Southern Trace Country Club, Shreveport, Louisiana

MAINE

Bethel Inn and Country Club, Bethel, Maine

▷ Brunswick Golf Club, Brunswick, Maine

▷ Kebo Valley Golf Course, Bar Harbor, Maine
One of the oldest courses in the country (1888), this remains a challenging seaside links-style course with fabulous, breathtaking scenery. At less than $40, this is a real bargain.

Sugarloaf Golf Club, Carrabassett Valley, Maine

Portland Country Club, Falmouth, Maine

Cape Arundel Golf Club, Kennebunkport, Maine
Built in 1901, this is an old links-style course just off the rocks and great cliffs that make Maine picturesque. The course is fun too.

North Harbor Golf Club, North Harbor, Maine

Waterville Country Club, Oakland, Maine

▷ Riverside Municipal Golf Course, Portland, Maine
Popular, wide-open course, nicely designed back in 1935. It's challenging and gets more difficult as you go.

Rockland Golf Course, Rockland, Maine
Great scenery and great price on this entertaining, old, well-maintained course.

▷ Sable Oaks Golf Club, South Portland, Maine
One of the newer courses in a state that features so many old ones. Tight, long course, interesting greens, some hills, and some tricks, but not much money to play at under $30.

MARYLAND

▷ Mount Pleasant Golf Club, Baltimore, Maryland

The Beach Club Golf Links, Berlin, Maryland

River Run Golf Club, Berlin, Maryland

Burning Tree Club, Bethesda, Maryland

Congressional Country Club, Bethesda, Maryland
Look out for Gerald Ford. You never know who you'll meet at this highly rated course. Facilities, from greens to locker rooms, are first class.

▷ Wicomico Shores Municipal Golf Course, Chaptico, Maryland

Columbia Country Club, Chevy Chase, Maryland

▷ Hog Neck Golf Course, Easton, Maryland
Long course, wide open and then tighter as you go. Sand, water, woods, and more. Highly rated by the golf publications.

▷ Black Rock Country Club, Hagerstown, Maryland
About ninety minutes from Baltimore, this is a fun, well-kept, inexpensive course. If President Clinton can play it, so can you.

The Golf Club at Wisp, McHenry, Maryland
This is a mountain course, with tight fairways and plenty of distance. Scenic and enjoyable.

Caves Valley Golf Club, Owning Mills, Maryland
It's an excellent course—if you can find it.

▷ Maple Run Golf Course, Thurmont, Maryland
Challenging, new, inexpensive course just outside Frederick.

Baltimore Country Club at Five Farms, Timonium, Maryland

▷ Queenstown Harbor Golf Links, Queenstown, Maryland
Sweeping views of the Chester River provide a spectacular backdrop for these two championship-caliber courses. About an hour from Baltimore and worth the trip. The scenic River Course is one of the top rated in the state.

MASSACHUSETTS

▷ New England Country Club, Bellingham, Massachusetts

▷ Crumpin-Fox Club, Bernardson, Massachusetts
A beautiful course cut out of the hills and woods in northern Massachusetts. Be on the lookout for moose, fox, and other four-legged visitors. Fun course with tough greens; very picturesque!

Industrial Golf Club, Bolton, Massachusetts
Flex those muscles, eat your Wheaties, and follow through! This is the longest course in the country at 8,325 yards. Industrial-strength golf and a good course to boot.

The Country Club, Brookline, Massachusetts

▷ Captains Golf Course, Brewster, Massachusetts

▷ Shaker Hills, Harvard, Massachusetts
Well-kept, tough course can fool you; get a Harvard degree in golf before playing this one . . . or just be at your best. Hilly, with a good layout. Intriguing.

▷ Cape Cod Country Club, Hatchville, Massachusetts
Up and down you go on this hilly, old, well-designed course from 1929. Still a real challenge and a great place to play on vacation at the Cape or in Boston.

Kittansett Club, Marion, Massachusetts
One of the best links courses in the country.

Nantucket Golf Course, Nantucket,
Massachusetts

New Seabury Country Club, New Seabury,
Massachusetts

Salem Country Club, Peabody, Massachusetts

Presidents Golf Course, Quincy,
Massachusetts
*For history buffs, this was home to John Quincy
Adams—the town, not the course. The short
course, at a reasonable $17–22, is a pleasant,
fun course in quaint surroundings.*

Country Club of New Seabury, New Seabury,
Massachusetts
*Winds, water hazards on half the holes, well-
placed greens, and sand traps. All the challenges you need.*

▷ Far Corner Golf Club, West Boxford,
Massachusetts
*Highly rated public course, not far from Boston.
Well-kept and challenging.*

Brae Burn Country Club, West Newton,
Massachusetts

▷ Bayberry Hills Golf Course, West
Yarmouth, Massachusetts
*At nearly 7,200 yards, it is the longest course
on the Cape. This is one of several enjoyable,
challenging Cape Cod courses with nice scenery.*

MICHIGAN

Grand Traverse Resort Village, Acme,
Michigan
*Resort home to great courses designed by great
players. The Palmer, Trevino, and Gary Player
courses provide all sorts of challenges.*

▷ Stonebridge Golf Club, Ann Arbor,
Michigan

▷ Elk Ridge Golf Course, Atlanta, Michigan
*Play this one carefully, as it winds through over
400 acres of woods. You get nothing for hitting
a deer or elk, but you could get five to ten for
striking a bald eagle (that's years not strokes),
so watch it. Bunkers, ponds, and more fun on
this scenic course.*

Point O'Woods Golf and Country Club,
Benton Harbor, Michigan

Oakland Hills Country Club, Birmingham,
Michigan

Boyne Mountain Resort, Boyne Falls,
Michigan
*Pack a mountain-climbing rope in your bag. The
two marvelous resort courses carved out of the
side of a mountain are fun, scenic, and well
worth the visit.*

Belvedere Golf Club, Charlevios, Michigan

Detroit Golf Club, Detroit, Michigan

▷ Rouge Park Golf Club, Detroit, Michigan

The Rock at Drummond Island, Drummond Island, Michigan
Off the beaten path, this is a very scenic resort course. Plenty of woods, and plenty of bear, deer, and other animals, so bring your camera.

Treetops Sylvan Resort, Gaylord, Michigan
Four fabulous resort courses, including a 9-hole, include woods and water in a town that has several highly rated courses. Robert Trent Jones and Tom Fazio designed two of these marvelous top-rated courses.

Wilderness Valley Golf Resort, Gaylord, Michigan
The two resort courses here are both highly rated. The Black Forest Course gives you an idea from the name what you're up against. Hit it straight or kiss it good-bye. Two tiered greens make for more fun if and when you get there. Good luck.

▷ Little Traverse Golf Club, Harbor Springs, Michigan

Boyne Highlands Resort, Harbor Springs, Michigan
Three championship-caliber courses here include the Ross Memorial Course, which pays tribute to Donald Ross with replicas of some of his great holes from courses like Seminole, Oak Hill, and Pinehurst.

▷ Faulkwood Shores Golf Course, Howell, Michigan

▷ A-Ga-Ming Golf Course, Kewadin, Michigan
This tricky, beautiful course has the oddest name in the state. Bring your camera for the views from this one.

▷ Rattle Run, St. Clair, Michigan
Highly rated, tough public course features water on most of the holes and sand all over the place. Aim, aim, and aim again.

▷ Orchards Club Golf Course, Washington, Michigan
A rolling woodland course from Robert Trent Jones Jr., less than an hour from Detroit. Only a few years old and already rated one of the best public courses by Golf Digest.

▷ Huron Golf Club, Ypsilanti, Michigan
Just 45 minutes from Detroit, Huron has its share of water, interesting greens, and a great view of Ford Lake. Popular course, because everyone loves to say they played at Ypsilanti!

MINNESOTA

Alexandria Golf Club, Alexandria, Minnesota

Madden's on Gull Lake, Brainerd, Minnesota

▷ Pine Meadows Golf Course, Brainerd, Minnesota
This course can be tricky, so pay attention. At under $30 it's a good deal.

Hazeltine National Golf Club, Chaska, Minnesota

▷ Bunker Hills Golf Course, Coon Rapids, Minnesota

Rutgers Bay Lake Lodge, Deerwood, Minnesota
Championship golf course built around a lake— after all this is Minnesota!

▷ Wildflower Golf Course, Fair Hills, Minnesota

▷ Pebble Lake Golf Club, Fergus Falls, Minnesota
This tough, hilly course will keep you on your toes. Fun, even if in the middle of nowhere.

▷ Minnewaska Golf Club, Glenwood, Minnesota
Flowers, prairie grasses, and lots of other foliage adorn this four-year-old course on a resort that's been around since 1928. Great prairie-links layout.

Pezheekee Golf Club, Glenwood, Minnesota
This thirty-year-old resort course is interesting, with plenty of hills and a challenging name.

▷ Grand National Golf Club, Hickley, Minnesota
This new course is already ranked as one of the top public courses in the state. It features lots of water in ponds, creeks, and marshes, not to mention a casino down the road in case your luck is better at the tables than on the course.

Izatys Golf and Yacht Club, Lake Millie Lacs, Minnesota
Alice and Pete Dye designed this gem, not far from the Twin Cities. Water on twelve of eighteen holes. Challenging, it makes you use every club in your bag. Moonlight golf available using glow-in-the-dark balls, fluorescent markers, and plenty of lights.

Rush Creek Golf Club, Maple Grove, Minnesota
Less than a half hour from downtown Minneapolis, this new course was designed to feature 18 unique holes on an array of bent grass, with all the usual amenities like bunkers, lakes, etc. Sits on 260 acres of everything from open prairie to marshes.

▷ Ortonville Public Golf Course, Ortonville, Minnesota

The Pines, Nisswa, Minnesota
A resort course that's highly rated by the top golf magazines. Challenging, championship course. Get there in the warm months.

The Wilds, Prior Lake, Minnesota

Rochester Golf and Country Club, Rochester, Minnesota

▷ Oak Glen Golf Club, Stillwater, Minnesota
There is lots of water on this tightly woven, interesting layout. Play accurately or you'll have a long day. A good value at under $30, and only about a half hour from St. Paul.

MISSISSIPPI

Diamondhead Country Club, Diamondhead, Mississippi

▷ Mississippi National Golf Club, Gautier, Mississippi
This thirty-year-old course is a good find at under $30.

▷ Timberton Golf Club, Hattiesburg, Mississippi

Considered one of the best in the state, this well-kept, long, beautiful course offers a host of challenges. About two hours from New Orleans and worth the trip if you're in the area.

Country Club of Jackson, Jackson, Mississippi

Colonial Country Club, Madison, Mississippi

St. Andrews Country Club, Ocean Springs, Mississippi

Less than an hour from Mobile, but very very far from Scotland.

▷ Mississippi State University Golf Course, Starkville, Mississippi

A solid, well-kept course with tough greens and long fairways, the more than 600-yard eighteenth is worth the $10–15 price alone.

Waverly Golf Club, West Point, Mississippi

MISSOURI

▷ Carthage Municipal Golf Course, Carthage, Missouri

Some woods, some open spaces, some tough holes, some easier ones . . . nice variety marks this sixty-year-old course near Joplin.

St. Louis Country Club, Clayton, Missouri

Bellerive Country Club, Creve Coeur, Missouri

Bent Creek Golf Course, Jackson, Missouri

About two hours from St. Louis, this tough but reasonable course will challenge you while letting you have some fun.

▷ Longview Lake Golf Course, Kansas City, Missouri

Popular and inexpensive, this links-style course is one of the best in the area.

Old Warson Country Club, Ladue, Missouri

Lodge of the Four Seasons, Lake Ozark, Missouri

North Port National Golf Club, Lake Ozark, Missouri

Long and demanding, this fairly new Arnold Palmer course is complete with hills and surprises. Popular, so plan ahead.

▷ Eagle Springs Golf Course, St. Louis, Missouri

Popular city course with a few tough holes. Enjoyable place to play if you're in St. Louis.

▷ Quail Creek Golf Course, St. Louis, Missouri

How often do you get to play a course designed by Hale Irwin? Popular and challenging.

▷ Tapawingo National Golf Club, St. Louis, Missouri

This course rated best in St. Louis by the magazines will keep you on your game. Over $50, but worth it. There are five tee choices on this long, new course.

Highland Springs Country Club, Springfield, Missouri

MONTANA

▷Big Sky Golf Club, Big Sky, Montana
Arnold Palmer course features a great view of the mountains and a nice variety of holes, all for under $40.

▷Eagle Bend Golf Course, Bigfork, Montana
One of the finest in the state, if not the finest. Woods, water, and photo opportunities abound. If you happen to be in Bigfork, check it out; if not, make the trip.

Meadows Lake Golf Resort, Columbia Falls, Montana

▷Hamilton Golf Club, Hamilton, Montana

▷Buffalo Hill Golf Course, Kalispell, Montana

▷Polson Country Club, Polson, Montana
This lakeside course with a more than sixty-year-old tree-lined back nine is relaxing and demands a variety of skills. If you can find Polson, you'll enjoy both nines.

Mission Mountain Country Club, Ronan, Montana

▷Whitefish Lake Golf Club, Whitefish Lake, Montana
Two scenic courses are highly rated by Golf Digest. *The old course features trees and magnificent scenery, while the newer course features a wide variety of holes. Both courses are inexpensive too!*

NEBRASKA

▷Indian Creek Golf Course, Elkhorn, Nebraska
You'll need your driver on this more than 7,200 yarder. Lift some weights and then go play this challenging course.

▷Grand Island Municipal Golf Course, Grand Island, Nebraska
Under $10 and worth the trip from anyplace. Nice layout, fun, and at the price, play it twice!

Country Club of Lincoln, Lincoln, Nebraska

Firethorn Golf Club, Lincoln, Nebraska

▷Highlands Golf Course, Lincoln, Nebraska
Long, wide-open, fairly new course is a pleasant excursion—very inexpensive too.

▷Highmark Golf Course, Lincoln, Nebraska

▷Applewood Golf Course, Omaha, Nebraska

▷Benson Park Golf Course, Omaha, Nebraska

Omaha Country Club, Omaha, Nebraska

Shadow Ridge Country Club, Omaha, Nebraska
This highly ranked new course is long, tough, challenging, and demanding. It's one of the toughest in the area.

NEVADA

▶ Eagle Valley Golf Club, Carson City, Nevada

Dayton Valley Golf Club, Dayton, Nevada
Arnold Palmer and Ed Seay put together this masterpiece around thirty-six acres of lakes. Prepare to hear the sound of your ball going splash unless you play with accuracy. Just an hour from Reno.

Red Lion Inn & Casino, Elko, Nevada

▶ The Golf Club at Genoa Lake, Genoa, Nevada
You'll use all your clubs on this course, which tests both distance and accuracy, while you have a fabulous view of the Sierra Mountains.

▶ Legacy Valley Golf Club, Henderson, Nevada
This resort course features a rolling layout and some lava rock to keep you from wandering too far off-course. This one is challenging.

Royal Kenfield Country Club, Henderson, Nevada

▶ Incline Village Golf Resort, Incline Village, Nevada
Championship course is a top-rated Robert Trent Jones Sr. layout from the early '60s. Not far from Reno or Tahoe. Also available is an excellent, short, mostly par-three course.

▶ Angel Park Golf Course, Las Vegas, Nevada

Desert Inn Country Club, Las Vegas, Nevada
Sitting on 176 acres of prime real estate, this popular resort course offers a nice diversion from the slots and the glamour of the strip. Trees, lakes, and a great, well-kept championship course that plays host to a PGA tournament—what more could you ask for?

▶ Las Vegas Golf Club, Las Vegas, Nevada

Las Vegas Hilton Golf Course, Las Vegas, Nevada

▶ Sahara Club Golf Course, Las Vegas, Nevada

Oasis Resort Hotel Casino Golf Course, Mesquite, Nevada
Oasis indeed—in the desert, in the middle of no place. Tough course, some water, and some long long holes. Get a cart or you'll die. Fun though.

▶ Northgate Golf Club, Reno, Nevada

▶ Edgewood, Tahoe Golf Course, Stateline, Nevada
This great public course sits 6,200 feet high by Lake Tahoe on a former cattle ranch. A Pony Express station from 1860 still stands on the course in case you want to send anyone a copy of your scorecard, especially if you birdie the 602-yard par-five third.

NEW HAMPSHIRE

▷ Amherst Country Club, Amherst,
New Hampshire
Hit it straight or hit a tree. Challenging, more than thirty-year-old course is well maintained and not very expensive. Good old New England golf.

▷ Souhegan Woods Golf Course, Amherst,
New Hampshire

▷ White Mountain Country Club, Ashland,
New Hampshire

▷ Wayside Inn, Bethlehem, New Hampshire

▷ Mount Washington Golf Course, Bretton
Woods, New Hampshire

▷ Beaver Meadow Golf Course, Concord,
New Hampshire
A tricky 101-year-old course. Not too long, but demands skill.

The Balsams Grand Resort Hotel, Dixville
Notch, New Hampshire
This hilly, well-kept old course is fun, demanding, and on a mountain.

Portsmouth Country Club, Greenland,
New Hampshire
This highly rated course is home to the New England Pro-Am and other tournaments; a challenging course in a marvelous setting.

▷ Hanover Country Club, Hanover,
New Hampshire
Very old (1899) hilly course will demand skills and stamina; not for beginners.

Manchester Country Club, Manchester,
New Hampshire

Sky Meadow, Nashua, New Hampshire
A highly rated semi-private course, within an hour from Boston. Only eleven years old but looks like it's been there longer. This strategically planned course fits in with the scenic surroundings nicely; an all-around good course.

▷ Sagamore-Hampton Golf Course, North
Hampton, New Hampshire

▷ Country Club of New Hampshire, North
Sutton, New Hampshire
Offering up some hills, some flatlands, some tricky holes, and some simpler ones, this forty-year-old course challenges all your skills like a course should and doesn't challenge your wallet, at around $30 per round.

Waterville Valley Conference Center,
Waterville Valley, New Hampshire

NEW JERSEY

Marriott's Seaview Resort, Abescon,
New Jersey
This pair of resort courses just north of Atlantic City will keep you on your toes. The shorter Bay Course is better for the average golfer, while the tough Pines Course will test all your skills.

Somerset Hills Country Club, Bernardsville,
New Jersey

▷ Green Knoll Golf Course, Bridgewater,
New Jersey
*Less than an hour from New York City, this is
your basic golf course for your average golfer;
open, well-designed, and fun.*

▷ Hominy Hills Golf Course, Colts Neck,
New Jersey
*A most difficult, Robert Trent Jones, over thirty-
five-year-old-course, complete with traps, bunkers,
rough, and greens. Basically, if you're a
beginner, steer clear of Colts Neck.*

Golden Pheasant Golf Club, Cream Ridge,
New Jersey

▷ Flanders Valley Golf Course, Flanders,
New Jersey

▷ Blue Heron Pines Golf Club, Galloway,
New Jersey
*This beautiful new course sits about thirty min-
utes from Atlantic City. So, if you're losing at
the tables, take a break and play. Well-planned,
classy course is challenging but not a killer.*

Galloway National Golf Club, Galloway,
New Jersey
Good, off-the-beaten-path course.

▷ Paramus Golf Club, Paramus, New Jersey
*A pleasant diversion from the plethora of shop-
ping malls in the area, sneak away and play
this one if you can. About a half hour from
New York City, this is a nice course for newer
golfers to have some fun.*

Ridgewood Country Club, Paramus,
New Jersey

Pine Valley Golf Club, Clementon,
New Jersey
*Ranked as one of the nation's best, but you'll
have to join an elite club to play.*

Plainfield Country Club, Plainfield,
New Jersey

Ron Jaworski's Eagle's Nest Country Club,
Sewell, New Jersey
*What do old NFL players do after they retire?
This one opened a golf course. Back nine has
hills and is tight, like a pass rush. Enjoyable if
you can find it and get on.*

Cherry Valley Country Club, Skillman,
New Jersey

▷ Quail Brook Golf Course, Somerset,
New Jersey
*Not far from NYC or Philly, this course will
challenge your game and your legs with hills on
the back nine.*

▷ Spooky Brook Golf Course, Somerset,
New Jersey

Baltusrol Golf Club, Springfield, New Jersey
*This top-ranked classic course has seen its
share of major championship events, including
seven U.S. Opens. Befriend a member so you
can play this course; it's worth it! See if you
can match John Daly, who reached the green
on two on the 630-yard seventeenth hole.*

NEW MEXICO

Rio Ranch Golf and Country Club,
Albuquerque, New Mexico

▷Arroyo Oso Golf Course, Albuquerque,
New Mexico

▷Paradise Hills Golf Club, Albuquerque,
New Mexico

▷University of New Mexico Golf Course,
Albuquerque, New Mexico
Three practice holes accompany this well-planned course with plenty of water hazards, gullies to clear, and hills to climb. Has hosted PGA and LPGA qualifying rounds, as well as state and NCAA tournaments.

▷Santa Ana Golf Course, Bernadillo,
New Mexico
Fairly new links-style course sits on farmlands and features three 9-hole layouts around eight lakes.

▷Cochiti Lake Golf Course, Cochiti Lake,
New Mexico
Just forty miles from Santa Fe, this Robert Trent Jones Jr. course sits on land owned by the Pueblo Indians. A mostly open course with sand, rocks, and great scenery, it is ranked as one of the best in the state by Golf Digest. Good bargain at only $25–30.

▷Pinon Hills Golf Course, Farmington,
New Mexico
At 5,900 feet high, this well-maintained course featuring all the desert terrain you could ever want. At only $13, how can you go wrong?

Inn of the Mountain Gods Golf Course,
Mescalero, New Mexico
This fabulous, scenic, resort course sits some 7,200 feet high on a 460,000-acre Indian reservation. Lots of ups and downs thanks to elevation changes. Ball will carry far, but you need accuracy to avoid hazards, traps, elk, bear, deer, and mountain lions.

Pendares Lodge Golf and Country Club,
Rociada, New Mexico

Taos Country Club, Rancho de Taos,
New Mexico
Where the desert meets the Rockies, you'll have to keep the ball on the fairways between desert brush. Kentucky bluegrass in New Mexico.

▷Links at Sierra Blanca, Ruidoeo,
New Mexico

NEW YORK

Bativia Country Club, Bativia, New York
Not a long drive from either Rochester or Buffalo, about 30 minutes from each city, this course requires a long drive on most holes.

Sagamore Golf Course, Bolton Landing,
New York
A scenic course in the mountains over Lake George, this Donald Ross classic demands accuracy to get by deep bunkers to small greens.

▷Dyker Beach Golf Course, Brooklyn,
New York
Golf in Brooklyn? Very much a city course (how many courses have an address of 7th Avenue and 86th Street?). Wide-open, hilly old course (1928) is a fun respite in the middle of the city.

▶ Central Valley Golf Club, Central Valley, New York

Leatherstocking Golf Course, Cooperstown, New York

Maidstone Club, East Hampton, New York
Highly rated links course in scenic surroundings.

▶ Bethpage State Park, Farmingdale, New York
Five top-notch public courses take up most of Farmingdale. Home to an upcoming U.S. Open, the Black Course is not only long, but hilly, scenic, and very tough. The other four are tricky, but the Black Course is the one to take on when you're ready to play with the best of 'em.

Concord Hotel Golf Course, Kiamesha Lake, New York
Forty-five holes of golf are featured at this legendary Catskill resort, including the famed "Monster" course, the longest in a state with a lot of courses. The name alone should challenge you.

Lido Golf Course, Lido Beach, New York

Loon Lake Golf Course, Loon Lake, New York
This old course from 1894 features short holes and tiny greens that will test your accuracy.

Winged Foot Golf Club, Mamaroneck, New York
Very famous, photographed often, and talked about by the pros, this private club is not easy to get on. Sorry.

Niagara-Orleans Country Club, Middleport, New York
Over sixty years old, the course has been recently refurbished and updated. Situated along the Erie Canal, this is a fun course that is well kept and can be difficult when it gets windy.

▶ Montauk Downs State Park Golf Course, Montauk, New York
Near the tip of Long Island, this one has a little bit of everything, and a lot of challenges for only $20–25. Scenic and top-rated besides!

▶ Clearview Golf Club, New York, New York
Basic golf for city dwellers who just want to get out of the office and play—and there are a lot of them, as this Queens course is crowded.

▶ Douglaston Golf Club, New York, New York
Only a few miles from downtown Manhattan. A popular, hilly public course that's not too long—you can spend more time in traffic on the Long Island Expressway than on the course.

▶ Kissena Park Golf Course, New York, New York
Short, fun course in Queens, with tricky greens.

▶ Van Cortlandt Golf Club, New York, New York
One of the oldest courses in the country, this Bronx course is a 3-wood from Yankee Stadium. A pleasant course that has some challenges, it is one of a few in the country that you can take the subway to.

▶ Saratoga Spa Golf Course, Saratoga, New York

▷ Cragie Brae Golf Course, Scottsville, New York
Popular, wide-open links course gets play all year, even in the snow. If you don't mind the thruway passing through, Cragie Brae is a pleasant, inexpensive course to play that caters to seniors.

National Golf Links of America, Southampton, New York

Shinnecock Hills Golf Club, Southampton, New York
Classic old course, home to many championship events.

▷ Oyster Bay Golf Course, Woodbury, New York

▷ Dunwoodie Golf Club, Yonkers, New York
Plenty of hills on this short but fun course; not far from New York City.

NORTH CAROLINA

The Grove Park Inn Resort, Asheville, North Carolina
The tree-lined fairways of this scenic course that opened in 1899 have seen the likes of Bobby Jones, Ben Hogan, Arnold Palmer, Jack Nicklaus, and many others. If that doesn't impress you, the mountain scenery and winding streams will.

Bald Head Island Golf Course, Bald Head Island, North Carolina
Accessible via ferry service, this remote-island course winds its way around dunes and lagoons and runs along a forest. Nice escape from the real world.

▷ Sugar Hollow Golf Course, Banner Elk, North Carolina

High Hampton Inn and Country Club, Cashiers, North Carolina
Picturesque, challenging course designed by George W. Cobb, who designed over 350 courses.

▷ Finley Golf Course, University of North Carolina, Chapel Hill, North Carolina

Ballantyne Golf Club, Charlotte, North Carolina

▷ Charlotte Golf Links, Charlotte, North Carolina
Deceptive four-year-old links-style course for under $30. Good value, if you don't spend too much on extra balls.

▷ Oak Hill Golf Course, Charlotte, North Carolina

▷ Tanglewood Park, Clemmons, North Carolina

▷ Westport Golf Course, Denver, North Carolina

Colony Lake Lure Golf Resort, Fairfield Mountains, North Carolina
A championship course nestled in the Blue Ridge Mountains, you'll want to play this one slowly as you spend time looking at the breathtaking scenery.

▷ Bel Air Golf and Country Club, Greensboro, North Carolina

▶Longview Golf Course, Greensboro, North Carolina

Linville Golf Course, Linville, North Carolina
If you like playing in the mountains, this is it. Donald Ross designed this one in 1924, and it's a top-rated course over seventy years later.

Country Club of North Carolina, Pinehurst, North Carolina

Pinehurst Resort and Country Club, Pinehurst, North Carolina
One hundred forty-four holes on eight courses make the legendary Pinehurst the largest resort golf complex in the world. Pinehurst has been home to the most prestigious pro tournaments in the game. It has also been designated a National Historic Landmark.

Deercroft Country Club, Wagram, North Carolina
Tucked away in the woods and about a half hour from Pinehurst is this little-known gem. PGA and PGA Senior qualifying events have been held here.

▶ Foxwoods Golf Course, Salisbury, North Carolina

▶ Homestead Golf Club, Winston-Salem, North Carolina

NORTH DAKOTA

▶ Riverwood Golf Course, Bismarck, North Dakota
One of the best courses in the state, accuracy is essential to avoid ending up in the trees or hitting deer or other animals.

▶ Tom O'Leary Golf Course, Bismark, North Dakota
This twenty-five-year-old course is short, open, relaxing, and inexpensive.

▶ Heart River Golf Club, Dickinson, North Dakota

▶ Edgewood Golf Course, Fargo, North Dakota
The pride of Fargo, this is a challenging, well-maintained, not too long, tree-lined, old (1915) course. Large greens and large fun.

Fargo Country Club, Fargo, North Dakota

Rose Creek Golf Course, Fargo, North Dakota

Lincoln Parks Golf Course, Grand Forks, North Dakota

▶ Prairie West Golf Course, Mandan, North Dakota
This new, nicely designed course is less than $20, and great if you're near Bismark.

▶ Souris Valley Golf Course, Minot, North Dakota

Bois de Sioux Golf Club, Wahpeton, North Dakota

The Links of North Dakota at Red Mike Resort, Williston, North Dakota
Native grasses and fresh air mark this marvelous, highly touted, sprawling links course with five sets of tees.

OHIO

▷ Yankee Run Golf Course, Brookfield, Ohio

▷ Blue Ash Golf Course, Cincinnati, Ohio
A popular course among better players in the Cincinnati area, this long course with large greens is a great deal at $20 a round.

Camargo Club, Cincinnati, Ohio

▷ The Vineyard, Cincinnati, Ohio
An excellent, scenic course for under $25. What more could you want?

Brookside Country Club, Columbus, Ohio

Ohio State Golf Course, Columbus, Ohio
Excellent collegiate course(s) with 36 holes; hard to get on.

Scioto Country Club, Columbus, Ohio

Quail Hollow Resort, Concord, Ohio
This top-notch course just outside of Cleveland sees the Nike Tour pass through. Hills and tough greens can make this one a real challenge.

Muirfield Village Golf Club, Dublin, Ohio

Double Eagle Club, Galena, Ohio
A new course; challenging, with an encouraging name.

▷ Apple Valley Golf Club, Howard, Ohio
A popular course, full of long par fours and inexpensive to boot!

▷ Pine Hills Golf Club, Hinckley, Ohio
Tough, hilly, wooded course just fifteen miles from Cleveland; not a long course, but don't let that fool you.

▷ Shaker Run Golf Course, Lebanon, Ohio
Play with accuracy or stay home. This course is highly rated by Golf Digest *and deservedly so. Long, scenic, and difficult, but fun if you're a low handicapper.*

▷ Beaver Creek Meadows Golf Course, Lisbon, Ohio
Short course with a lot of water; a really good price at $11–15 per round.

▷ Indian Springs Golf Club, Mechanicsburg, Ohio

Inverness Golf Club, Toledo, Ohio
This old course has been home to many major tournaments. Also where Jack Nicklaus grew up.

▷ Pine Ridge Country Club, Wickliffe, Ohio

▷ Eagle Sticks Golf Course, Zanesville, Ohio

OKLAHOMA

Dornick Hills Golf and Country Club, Ardmore, Oklahoma

White Hawk Golf Course, Bixby, Oklahoma

▷ Forest Ridge Golf Course, Broken Arrow, Oklahoma
Not far from Tulsa, this highly rated eight-year-old course will test all your skills.

Golf Club of Oklahoma, Broken Arrow, Oklahoma

Cedar Ridge Country Club, Broken Bow, Oklahoma
If you can find Broken Bow, you can play this course for around $10. Not a bad deal. This more than twenty-year-old course has some trickery.

▶ Heritage Hills Country Club, Claremore, Oklahoma

▶ Cushing Golf Course, Cushing, Oklahoma

▶ Kickingbird Golf Club, Edmond, Oklahoma
This pleasant, inexpensive course is less than thirty minutes from Oklahoma City. Challenging, and no, you can't kick any birds, just hit birdies.

▶ John Conrad Golf Course, Midwest City, Oklahoma

▶ Lincoln Park Golf Club, Oklahoma City, Oklahoma
These two public courses are highly rated by Oklahoma golfers.

▶ Karsten Creek Golf Course, Stillwater, Oklahoma
One of the top-ranked courses in the state, this championship course offers six tee-off choices. Scenic and challenging.

Stillwater Country Club, Stillwater, Oklahoma

▶ LaFortune Park Golf, Tulsa, Oklahoma
A popular city course with a neighboring 18-hole par three. Long, not too tough, but a fun city course nonetheless.

Mohawk Park Golf Course, Tulsa, Oklahoma

Southern Hills Country Club, Tulsa, Oklahoma
Founded in 1936, it has been home to the U.S. Open, PGA Championship, and most recently, The Tour Championship. If it's good enough for Raymond Floyd, Dave Stockton, Corey Pavin, and so many others, it's good enough for you. Three courses in all.

OREGON

Awbrey Bend Golf Club, Bend, Oregon
A long, interesting, hilly new course with great scenery. It will test your game, so be prepared.

▶ Riveridge Golf Course, Bend, Oregon

Sunriver Golf Course, Bend, Oregon
Two 18-hole, sprawling, challenging resort courses offer snow-capped mountains as a spectacular backdrop.

▶ Tokatee Golf Club, Blue River, Oregon
Not far from Eugene and worth the trip. This is a well-maintained, challenging mountain course that will have you stopping for Kodak moments. Not expensive; you'll spend more on film than on greens fees.

▶ Pumpkin Ridge Golf Club, Cornelius, Oregon

Eugene Country Club, Eugene, Oregon

▶Sandpines Golf Course, Florence, Oregon
This sprawling new course was ranked among one of the best public courses by Golf Digest *in 1993. There are plenty of pines, sand dunes, and water on this Rees Jones layout.*

▶Broadmoor Golf Course, Portland, Oregon

Columbia-Edgewater Country Club, Portland, Oregon

▶Eastmoreland Golf Course, Portland, Oregon
A very tough old course with lots of trees and some water too. This scenic city course can be tackled for around $20; well worth it.

Portland Country Club, Portland, Oregon

Waverly Country Club, Portland, Oregon

PENNSYLVANIA

Merion Golf Club, Ardmore, Pennsylvania
A popular USGA tournament course, this old course is great for those who like a touch of golf history. Bobby Jones completed his grand slam here in 1930.

Sacun Valley Country Club, Bethlehem, Pennsylvania

▶Tom's Run Golf Course, Blairsville, Pennsylvania
Lots of sand on this beautiful new course that's not far from Pittsburgh.

▶Champion Lakes Golf Course, Bolivar, Pennsylvania
A championship-caliber course with a unique layout. About an hour from Pittsburgh and only in the $20–25 range. Dick Groat of the Pirates used to own it; a must for Pirate fans.

Mill Race Golf Course, Brenton, Pennsylvania
If you're near Wilkes-Barre and you really like water, try this short resort course.

▶Center Valley Golf Club, Center Valley, Pennsylvania

▶Erie Golf Club, Erie, Pennsylvania

Hershey Country Club, Hershey, Pennsylvania
Three classic courses including The West, with back-to-back par fives and a host of gorgeous trees to avoid; The East, host of a recent Nike Tournament; and the South, formerly known as the Hershey Parkview, dating back to the 1920s. Among the best courses in the large state.

Golf Club at Hidden Valley, Hidden Valley, Pennsylvania

Laurel Valley Golf Club, Ligonier, Pennsylvania

Mount Airy Golf Course, Mount Pocono, Pennsylvania
You've heard about the resort, so try out the course. Long, scenic, hilly, but not so tough it'll ruin your vacation.

Aronomink Golf Club, Newton Square, Pennsylvania

Oakmont Country Club, Oakmont, Pennsylvania
Home to major tournaments, watch this one on TV, as chances are you'll never get to play it. You need to be a member, which means knowing another member very well.

Wyncote Golf Club, Oxford, Pennsylvania
This is one of those tough courses that will have you using every club in your bag. Designed like the courses in Scotland, but much closer to East-Coasters at only an hour from Philly.

▷ Wilkes-Barre Golf Club, Wilkes-Barre, Pennsylvania
Scenic, woodsy, somewhat challenging course gives you something to do while in Wilkes-Barre, and only around $20 to play.

Coolcreek Country Club, Wrightsville, Pennsylvania
Challenging, hilly course near Lancaster; almost fifty years old.

Heritage Hills Golf Resort, York, Pennsylvania

RHODE ISLAND

▷ Exeter Country Club, Exeter, Rhode Island
Challenging, yet reasonable enough for the average golfer, a terrific layout puts this as one of the top in a small state.

▷ North Kingstown Municipal Golf Course, Kingstown, Rhode Island
This fun course, not far from Providence, will keep you on your game and won't cost you much, either, with its $20 greens fee.

Newport Country Club, Newport, Rhode Island

Pawtucket Country Club, Pawtucket, Rhode Island

Metacomet Country Club, Providence, Rhode Island

▷ Triggs Memorial Golf Club, Providence, Rhode Island

▷ Richmond Country Club, Richmond, Rhode Island
A very well-designed and well-kept, beautiful new course. Good for all levels, provided you hit straight!

Misquamicut Club, Watch Hills, Rhode Island

Rhode Island Country Club, West Barrington, Rhode Island

SOUTH CAROLINA

Ocean Creek, Fripp Island, South Carolina

Harbour Town Golf Links, Hilton Head Island, South Carolina

Palmetto Dunes Resort, Hilton Head, South Carolina

The Westin Resort, Hilton Head, South Carolina
The three courses available, including one recently remodeled by Pete Dye, are all challenging and beautiful. Stay at the resort long enough to play them all and enjoy some tennis too.

Arcadian Shores Golf Club, Myrtle Beach,
South Carolina
*Designed by world-famous golf architect Rees
Jones, this well-designed course features over
sixty bunkers, natural lakes, and lush Bermuda-
grass greens.*

▷ Bay Tree Golf Plantation, Myrtle Beach,
South Carolina
*Three 18-hole courses on sprawling grounds
should keep you busy for a while. These
courses have featured an LPGA Championship,
PGA qualifiers, and other tournaments. George
Fazio and Russell Breeden did a nice job cre-
ating these spectacular courses.*

▷ Buck Creek Golf Plantation, Myrtle Beach,
South Carolina

▷ Caledonia Golf and Fish Club, Myrtle
Beach, South Carolina
*Sitting on a historic rice plantation, complete
with century-old oak trees and views of the
river, Caledonia makes for a great day of
golfing.*

▷ Gator Hole Golf Course, Myrtle Beach,
South Carolina
*Oak trees, rolling hills, sand dunes, and mar-
velous scenery make this Rees Jones course
most interesting. Don't let the name fool you;
the natural gator marsh may take "a bite" out
of your game.*

▷ Glen Dornoch Golf Links, Myrtle Beach,
South Carolina
*Set on 260 acres, this course is a tribute to the
links courses of Scotland. Located along the
river, this new course is already making a
name for itself among the multitude of Myrtle
Beach courses.*

▷ Heather Glen Golf Links, Myrtle Beach,
South Carolina

The Long Bay Club, Myrtle Beach,
South Carolina
*Jack Nicklaus–designed course features the
amazing tenth hole with a horseshoe-shaped
sand bunker that has to be seen to be believed.
A challenging course you'll be talking about for
some time.*

Myrtle Beach Hilton, Myrtle Beach,
South Carolina

Tidewater Gold Club, North Myrtle Beach,
South Carolina
*This top-rated course sits on a peninsula and
offers you every opportunity to hear your ball
go splash while playing a challenging round of
golf.*

Waterway Hills, Myrtle Beach, South Carolina

Wicked Stick Golf Course, Myrtle Beach,
South Carolina
*This is the first John Daly signature course.
Dunes like mounds and lakes will make this a
fun, challenging course for all-level golfers.*

▷ The Heritage Club, Pawleys Island,
South Carolina

Pawley's Plantation, Pawleys Island,
South Carolina
*This spectacular Jack Nicklaus course includes a
double green, split fairway, marshes, and spec-
tacular views. Don't miss this one on your
Myrtle Beach golf-obsession vacation.*

▷ Indigo Creek Golf Course, Surfside Beach, South Carolina

SOUTH DAKOTA

▷ Moccasin Golf Club, Aberdeen, South Dakota
A long course from the back tees with plenty of well-placed trees to smack along the way. One of the best in the state.

▷ Southern Hills Golf Club, Hot Springs, South Dakota

Meadowbrook County Club, Rapid City, South Dakota

Minnehaha Country Club, Sioux Falls, South Dakota

Westward Ho Country Club, Sioux Falls, South Dakota

▷ Willow Run Golf Course, Sioux Falls, South Dakota
Possibly the best in the state, this public course offers a host of challenges at a very inexpensive rate. Hit it straight!

▷ Watertown Municipal Golf Course, Watertown, South Dakota

▷ Fox Run Golf Course, Yankton, South Dakota

Hillcrest Golf and Country Club, Yankton, South Dakota
A good forty-five-year-old course, still ranked highly. Not far from Sioux City.

TENNESSEE

▷ Henry Horton State Park Golf Course, Chapel Hill, Tennessee
Top-notch, well-kept, inexpensive park course. This one is l-o-n-g!

▷ Brown Acres Golf Course, Chattanooga, Tennessee

Honors Course, Chattanooga, Tennessee

Holston Hills Country Club, Knoxville, Tennessee

▷ Willow Creek Golf Club, Knoxville, Tennessee
A long course that tests all aspects of your game, it is one of the best in the area.

▷ River Islands Golf Club, Kodak, Tennessee
Located on Kodak Road in Kodak, you have to know this is a "picturesque" course. Tough Arthur Hills course with some tricky holes and plenty of water. Well-planned, it keeps you on your game.

Memphis Country Club, Memphis, Tennessee

▷ Stoneridge Golf Course, Memphis, Tennessee
This tough course with lots of water will give you the Memphis blues if you're not careful.

Belle Meade Country Club, Nashville, Tennessee

Opryland Hotel, Nashville, Tennessee

▶Fall Creek Falls State Park Golf Course, Pikeville, Tennessee
A marvelous, off-the-beaten-track course in a beautiful setting. Woods, wildlife, sand, and all sorts of challenges make this one of the best in the state.

The Country Inn, Seymour, Tennessee

TEXAS

▶Andrews County Golf Club, Andrews, Texas

Horseshoe Bay Country Club, Applerock, Texas
Within an hour from Austin sit three challenging courses complete with creeks, oak trees, hills, lakes, and a 100-foot-high waterfall backdrop to the fourteenth hole on the Slick Rock Course. A top-notch golf-resort destination.

The Austin Country Club, Austin, Texas

▶Circle C Golf Club, Austin, Texas

▶Lion Mountain Golf Course, Austin, Texas

Hyatt Bear Creek Golf and Racquet Club, Dallas/Ft. Worth Airport, Texas
If you don't mind the planes, this popular, top-notch course features mostly elevated Bermuda-grass greens and lots of bunkers and is home to PGA qualifying events and many charity and corporate outings.

Preston Trail Golf Club, Dallas, Texas

▶Tension Park Golf Club, Dallas, Texas

▶Galveston Island Municipal Golf Course, Galveston, Texas

Four Seasons Resort and Club at Las Calinas, Irving, Texas
The TPC at Las Calinas was built with some consulting help by Byron Nelson and Ben Crenshaw. Annual home to the PGA GTE Classic. A top-notch course, and even more fun to play if you like being in the immediate neighborhood of the Dallas Cowboys.

Crown Colonial Country Club, Lufkin, Texas

▶Clear Creek Golf Course, Houston, Texas

▶Buffalo Creek Golf Club, Rockwall, Texas

▶Pecan Valley Golf Course, San Antonio, Texas
One of the best public courses in the country, Pecan Valley sits among 200 wooded acres. Lots of water and lots of trees, including an 800-year-old oak that has seen more golf balls than you could ever imagine.

▶Cedar Creek Golf Course, San Antonio, Texas

▶The Quarry Golf Club, San Antonio, Texas

Hyatt Regency Hill Resort, San Antonio, Texas
A fabulous Arthur Hills course sits on this 200-acre property. It's rated as one of the best golf resorts in the state . . . and it's a big state!

▷ La Cantera Golf Course, San Antonio, Texas
Accompanied by a golf academy offering a wealth of courses and programs for all golfers, this new Tom Weiskopf/Jay Morrish course is a 7,000-yard gem that is both scenic and challenging.

San Antonio Hill County Golf Club, San Antonio, Texas
Scenic views, tree-lined fairways, Bermuda greens, and a par five 549-yard finishing hole make for a solid golfing experience.

▷ San Sabo Municipal Golf Course, San Sabo, Texas

Woodland TPC, The Woodlands, Texas
Just outside of Houston by Lake Harrison, the water on nine of eighteen holes will have you playing carefully on your way to large, fast, Bermuda-grass greens.

UTAH

▷ Bountiful City Golf Course, Bountiful, Utah
This beautiful, scenic, wooded course has plenty of elevation changes and offers plenty of challenges. Inexpensive, well-maintained, and worth the "trip to Bountiful."

▷ Eagle Mountain Golf Course, Brigham City, Utah
About an hour from Salt Lake City, inexpensive, and challenging, this scenic, wide-open course affords a great view of the mountains.

▷ Davis Park Golf Club, Fruit Heights, Utah

▷ Valley View Golf Course, Layton, Utah

▷ Logan Run Golf Course, Logan, Utah
If you like water in Utah, this is your course. Challenging, narrow fairways will test your accuracy as you play along the river on this relatively new, scenic course.

Jeremy Ranch Golf Club, Park City, Utah

▷ Park City Golf Course, Park City, Utah
Only a half hour from Salt Lake City, this more than thirty-year-old layout features eighteen very distinctive holes. Worth the ride from Salt Lake.

▷ Park Meadows Golf Club, Park City, Utah
Considered by some as the best in the state, this long course features plenty of hazards and great scenery, and like the Park City course, it is a short drive from Salt Lake City.

▷ Gladson Golf Club, Payton, Utah
Canyons and lots of high and low scores and elevations make for an interesting day on this mountain course.

Willow Creek Country Club, Sandy, Utah

▷ Bonnerville Golf Course, Salt Lake City, Utah
A very popular one from 1929, this easy-to-walk course is pleasant, and at only $15–20, it is an excellent value.

▷ Eaglewood Golf Course, Salt Lake City, Utah

▷ Hobble Creek Golf Club, Springville, Utah
This beautiful course will have you using every club in your bag. Great scenery in a canyon course.

▷ St. George Golf Club, St. George, Utah

▷ Sunbrook Golf Club, St. George, Utah
Tough to play but with a great view of the mountains, this highly ranked course features a wide array of challenges.

▷ Green Springs Golf Course, Washington, Utah
Green Springs is possibly the toughest in the state. Everything from desert, to jungle, canyons, and fabulous mountain views make this a course worth visiting.

VERMONT

▷ Country Club of Barre, Barre, Vermont
A fun old course—not too long, but tricky. It's very scenic, and a pleasant New England atmosphere abounds.

Burlington Country Club, Burlington, Vermont

Ekwanok Country Club, Manchester, Vermont

Gleneagles Golf Course, Manchester, Vermont
Nestled in the Green Mountains, this seventy-year-old course features a breathtaking thirteenth par four with a hilltop green that you'd better reach.

Manchester Country Club, Manchester, Vermont

Quechee Club, Quechee, Vermont

Rutland Country Club, Rutland, Vermont
Golf Digest rates this short, old course very highly. Well-kept and challenging.

Sugarbush Golf Course, Warren, Vermont
Forget a cart; have a mountain goat carry your clubs. Bring your camera and your best game to this entertaining resort course.

Mount Snow Golf Club, West Dover, Vermont
Hills, hills, and hills. With the name snow in the title, you have to think skiing in the winter months. Challenging, beautiful resort course.

VIRGINIA

Birdwood Golf Course, Charlottesville, Virginia

▷ The Crossings Golf Club, Glen Allen, Virginia
This interesting course challenges average players and high handicappers alike and is not far from Richmond.

▷ Woodlands Golf Course, Hampton, Virginia

The Homestead Resort, Hot Springs, Virginia
Of three resort courses, the Cascades Course is the most challenging. The other two courses are easier, but still challenging and great fun.

▷ Newport News Golf Club, Newport News, Virginia

Country Club of Virginia, Richmond, Virginia

▷ Hanging Rock Golf Course, Salem, Virginia
The fairly new, long, scenic course will test your entire game.

Stoney Creek at Wintergreen, Stoney Creek, Virginia

▷ Sleepy Hole Golf Course, Suffolk, Virginia

▷ Hell's Point Golf Course, Virginia Beach, Virginia
This Rees Jones course is difficult and scenic, and features eighteen distinctive holes.

Honey Bee Golf Course, Virginia Beach, Virginia
A basic course that can sting you at times. Short and enjoyable.

The Colonial Course, Williamsburg, Virginia
Old town, new course; already has character and is highly touted.

Golden Horseshoe Golf Club, Williamsburg, Virginia
The Gold Course from Robert Trent Jones Sr. is a beautiful one, immaculate and known for some tough par threes. Not easy, but a must if you're vacationing in the neighborhood. The Green Course is much newer and longer, an excellent Rees Jones design.

Wintergreen Resort, Wintergreen, Virginia

WASHINGTON

▷ Lake Padden Golf Course, Bellingham, Washington
Near a lake, in the forest, with hills; challenging and very inexpensive.

▷ Gold Mountain Golf Course, Bremerton, Washington
Not far from Seattle, this popular public course is said to play like a country-club course. Challenging and well-kept.

▷ Shuksan Golf Club, Bellingham, Washington

Canterwood Golf and Country Club, Gig Harbor, Washington

▷ Canyon Lakes Golf Course, Kennewick, Washington
Water, sand, and more water; lots of challenges and lots of variety.

▷ Capitol City Golf Club, Olympia, Washington
This top-rated public course is worth checking out if you're anywhere nearby.

▷ Desert Canyon Golf Course, Orondo, Washington
Among the best in the state according to Golf Digest, *it is challenging and sometimes the wind will play tricks with your shots. Great scenic views.*

▷ McCormick Woods Golf Course, Port Orchard, Washington
Wildflowers, woods, pine trees, various types of foliage, deer, elk, and even a tough, challenging, highly rated public golf course.

Sahalee Country Club, Redmond, Washington

▷ West Seattle Golf Club, Seattle, Washington
Possibly the best city course and very popular, it is wet, hilly, and entertaining at a variety of levels.

Classic Country Club, Spanaway, Washington
This fairly new course sits within a short drive from Seattle, near Tacoma. Long, narrow fairways test your abilities. Great view of Mount Rainier.

▷ Downriver Country Club, Spokane, Washington

▷ Hangman Valley Golf Resort, Spokane, Washington
Fast greens, challenging holes, and a great layout that demands you stay on the course. Prices range from $13 to $18 for this one built at the end of the '60s.

▷ Kayak Point Golf Course, Stanwood, Washington
Less than an hour from Seattle, this great municipal course is hilly, challenging, narrow, highly rated, and offers great views. Take an umbrella—it is near Seattle.

▷ Lake Spanaway Golf Course, Tacoma, Washington

▷ Apple Tree Golf Course, Yakima, Washington
A great layout, with five sets of tee areas that play through an apple orchard. The seventeenth hole features an apple-shaped green.

WEST VIRGINIA

Pete Dye Golf Club, Bridgeport, West Virginia

Glade Springs Resort, Daniels, West Virginia

▷ Woodridge Plantation Golf Course, Mineral Wells, West Virginia
Probably the toughest course in Mineral Wells. Fairly new, fairly short, well-maintained, and hard to find.

Lakeview Resort, Morgantown, West Virginia

Hawthorne Valley Golf Course, Snowshoe, West Virginia
Carved out of the mountainside, this Gary Player course demands accuracy. New and long.

Williams Country Club, Weirton, West Virginia

▷ Oglebay Park Golf Courses, Wheeling, West Virginia
Two courses, one long, one short. One is for newer players, and one has hosted LPGA Tournaments. Both are an hour from Pittsburgh, PA.

Speidel Golf Course, Wheeling, West Virginia

The Greenbrier Resort, White Sulphur Springs, West Virginia

WISCONSIN

▷ Country Club of Wisconsin, Grafton, Wisconsin
Long, fairly new course keeps you on your toes with blind shots. About a half hour from Milwaukee.

Oneida Golf and Riding Club, Green Bay, Wisconsin

▷ Blackwolf Run Golf Course, Kohler, Wisconsin
This 36-hole complex is one of the best public facilities in the country. The River Course flanks the Sheboygan River and, like the accompanying Meadows Valley Course, has an incredible layout.

Geneva National Golf Club, Lake Geneva, Wisconsin
The two solid, long, resort courses on Lake Geneva are full of challenges!

Grand Geneva Resort and Spa, Lake Geneva, Wisconsin

▷ Yahara Hills Golf Course, Madison, Wisconsin

▷ Brown Deer Golf Course, Milwaukee, Wisconsin
This city course has seen its share of tournaments. Very demanding, fun, and well-maintained.

Milwaukee Country Club, Milwaukee, Wisconsin

▷ Lake Arrowhead Golf Course, Nekoosa, Wisconsin

▷ Brown County Golf Course, Oneida, Wisconsin

Sentry World Golf Course, Stevens Point, Wisconsin
This par seventy-two features the famed "Flower Hole," with one of the most beautiful hazards.

Just don't try to pick any flowers or play through; the manager won't be pleased!

▷ University Ridge Golf Course, Verona, Wisconsin

WYOMING

▷ Buffalo Golf Club, Buffalo, Wyoming
A hilly old course at the base of a mountain. When they say buffalo, they may mean buffalo!

▷ Casper Municipal Golf Course, Casper, Wyoming
A basic old course at good prices.

Cheyenne Country Club, Cheyenne, Wyoming

Olive Glenn Golf and Country Club, Cody, Wyoming

Teton Pines Golf Club, Jackson, Wyoming

Jackson Hole Golf and Tennis Club, Jackson Hole, Wyoming
Perhaps the best in the state, this very highly rated course is long and scenic and demands that you concentrate.

▷ Rock Mountain Golf Course, Rock Springs, Wyoming

Old Baldy Club, Saratoga, Wyoming

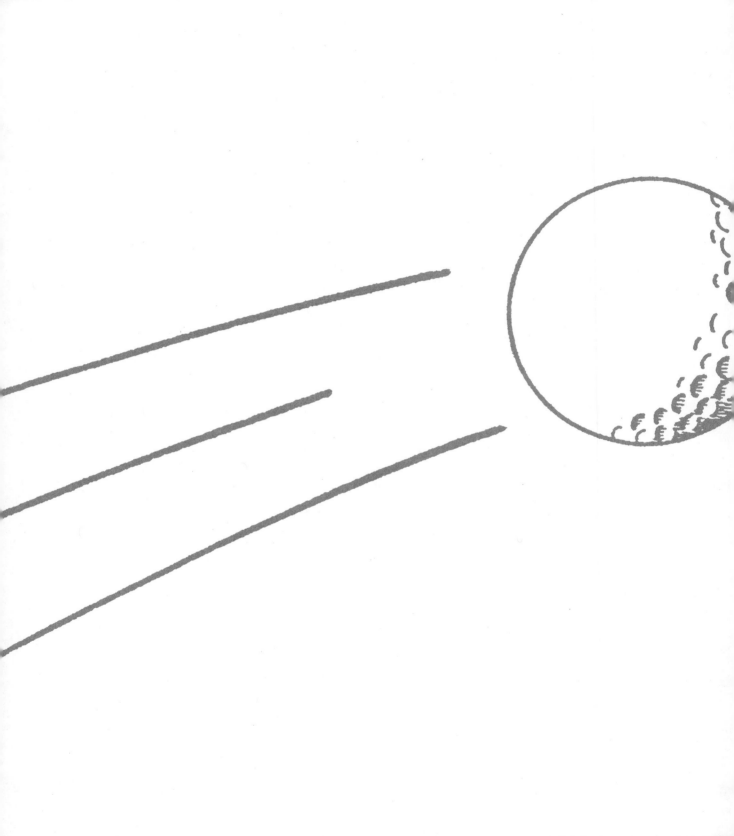

ARCHITECTURE AND THE ENVIRONMENT

To any ardent golfer, the idea of designing a course is titillating. Imagine a course built for your game, with dramatic doglegs off the tee area to account for your slice, no sand, greens that come with built-in instructions on how to read them, and so on. For those who design courses, it's a marvelous feeling to envision and complete a course. Architects refer to the course as their new baby, having taken more than nine months to put together and years for it to grow and mature.

Architects come from a variety of backgrounds, including the ranks of professional golfers. They need to have not only an astute knowledge of the game, but of the land on which it is played. They know the way a course should look and feel. They design based on a combination of that feeling for the course and mathematical precision, taking into account numerous factors and elements.

Once little things like financing and locating a potential site have been worked out, the design and construction of a golf course is a highly specialized field and has been since the early links courses of Scotland. There are numerous factors today that the early European course designers never would have dreamed of. Course architects must now be familiar with factors such as the integration of the course with the environment and, where applicable, associated real estate developments. Today's premier architects must draw from many disciplines—landscape architecture, land planning, engineering, agronomy, turf maintenance, and irrigation—to turn 140 to 200 acres into a challenging course that is aesthetically pleasing and utilizes the natural aspects of the land to the fullest.

One of the premier architects in the game today is Dr. Mike Hurdzan who, for some forty years, has been found on or nearby golf courses, beginning with his boyhood days working for golf-course builders. Hurdzan, who has built courses from coast to coast and in Canada, says that if his son is going to follow in his footsteps he's going to need a degree in civil engineering. "Courses have become complicated enough. Engineering requirements are placed on us, and there are so many variables when you build a course today that a degree in landscape architecture is no longer sufficient. Since there are so many factors involved, much of the work is being engineered today."

On the other hand, architect Rees Jones, who has worked on many of the legendary courses throughout the country by building or redesigning them for top tournament play, worries about too much engineering getting into golf. Jones adds, "We have to be careful that we don't end up with computers designing our golf courses. The emulation of nature is what the courses are about, and if we start getting too engineered we're going to have sharp lines and straight edges. You have to make sure you are designing in concert with the area around you, and you're designing in concert with nature."

THE BUILDING PROCESS

Dr. Mike Hurdzan describes, in brief, the process an architect goes through when initially planning a course. "The first thing you have to do is a sight assessment to figure out everything that will be important to the development of that site and the long-term maintenance that a golf course on that site will require. You look at things like soil, climate, winds, vegetation, water (both quality and quantity), habitat, wetlands, wildlife, and so on. It usually takes a team to look over all those factors. Then you prioritize what you find on that sight to determine what is of greater value and what is of lesser value. For instance, a habitat is of very high value. Areas of lesser value are the ones you're going to look at for the course, providing that they are usable. Together with a team you will determine where all the natural resources are on that site, and then it becomes an engineering thing. Often your next move is dictated by the highway department, who will determine what kind of access there is to the site and what roads can be built. They'll tell you where you can and

cannot build an access road, then you can determine where the clubhouse can go. Many times there are engineering decisions based on sewage and water and fire protection and elevation as far as visual height. Some places simply don't want to see the clubhouse, and other places don't care. There are various decisions before you start, including parking facilities, whether or not you'll need to leave room for a tennis court or a swimming pool, and so on."

Once the groundwork has been set, the planning of the actual course evolves. Different designers have their indelible styles. Rees Jones says that his style emphasizes definition. He believes in giving the golfer a concept when he or she stands over the ball. Like a chess master, Jones starts with the mental approach. He's not out to deceive or trick the player, only to challenge him or her. "I want them to be able to see the intended target and visualize the shot," explains Jones. To achieve this, he elevates tees, grades fairways, and adds bunkers, pockets, and mounds around a carefully crafted green. According to Jones, "A properly contoured and fortified green, more than any other feature, is the place where par is preserved as a standard of excellence."

Several top golf architects say they plan courses by

mentally thinking through the game as it's being played. Rees Jones wants the player to be able to create a plan of action for himself, or herself, from the moment he or she steps up to the tee area. Explains Jones, "I concentrate on the golfer having signals so he can think the shot out. If it looks like there is nowhere you can hit the shot, if there are bunkers all over the place, then you have a blank screen in your head and you can't plan your shot. I try to give the golfer a target to aim at or aim away from. The problem with a course that is too penal or bunkered all over the place is that you stand up there with no concept of what you want to do. The same holds true with a green; if it's blind or there are bunkers everywhere, you can't come up with a strategy. I like to give golfers options, but I like them to be able to plan and be strategic."

WHO ARE COURSES BUILT FOR?

As Curtis Strange said after he won at Brookline, "Isn't it great that the U.S. Open can be played here and won by 6 under par, and the next day the club members can go out and enjoy the course?" Rees Jones noted, "You don't want to build for the top players only; they only come around once a year."

Building courses for the ardent golfer is the goal of many architects. Pete and Alice Dye look to make a course interesting and challenging for the people who will be playing it every week. Alice Dye explains, "You have to make it interesting for the players who will be there often. We put in a lot of angles, do a lot of bunkering around

the green and a lot of contouring the green. We do all of these things for the person who is going to play it two or three times a week. That's the player for whom we're trying to create a challenging course. When the PGA tour comes in for four days, they don't dare gamble like the average person having fun. They don't really want a course that's too hard, since they're playing tournaments every week. They're tired and don't want to be worn out by the course. But since the pros only come to a course maybe one week a year, and the rest of the time the course is played by the club members or the public, we want to design it to be challenging for them."

Rees Jones says he builds not only with the ardent golfer in mind, but also likes to feel that his courses will stand the test of time. "I consider the real critics to be the members or frequent players. They are the ones who will play all the time and the ones who need to be challenged again and again. When you redo a course, those are the people that see the improvements."

Jones's philosophy is to "create an environment for the game of golf that is challenging, fair, and aesthetically pleasing." Jones prefers to build a course that best blends in with its natural surroundings than to overload a course with gimmicks that only serve to frustrate and discourage the average golfer.

TOUGH COURSES FROM THE BUILDER'S PERSPECTIVE

According to Dr. Mike Hurdzan there are two types of tough courses to build, mentally tough and physically tough. "There are

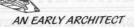

AN EARLY ARCHITECT

To give you an idea of how far course architecture has come with planning teams and engineering concerns, here is a tale that has been passed down for years about one of golf's early architects.

Tom Bendelow was an early golf-course architect, to use the term loosely. Honing his skill and love of the game in his native Scotland, the charismatic Bendelow came to America when the game was first developing here in the late nineteenth century. He would, by appointment only, inspect the grounds on which the proprietor wished to build a course. He would always make sure to compliment all town officials and interested parties on their choice of location for the course.

Once it was established that there was indeed enough room for a golf course, Tom would get to work. He would pick out an appropriate site, put down a stake, pace 100 yards, and put down another stake where a bunker would sit. He would then pace off yardage to the green, being another 100 or 200 paces, and plant another stake in the ground. He would complete the course in this manner in only one day, receive a fee of $25, and leave instructions for the builders. Then he'd be on his way. He'd always let the course owners know that they would, if everything was built correctly, have a very fine course when the work was completed.

Bendelow designed, or paced, numerous courses. Needless to say, golf-course design has come a long way since.

courses where you need to think through perplexing situations and numerous factors before making your final plans, and courses where you just have a battle with the land," says Dr. Hurdzan.

One of the most physically challenging courses for Hurdzan was in Vancouver, Canada. The course, called Westward Plateau, was built into the foothills of the Canadian Rockies, and that site was home to huge, old trees and plenty of granite. Lots of rock blasting was required, and there was almost no topsoil to work with. There were also environmental areas to work around and plenty of wildlife to keep clear of in the building area, like deer and bears. It was a physically challenging process that resulted in a challenging course in an incredibly scenic area.

Naples, Florida, provided Hurdzan with a more cerebral challenge as he and his team of builders tried to figure out what to do with a huge wetland area. The question was how to build a course and preserve the wetland environment. They managed to work their way through the wetlands, carefully preserving the vegetation land while figuring out how to make an interesting, playable course around it.

Sometimes course building is just plain aggravating. One Hurdzan course sits in the Palm Desert region of California. According to Hurdzan, "What made building that course challenging was the short time frame we had to work with and the conditions. It seemed that every time we would get something finished, the winds would come up at night and blow away most of what work we'd done the day before. It was a difficult process to outmaneuver the desert winds. Somehow we got it built."

REDESIGNING COURSES

Some courses get old; some are reconstructed in an effort to "modernize"; and some are changed for aesthetic purposes, others because some new owner had some new vision. There are a host of reasons why courses need to be redone.

Rees Jones, besides being one of the premier architects in golf today, is the master of redesigning, rebuilding, and restoring great courses. Called the "Open Doctor," Jones has been called in on half a dozen occasions to redesign courses for the U.S. Open.

Jones enjoys the hands-on approach, walking the courses while figuring out exactly how to re-create the original creation. "We try to incorporate in the changes and improvements the original style of the original architects as much as possible." Jones is not looking to reinvent the wheel, just make subtle changes in line with how the course was designed to be played. "After we worked on Brookline, people used to look at the course then come up and ask me what I did, and I'd say thank you very much because people didn't notice the changes."

In redesigning Jones looks to re-create the subtleties that you don't see the first time you play. According to Jones, "The subtleties you find the second, third, and fourth time you play are the mark of a great course."

Courses today are often being redesigned to look like the courses of yesteryear. Being a game of great tradition, golf,

BUILDING COURSES FOR WOMEN GOLFERS

A Conversation with Golf Architect Alice Dye

"We try to make our courses more manageable for women. We have to shorten them and go into shortened tees since courses are watered a lot these days. Courses were built with the idea that the ball was going to roll, but since the end of the '60s there have been watered fairways, which has eliminated the roll. A shot that was hit 150 yards in the air would roll 50 yards; now that ball won't roll, so the hole becomes 50 yards longer. So golf courses can become very long and pretty unmanageable for women.

"So on our courses we have added shortened tees to take into consideration the lack of roll. Also, we are very careful about forced carries except on the par threes. On a par three we know where you are hitting the shot from and that you can reach the green. On a par four or a par five we do not have a forced carry because we don't know where the second shot is going to be hit from. Maybe she hit it 140 or 150 or 180 yards, but we don't know how far she's going to have to hit it. If we put a pond in front of the green, we don't know if she's going to need a short chip shot to get in front of the pond and then try to carry over it. Therefore we put our water to the sides, not forcing her to have to go over it from wherever she is on the course. We try to put our hazards to affect the low handicapper and not the person of less strength. The challenge is to hit a good shot, and not simply a matter of rewarding the stronger golfer."

not unlike baseball with Camden Yards in Baltimore, wants to preserve that heritage. "Sometimes it's a matter of taking old photographs and trying to put the course back into the style and shape it was in before being worn down by overuse or weather conditions," explains Jones. "Each one is different. Many are sacred grounds that were

GRASS FACTS AND INFORMATION

Bermuda grasses are slower on the green than bent grass, but they withstand heat better.

All grasses are tested before they are released for course use.

Bent grass in the north is an example of a cool-season grass that cannot take the summers in Florida and the Deep South.

Greens are now cut at 1/32 of an inch today, making the greens faster than before. Higher grass made for slower greens.

The modern grass can withstand closer cuts and even stays healthier with the "cropped" cut.

The USGA has sixteen agronomists, located in different regions of the country, who visit 1,600 courses to help with golf-course maintenance or problems. They are trained to know what is best for their regions.

lost, such as Brookline which was changed without any reference to the old design. We took out all the changes that were made over the last thirty years with modern styles and put the old style back."

Another example of designing with the past in mind comes from the legendary Pinehurst courses. "At Pinehurst #2 we rebuilt the greens in old Donald Ross style, using old walking mowers to restore some of the old feel and old slopes that had been lost. There we restored it as we did with Brookline."

GOLF AND THE ENVIRONMENT

Environmental issues are an ongoing concern of the modern golf architect. The 1990s have brought a greater consciousness than ever before and have put golf courses under attack for being harmful to the environment. Since golf courses take up some 2.5 million acres in the United States alone, the concern is significant. The golf architectural community has heard the complaints and concerns and is taking action, and in some cases using their skills to better the environment. The problems of pesticides, water use for golf courses, wildlife, and loss of natural areas is being studied in grant-funded programs coast to coast. The ongoing tasks that will take researchers into the next century will be to better understand the impact of golf courses on the environment, minimize negative effects, educate course superintendents and officials, and determine what the game can do to protect the environment.

While golf courses do alter the shape and topography of the natural environment, they often beautify the setting while preserving wildlife and provide an ongoing, well-maintained green area. They preserve many natural spaces that might otherwise become mini-malls.

Courses have been built on landfills, around volcanoes, over marshland, and in other areas that have seen much of their natural resources disappear. Those in the business of building courses are learning about grass and trees, which can prove beneficial beyond just the building of the course. As one golf enthusiast points out, "sick trees, drying up streams, polluted waters, and grass with diseases are not found on golf courses because courses are well maintained. There is a dedication to taking care of the land."

THE USGA'S ROLE

The USGA supports the largest research effort in the world concerning turfgrass for courses. Their Turf Green Program and

Green Section, founded in 1920, is sponsored in cooperation with the Golf Course Superintendents of America. Their primary goals are to develop turfgrasses for golf courses that substantially reduce water use, reduce pesticide needs, and lower maintenance costs; create and develop management practices for new and established turf that protect the environment while providing quality playing surfaces; and encourage young scientists to become leaders in turfgrass research through education.

With pesticide use and water use becoming significant environmental issues, there is a need for grasses that look good and play well but are resistant to pests and diseases, and that require less water. Plot by plot, literally, the USGA Green Section, and scientists nationwide and even worldwide are working to develop better grasses for golf courses, neighborhood parks, lawns, and other uses.

RESEARCHING THE TURF

Since the 1960s new grass varieties have been developed that favor courses in different parts of the country. Bent grass, Kentucky bluegrass, Bermuda grass, zoysigrass, and buffalo grass are among those studied closely by the USGA Green Section. Each year the USGA publishes a report called the Turfgrass Research Summary, which can be yours by writing to the USGA Green Section at P.O. Box 708, Far Hills, New Jersey 07931, or by calling (908) 234-2300.

THE USGA MEETS THE ACSP

The concern about golf courses and their effect on wildlife has prompted the USGA and the Audubon Society of New York to establish the Audubon Sanctuary Program for golf courses (ACSP) across the country.

The society helps to promote the idea of a golf course as a wildlife sanctuary, thus providing a safe haven for players and animals alike from predators such as developers. Over 1,900 courses were signed up to the program within the first five years since its inception in 1991. For $100 a year the society studies a course and prepares a report recommending conservation and habitat-enhancement projects. The seven categories included in the program's study are: environmental planning, wildlife food enhancement, wildlife cover enhancement, public involvement, integrated pest management, water conservation, and water enhancement. Courses are certified in these seven areas.

SOME "HOLE-IN-ONE" ENVIRONMENTAL COURSES

Below are a few examples of the many courses that are doing something special for the environment and the world around the golf course.

St. Charles Country Club. The 60 acres above the course are maintained as a nature walk, providing a 2.5-mile trail of natural woodlands, wetlands, and prairie, all secured with wildlife preservation in mind. Cub Scouts, Boy Scouts, Girl Scouts, and grade schoolers are frequent touring visitors of this wildlife preserve, learning about the natural surroundings and the animals that inhabit the area.

Bridgehampton Golf Club, Bridgehampton, New York. Sometimes the problem not only is solved, but provides far more gratifying results. The Bridgehampton Course has long been home to Potash Pond, a drainage area near the first hole that had gone from a fine skating pond many years ago to a somewhat polluted, aesthetically unpleasing eyesore. With its being listed as a wetland by the Department of Environmental Conservation, however, little could be done to change this situation. After a lot of paperwork, planning, digging, and restructuring, to the tune of $12,000, the pond today is a haven for ducks and other local wildlife, thanks in part to the seeding efforts of the local elementary school.

Egypt Valley Country Club, Grand Rapids, Michigan. This course is for the birds, literally. A marvelous course unto itself, it is home to finches, goldfinches, sparrows, woodpeckers, hummingbirds, and numerous other species of birds. One of sixty-seven recognized Audubon sanctuary golf courses in the nation, Egypt Valley provides nesting and feeding sites, stands of thistle, areas of dense vegetation, and other plant configurations where birds can perch and nest. There are bird houses, boxes, and several natural islands that provide food sources for the birds. Egypt Valley is one course that has worked hard and succeeded in increasing the number of "birdies" in the area.

Minikahada Club in Minneapolis, Minnesota. Vegetative buffers are the mode of the day around the water areas of this Minnesota course. They provide both valuable cover and food supplies for wildlife, as well as filtering any runoff from the course before entering the water features. For 500 yards, along three ponds and a creek, the buffers provide a corridor for wildlife and protect a local swimming area from any contaminants. The Baker National Golf Course in Medina, Minnesota, also utilizes such vegetative bunkers that interconnect wetlands and provide valuable travel routes for wildlife. The Medina course maintains wetlands and tests water quality along the 70-acre Spurtzen Lake.

Gull Lake View Golf Club, Augusta, Michigan. Spanning over 860 acres of northern hardwood habitat, this five-course complex includes woodlands, tall grass, lakes, ponds, freshwater wetlands, and a creek. Beyond all of that is a substantial wealth of wildlife, including nearly fifty varieties of birds, plus mammals, reptiles, and amphibians. In conjunction with the Kellogg Bird Sanctuary, the club has also been

instrumental over the past fifteen years in Canada-geese banding research. The courses provide feeding and nesting boxes for birds and raised sites around ponds to help provide additional cover for wildlife.

Morro Bay Golf Course, Morro Bay, California. This fully sanctioned Audubon Cooperative Sanctuary is renowned for incorporating member involvement into the ecological efforts. The Boy Scouts of America, California Conservation Corp, Santa Monica Community College, California Parks Service, and other groups have taken part in keeping this one of the most highly recognized, environmentally involved courses in the country. Programs include mounting and maintaining nest boxes, protecting and improving Monarch butterfly sites, and native tree reestablishment.

STUDYING THE ENVIRONMENT

Changes have come about due to irrigation technology, equipment technology, willingness of courses to spend more money on maintenance, and better control over water and hazards, but the studies continue. Golf-architect legend Pete Dye donated his time to build a new 36-hole course at Purdue University in exchange for a university program to study these issues. Dye helped raise the money for this major

project to ensure that accurate studies would be done on golf and the environment from a nongolf source.

Pete's wife Alice, also a golf architect, explained the project. "All of the information that is coming out about golf courses being good for the environment are coming from sources inside the industry, and this would be coming from a university which would not have anything to gain by putting out only positive information. So Pete has helped raise the money to build new buildings so students could study the turf, pesticides, and everything that has to do with a golf course. It's a very big environmental project for the golf industry."

Another recent Pete Dye environmental project was a new 36-hole course in Kohler, Wisconsin, on the edge of Lake Michigan. The spectacular golf course has manufactured huge sand dunes on the site of an old army base with an old runway and buildings. The area needed to be cleaned up, as required by the department of health. Whistling Straits Golf Course was the result of the project, a marvelous example of turning an environmental disaster into a fertile area of growth and greenery.

TURNING LANDFILLS INTO GOLF COURSES

The idea that a landfill can become a golf course is, for many people, a stretch of the imagination. Then again, so was man walking on the moon and hitting a golf ball. The modern credo of course architects in the '90s and into the next century should be: If it's there we can build a course on it.

THE ASGCA

Many if not most of the nation's premier architects belong to the American Society of Golf Course Architects, an organization active in environmental issues and funding for research projects and responsible for numerous first-rate publications pertaining to course design and course building. Based in LaSalle, Illinois (near Chicago), the ASGCA is the ideal place for anyone planning to build or refurbish a golf course at their resort or club, to gather the latest information and even begin to locate the top architects in the world.

Courses have been built on all possible sites. If you look closely at Mount Rushmore, Washington has a flag for the sixth hole somewhere on his forehead—well almost.

Landfills are certainly not the first choice of golf architects, but they are definitely a challenge that is very rewarding. It is a sign of golf's giving something back to the environment, beauty where there was nothing.

Building on landfills is difficult for three main reasons, leachates, gas, and settling. Landfills have been capped, and that cap has to stay intact so as not to let any contaminants, or leachates, spill out. Landfills also contain methane gas, which is flammable and dangerous for plants and wildlife. There's also a problem of subsidence, or settling. As the garbage rots down it settles, and since gravity wants to pull it down, you will get some degree of sinking.

Keeping things level, such as tees and greens, is a main concern when building on a landfill. Course designers take extra precautions, testing the soil more carefully to determine that the ground won't start to sink. One method is to experiment. Golf architect Mike Hurdzan explains that his building team does what is called preloading. "We try and compress the landfill and do what is called preloading, where you pile on dirt then leave it there for a period of time. You put down a settling plate, which is a surveyor measure. Essentially what you're doing is trying to see how much the ground will settle. You stack the dirt up maybe ten feet high, then pull seven feet of dirt off the pile and let it rebound a

little . . . then you can put a tee or green on it if it's not going to settle too much. Another thing we do is we put fabric underneath it, an engineering cloth that helps it from settling as well. There are a lot of special techniques that you have to do. Landfills have their own unique problems which can cost the course 50 to 100 percent more than a normal golf course."

Landfill courses are indeed more costly. Rather than moving the dirt and trees around and working with the natural area that is already there, these courses require that materials be brought in from another site, since there is nothing usable to start with.

Courses on landfills change the scope of the community and bring a whole new look, smell, and feel to the area, not to mention improving the value of the homes nearby. So the next time you see the modern landfill of today, think: here may lie the golf course of tomorrow.

GOLF OFF THE COURSE

RANGES AND GOLF CENTERS

Ranges have become more sophisticated over the years. Some offer family fun and miniature golf, and others have pro shops, while most have teaching and training available. Below are some of the top-ranked golf courses in the country through 1996 by the Golf Range and Recreation Association of America. They are rated according to overall design, landing area, tee line, targets, facilities available, teaching and training, and customer service.

NORTHEAST

Atlantic Golf Center—South Attleboro, Ma.
Big Oak Driving Range—East Rochester, N.Y.
Bumble Bee Hollow—Mechanicsburg, Pa.
Chantilly Golf Center—Chantilly, Va.
Closter Golf Range—Closter, N.J.
Commack Golf Center—Commack, N.Y.
Fairway Golf—Piscataway, N.J.
Family Golf Center—Flemington, N.J.
Garden State Golf Center—Somerville, N.J.
Golden Bear Golf Center—Elmsford, N.Y.
Golden Bear Golf Center & Dome—
    Liverpool, N.Y.

Golden Bear Golf Center—Rochester, N.Y.
Golf Club at Chelsea Piers—New York, N.Y.
Golf Country—Lynn, Ma.
Heartland Golf Park—Deer Park, N.Y.
Hiland Family Golf Center—Queensbury, N.Y.
Indian River Family Golf Center—Virginia
    Beach, Va.
Lancaster Golf Center—Lancaster, Ma.
McDain Golf Center—Monroeville, Pa.
McGolf—Dedham, Ma.
Oakdale Golf Center—Oakdale, N.Y.
Owl's Creek Family Golf Center—Virginia
    Beach, Va.
Pine Canyon Golf—Voorhees, N.J.
Somerton Springs South Jersey Golf
    Campus—Sewell, N.J.
Spring Rock Golf Center—New Hyde
    Park, N.Y.
Sun 'N' Air Driving Range—Danvers, Ma.
Sunnybrook Golf—Manassas, Va.

SOUTHEAST

Alamo Country Club—San Antonio, Tx.
Blockbuster Golf & Games—Ft. Lauderdale, Fl.
Fair Oaks Golf Park—Fairfax, Va.
Fox Creek—Atlanta, Ga.
Frasch Park Range—Sulphur, La.
Golf Atlanta—Lithia Springs, Ga.
Golf World—Edmond, Ok.
Golfsmith Learning Center—Austin, Tx.
Hank Haney Golf Center Cityplace—Dallas, Tx.
Harbour View Golf Complex—Little River, S.C.
Heritage Hills Golf Center—Austell, Ga.
John Jacobs Golf Center—Tulsa, Ok.
John Prince Golf Center—Lake Worth, Fl.
Legend Sports—Altamonte Sp., Fl.
Leonard Golf Links—Fort Worth, Tx.
Man o' War Golf—Lexington, Ky.

Meyer Park Golf Center—Houston, Tx.
Mooresville Golf Center—Mooresville, N.C.
Northcrest Golf Range—Atlanta, Ga.
Pop's Golf Range—Palm Beach Gardens, Fl.
Precision Golf—San Antonio, Tx.
Range at Maitland Center—Orlando, Fl.
Sundance Golf Range—New Brunfels, Tx.
Sunnybrook Golf—Manassas, Va.
Tour Golf's Practice Tee—Birmingham, Al.
Wedges 'N' Woods—Augusta, Ga.
Wendell Coffee Golf Center—Tyrone, Ga.

MIDWEST

Carl's Golfland—Bloomfield Hills, Mi.
Cincinnati Golf Academy—Cincinnati, Oh.
Cog Hill Driving Range—Lemont, Il.
Family Golf Center at Cincinnati—
    Fairfield, Oh.
Family Golf Center at St. Louis—
    St. Louis, Mo.
Harborside International—Chicago, Il.
Illinois Center—Chicago, Il.
Maumee Sports Mall—Maumee, Oh.
Meadow Links Golf Academy—Cincinnati, Oh.
Michael Jordan Golf Center—Aurora, Il.
Missing Links—Mequon, Wi.
Silver Springs Golf Center—Menomonee
    Falls, Wi.
Smiley's Golf Complex—Llenexa, Ks.
The Range—Hudson, Oh.

WEST

Birdies Golf—Spokane, Wa.
Boulders Golf Center—San Leandro, Ca.
Crackerjack Family Fun Park—Scottsdale, Az.
Eagle View Golf Center—Olympia, Wa.
Family Golf Center—Mesa, Az.
Fiddlesticks—Tempe, Az.

Golf Park—Kent, Wa.
Green Valley Golf Range—Henderson, N.V.
Harborside Golf Center—San Diego, Ca.
Hound Hollow—Wood Village, Or.
The Islands Golf Center—Anaheim, Ca.
The Lakes at El Segundo—El Segundo, Ca.
MacArthur Park—Santa Ana, Ca.
Mariners Point Golf Links—Foster City, Ca.
McInnis Park Golf Center—San Rafael, Ca.
Mission Bay Golf Center—San Francisco, Ca.
Park Hill Golf Course—Denver, Co.
Pin High Family Golf Center—San Jose, Ca.
RangeLand USA—San Jose, Ca.
Redwood Golf Center—
    Redmond, Wa.
Wailea Golf Center Training
    Facility—Maui, Hi.

GOLF SHOWS

Commonly at commercial golf shows, you will find vendors selling golf equipment, books, and instructional videos; promoting golfing organizations; and hyping their resorts. There are usually plenty of contests, a lot of free information, and a marvelous golf atmosphere. Many shows feature the latest in computerized technology for you to play some indoor golf. Some shows set up mini-driving ranges to check out new clubs, while most have putting areas where you can try your skills on artificial turf and possibly win prizes in putting contests.

Shows are held throughout most of the country between January and March, with a few after the golf season in November and December, when the winter weather doesn't allow for much play. They are usually two- or three-day weekend events. Below are some of the popular shows to look for. Fees are usually moderate, and in most cases you generally do not need to buy tickets in advance.

The trick to getting the most out of a golf show is to take in as much as you can early in the day and then return to the areas you wish to spend more time at later in the day. Most shows are crowded early in the morning and less crowded late in the afternoon. Apparently golfers coming to a commercial show are on a similar schedule as when they are on the course. Golf shows vary in size and set-up, but in general they attract vendors from the major equipment manufacturers and resorts, particularly in and around the area in which they are being held.

The following list is culled from the 1997 schedule of events, in approximate order of their appearance throughout the year. Locations, where listed, may vary, but these are among the premier annual shows to look for:

Great American Golf Shows, Kentucky Golf
Show, Louisville, Ky.
North Coast Golf Shows, Cincinnati, Oh.
The Great Kansas City Golf Show, Kans.
The Great St. Louis Golf Show, Trans
World Dome
Greenville Golf Show, Greenville, S.C.
The Cincinnati Golf Show, Dr. Albert B.
Sabin Convention Center
The Cincinnati Golf Show, Cincinnati
Convention Center
Great American Golf Shows, Tennessee Golf
Show, Nashville, Tenn.
The Great Michigan Golf Show, Pontiac
Superdome, Mich.
North Coast Golf Shows, Philadelphia, Pa.
The Tennessee Golf Show, Opryland Hotel,
Nashville
Washington, D.C.'s Premiere Golf Expo,
Capitol Expo Center
Chicago Golf Show, Rosemont Convention
Center, Ill.
North Coast Golf Shows, Buffalo, N.Y.
Charlotte Golf Show, Charlotte Merchandise
Mart, N.C.
The Spring Indiana Golf Show, Indiana
Convention Center, Indianapolis
The Super Show, Georgia World Congress
Centre, Atlanta
Denver Golf Expo, Merchandise Mart Pavilion
Richmond Golf Show, Fairgrounds on
Strawberry Hill, Va.
The New Jersey Golf Show, Meadowlands
Expo Center, Secacus, N.J.
The Minnesota Golf Show, Hubert H.
Humphrey Metrodome, Minn.
North Coast Golf Show, Suffern, N.Y.

North Coast Golf Show, Washington D.C.
Toronto Golf & Travel Show, Metro Toronto
Convention Centre
Boston Golf Expo, Bayside Expo Center
Greater American Golf Shows, Lexington Golf
Show, Ky.
Mid-Atlantic Golf & Travel Show Inc., Show
Palace Arena
Michigan Novi Golf Expo, Novi, Mich.
World Golf Expos, Dallas Morning News,
Market Hall
Tennessee Golf Show
Montreal Golf & Travel Show, Montreal
Convention Centre
North Coast Golf Shows, Pittsburgh, Pa.
The Northern Ohio Golf Show, Kent State
University, Akron
New York Golf Show, Westchester County
Center, White Plains, N.Y.
Great American Golf Shows, Northern Ohio
Golf Show. Columbus, Ohio
Great American Golf Shows, Fall Indiana
Golf Show
Golf & Ski Expo North, Valley Expo Center
Chesapeake Golf Shows, Oriole Park at
Camden Yards, Baltimore, Md.
North Coast Golf Shows, I-X Center,
Cleveland, Oh.

Along with these annual shows are PGA
events such as the PGA Merchandise Show in
January and the PGA International Golf Show
in the fall. The Merchandise Show, billed as
the Disney World of Golf Shows, takes place
in Orlando and features over 1,000 vendors.
The fall international show takes place in Las
Vegas and is also for golf merchandisers.

GOLF ASSOCIATIONS AND GROUPS

If you're in the market for more information, there is an organization for practically every aspect of golf from which you can get assistance and answers. Below are some of the key golf-related organizations and associations.

American Junior Golf Association
(770) 998-4653

American Senior Golf Association
(561) 863-3638

American Society of Golf Course Architects
(312) 372-7090

American Society of Landscape Architects
(202) 686-2752

Amateur Golfers' Association International
011-603-245-5001

Association of Disabled American Golfers
(303) 220-0921

Association of Golf Merchandisers
(602) 373-8564

Business and Charity Golf Link (805) 322-5601

Canadian Golf Association, Inc. (905) 338-5232

Canadian Golf Foundation (905) 849-9700

College Golf Foundation (Roex Tour)
(609) 252-1561

Golf Collectors Society (513) 256-2474

Golf Course Builders Association of America
(913) 841-2240

Golf Course Development Association
(416) 444-5422

Golf House (museum and home of the USGA) (908) 234-2300

Golfaholics Anonymous (408) 624-4386

Indoor Golf Association of America
(619) 273-0373

Junior Golf Alliance (904) 893-2991

Junior Golf Association of the USA
(216) 823-7406

LPGA—Ladies Professional Golf Association
(904) 274-6200

Miniature Golf Association of America
(904) 781-4653

Minority Golf Association of America
(516) 288-8255

National Association of Junior Golfers
(207) 935-7080

National Golf Foundation (506) 744-6006

National Mini-Tour Association (402) 484-8687

PGA of America—Professional Golf
Association (561) 624-8400

Professional Clubmakers Society (502) 241-2816

Senior Golfers Association of America
(803) 626-8100

U.S. Golf Federation (818) 595-1099

U.S. Golf Society (617) 369-1396

USA Junior Golf Association (847) 394-5014

United States Golf Association (908) 949-9411

United States Putting Association
(301) 791-9332

World Golf Hall of Fame (904) 273-3350

Worldwide Women's Golf (617) 262-1929

Worldwide Golf Marketers Association
(407) 321-6322

GOLF COLLECTIBLES

As golf becomes more popular, its treasures of the early years become more valuable. Items such as old feathery balls and long-nose woods from the 1800s are among the valued equipment that are part of the game's great history. Feathery balls, depending on the signature and condition of the ball, can go for as high as $15,000. Books from the nineteenth century and earlier that talk about the game, as well as artwork, are rare and command a high asking price at collectibles shows and auctions.

According to George Lewis, Director of the Golf Collector's Society, there are a great number of golf collectibles, including: balls, tees (of which there are thousands of varieties), golf comics from the '40s and '50s, autographs and letters from the top pros, advertisements of the tournaments as well as programs and posters, golf postcards from the early 1900s up through the 1930s, and even golf pencils with course names on them. Lewis also notes that ceramic, glass, and bronze statues made of golfers around the turn of the century are very collectible. The 1743 Thomas Mathison poem "Goff" (not Golf), the first book published on golf, also commands top dollar, selling for several thousand dollars in its original form.

The Golf Collectors Society, in Dayton, Ohio, offers a $40 ($45 in Canada) yearly membership, which includes their quarterly publication *The Bulletin*, a membership directory featuring the names and numbers of other collectors, and participation in their annual meeting and Hickory Hacker Golf Tournament. They also sponsor regional shows including the annual Trade Show at the Golf House (USGA Headquarters and Museum) in Far Hills, New Jersey.

Golf shows, sales, and auctions have become big business, with top auction houses selling items at substantial prices. Clubs belonging to either great golfers or celebrities can be very pricey items. As Lewis puts it, "Different collectors are interested in different things; they have preferences as to what they collect." Richard (Dick) Donovan of Endicott, New York, for example, is one of the foremost golf-book collectors in the world. For nearly twenty years he has been amassing an astounding collection of golf books. He is an authority on what is out there in print and where to find it.

Beyond books, there are collectors of scorecards and even trading cards. Like anything else, collecting has its specialties.

If there is some golf-related item of importance to you, it may be the start of a collection. For many, watching the auctions, checking out the golf collectibles shows, or visiting a golf museum is enough to put them in touch with the great history of the game.

Besides the golf museum at the USGA Golf House, in Far Hills, New Jersey, there are other museums around the country, including the James River Museum at the James River Country Club in Newport News, Virginia, near Norfolk, and the Ralph Miller Golf Museum in City of Industry. Located in

SOME GOLF STATISTICS

There are currently around 500 million rounds of golf played in the United States in a given calendar year on nearly 15,500 courses.

Seventy percent of the rounds played are at courses open to the public, and seventy percent of the courses around the country are now open to the public.

Nearly half of all golfers are between the ages of eighteen and thirty-nine, dispelling the notion that golf is primarily played by an older generation. This group of golfers plays twelve to thirteen rounds per year, while senior golfers (25 percent of the golf population, or 3.6 million players) average over thirty-six rounds of golf a year.

The typical golfer today is male, is 39.6 years old, has a household income of just under $57,000, and plays about twenty rounds of golf per year.

Women make up 21.5 percent of the golfing population.

About 2 million people try the game each year, nearly 60 percent of which are between the ages of eighteen and twenty nine. Nearly 40 percent are women.

Golfers spend more than $15 billion a year on equipment, related merchandise, and playing fees.

southern California, Ralph Miller Golf Museum houses a 5,000-book golf library, including a copy of the 1743 edition of "Goff."

For those traveling abroad, you might duck into the BC Golf House Society in British Columbia, Canada. In Japan you might visit the Japan Golf Association Golf Museum in the Palace Building in Tokyo, while in Scotland, you might make a special appointment to visit the Heritage of Golf in East Lothian, which features some of the earliest golf paintings.

GOLF COMMUNITIES

Golf communities continue to open around the country, especially in warm climates rich with courses such as Florida, Arizona, Texas, and California. Communities are geared primarily for retirees and are often mentioned in senior and retirement magazines such as *Senior Golfer*. Family communities with golf courses are also becoming prominent.

Depending on the size of the community, these real estate developments can have anywhere from one to five courses and include athletic and social amenities such as community centers, fitness centers, swimming, tennis, and other activities commonly found at vacation resorts.

As for the real estate itself, homes run the gamut from townhouses to custom-built ranch houses. From $100,000 to $2 million, you can find any type of home you desire. For those who still enjoy a little change of season, or want to stay close to family and

friends, other parts of the country such as the Northeast have communities as well.

When looking to move to a golf real estate community it's important to check out all that is available. Questions you might consider include:

How big is the population? You want to know how crowded the course (and other) activities will be.

How many courses are there? Variety is nice.

What other activities are there? You can't always be on the course.

What is security like?

How far is the community from local shopping?

What kind of services and amenities are available?

What is the average age? This is important, as some communities are retirement while others sport a semi-retired, younger crowd and some are even geared for family living.

How long will it be before your home is ready? (if you are having a home custom built)

What styles of homes are offered?

Do you have an approved builder list? Check out who the builders are.

Can you rent a home to see if you like living there?

Who owns the facilities and the course? Some communities, like condominiums, have ownership of the facilities by the residents, which may be advantageous in assuring that the property won't be sold in years to come.

Don Langden, sales director of Palm Beach Polo Golf Country Club, emphasizes that people should try to assess the lifestyle first. "Typically golfers are concerned about how crowded the course or courses will be and what houses are available, but I think what you're really buying in most of these communities are the people and the lifestyle. The sticks, the bricks, and the homes can be built anywhere, but the people that you play and do things with are the most important element. The homes are usually built by a similar list of approved builders regardless. It's the community and lifestyle that matter most."

There are also communities where people are buying for part-time living. If you are buying to escape the cold weather for the winter months, you will be more concerned about security since you won't be there for part of the year. You want to be sure that you are notified in case of an emergency and that the property is safe and well built. From the opposite side of the coin, you

may be concerned that too many of your neighbors won't be your neighbors much of the year, which is a plus for getting tee times, but may leave you feeling a bit deserted.

Here are just a few examples of what these communities offer. For those interested, you might first determine whether Florida, California, Texas, Arizona, or another locale suits you best in regard to family, friends, and health concerns. Then you can seek out communities in that part of the country.

Sun City Georgetown. This 5,300-acre Texas community has recently opened up for adults over the age of fifty-five and features four golf courses: three championship courses and a par-sixty executive course. Homes are priced from $108,000 to $237,000. A large community and activity

center offers swimming, a first-rate fitness center, tennis courts, and other activities. This Sun City sits near Austin, Texas, but there are others in Phoenix, Las Vegas, Palm Desert, California, and one in northern California as well. (800) 833-5932

Lost Lake Golf Club. Lost Lake offers golf mavens a 355-acre community surrounded by a marvelous Tom Fazio par-seventy-two golf course. With homes to be had in the $135,000 to $200,000 range, the creators of Lost Lake hoped to keep costs down and affordable. Amenities include a swimming and tennis center, 175-seat dining room, terrace grille, lounge, and clubhouse. Lost Lake is in sunny Florida. (800) 253-9122

Winston Trails. In the heart of Palm Beach County, Florida, at Lake Worth, sits a prominent community with homes starting in the low $100,000s. Surrounded by an 18-hole Joe Lee course, is a wide selection of single family homes. Swimming pools, wading pools for children, and lighted tennis courts offer various activities at a recreation center. Not strictly a retirement community, Winston Trails also has a new state-of-the-art clubhouse and fitness center that offers aerobics classes, weight room, and golf lessons from an on-staff PGA professional. (561) 433-2220

Palm Beach Polo Golf and Country Club. The weather is always marvelous in West Palm Beach, and this community offers a variety of housing styles to enjoy life near the course. Villas, townhouses, and custom-designed homes start at $185,900 and sit in

seven new neighborhoods. The Pete Dye 18-hole Cypress Course, the Ron Garl/Jerry Pate 18-hole Scottish links-style Dunes Course, and the George Fazio 9-hole Olde Course provide three very different golfing experiences. A brand-new putting course, lit for night play, twenty tennis courts, a health and fitness center, spa, swimming pools, and world-class polo and equestrian facilities give you more choices of activities at this very sporting club. Twenty-two hundred acres allows for a lot of activities and up to 1,500 homes without a crowded living situation. (800) 257-1038

PGA National. Why not move in with the pros? The PGA National offers condos, villas, and estates ranging from $160,000 to nearly $800,000, and features five championship golf courses. A host of activities include bicycle paths, jogging trails, swimming pools, and an aerobics and dance studio. Tennis courts, a health and fitness club, shopping, schools, and beaches sit nearby the PGA National, which is located on a spacious settlement in Palm Beach Gardens, Florida. (800) 226-6900

Heritage Highlands in Marana, Arizona, is a brand-new community with its own Arthur Hills championship golf course flanking nearly 1,300 homes on some 5,500 acres of prime real estate. Homes vary in style and range from around $100,000 up to $300,000. A large community center offers a health center, swimming, tennis, and other amenities. (888) FUN-BEGINS

INTERNATIONAL GOLF

Golf is played in more countries than any other sport. It is truly a universal game. History traces the roots of the game back to Belgium, Ireland, and of course, Scotland, where the game's official birthplace sits on the windswept links courses that hug the ocean. The game has since grown in prominence throughout the British Isles, where today there are over 2,000 courses in England, Scotland, Wales, and Northern Ireland. Closer to home, Canada has some 2,000 courses, while Mexico is seeing new resort courses built at an impressive rate.

Across the Pacific, Japan is home to some phenomenal mountain courses and numerous driving

ranges, some standing two and three tiers high, as the game has become a significant part of the Japanese lifestyle. China is a prospering golf community, as the Asian tour promotes the game to millions of new golf enthusiasts. And in Australia, home of several world-renowned players and courses, golf holidays are a way of life.

PGA and LPGA members now hail from more than thirty nations worldwide. American tours and tournaments have now reached as far as the mainland of China, and the competition in many international championships is now at a higher level than ever before. Satellite capabilities now beam golf into more than 100 countries, and the sport continues to grow into new and uncharted territories.

THE BRITISH ISLES

For centuries Scotland has been home to classic links courses that are as indigenous to the area as kilts and bagpipes. The links courses have been windswept courses along the water, with a host of natural and man-made challenges. Various types of courses

now sit alongside century-old manors and castles as well as the newer luxurious resorts. From private clubs to public courses run by local authorities, the game has long attracted Brits. Fees range from £6 for public courses to over £40 for the more exclusive clubs such as the courses at St. Andrews. Some areas in Scotland offer packages for weekly play, while other clubs offer a ticket enabling golfers to play two rounds in one day.

To play on some of the classic old courses, it's a good idea to bring a signed proof of handicap. It's also suggested that if you're traveling to Britain, you might call ahead to find out the availability of the courses you wish to play. Naturally, hotel guests have priority at resort courses. However, if you are determined to make golf a primary concern, you might choose a specific holiday organizer or golf-tour package for England, Scotland, Wales, or Northern Ireland. Many touring companies in the United States offer packages that include golfing throughout Britain, especially Scotland. The British Tourist Authority in New York City can be helpful if you're looking for such a tour.

As for the game itself, it is played in much the same manner as it is in the United States. The Royal and Ancient acts in harmony with the USGA on almost all rulings. There are less trollies, or electric carts as we know them in the States, but otherwise the basic idea remains unchanged. Throughout the British Isles, however, golfers are predominantly purists. Says architect Jay

Morrish, "I've never heard of a golfer in Scotland picking up the ball and moving it in any circumstance. They just don't do it no matter what. In the United States we play winter rules and use other variations, but in Scotland, they play it no matter where it lies. They are golf purists."

It might also be noted that one of the significant differences between courses in the United States and in the British Isles is in the maintenance and appearance of the courses. Greens may have weeds on them; there may be brown on the leaves or on patches of the fairway. This is not for lack of upkeep, it is simply the tradition of golf in Scotland. The natural look and growth of a course is part of the beauty and majesty of the English and Scottish courses. There is less emphasis on fertilizer and pesticides, or on everything being green at all times. The natural beauty is allowed to include the natural changes in greenery. Several American architects note that rather than making American courses camera ready, with the perfect green look and tightly cropped greens, they like the idea of letting the course mature naturally. It often makes for a more interesting, challenging course.

The more than 2,000 courses in the British Isles include many classics well known to golf enthusiasts, vacation planners, and tournament officials. These courses see their heaviest crowds in the spring and summer months, and not unlike the United States, can be hellish in winter, if one dares to be so bold. Some of the premier courses in Scotland include:

Gleneagles, Scotland's premier inland golf venue, is one of Europe's finest resorts. The King's, Queen's, and Monarch Courses offer championship-caliber play, and there is also a 9-hole course and driving range to boot. They all flank the fabulous Gleneagles Hotel resort, which sits on some 830 acres. The resort is home to everything from a modern health spa to a shooting school and equestrian centre.

Royal Dornoch in Dornoch, Sutherland, Scotland, has seen golf balls bound down the fairways since 1616, so nothing you do on the course hasn't been done before. Featuring raised plateau greens and plentiful mounds and hilltops, this windswept course is a walk on sacred and hallowed ground.

St. Andrews, the official home of golf, sits on the links between the ocean and the farmlands. Five courses now make up the legendary St. Andrews, including the historic Old Course. Home of the Royal and Ancient Golf Club, the sacred governing body of golf in the British Isles, St. Andrews has been home to countless tournaments. It is a perennial favorite stop for tours from all over the world. Getting to play this magnificent homage to the great game is not easy. St. Andrews features the Old Course Hotel, situated by the famed seventeenth, the Road Hole.

Turnberry, on the Ayrshire Coast, has been home to the British Open since the holes were first designed back in 1903. Remodeled after the Second World War, this classic seaside links features long, sweeping sands along the two courses known as Alish and Aaron. The accompanying resort, overlooking Turnberry Bay, is one of the finest, most elegant in the world.

Other premier courses in Scotland include the course at the phenomenal **Cally Palace Hotel** in Kirkcudbrightshire, the new **Lagganmore** course in Wigtownshire, the classic **Royal Troon** and **Muirfield**. **Lock Lomond**, near Glasgow, is a new favorite and is the first American-designed course in Scotland. The Tom Weiskopf/Jay Morrish course is well kept in the American maintenance tradition and offers a host of traditional Scottish challenges. A private club, Lock Lomond sits on vast acreage that surrounds the Rossdhu House, a lavish estate from 1773. The natural beauty and championship-caliber course combine for a marvelous experience for club members or invited guests.

In England, an outstanding golfing experience can be found at **Sunningdale**, in Berkshire. Two courses, Old and New, are equally tricky, although not necessarily long. Since the turn of the century, championships have graced the Old Course, which offers exquisite panoramic views. The New Course lacks some of the scenic majesty but will certainly see its share of noteworthy events in years to come.

Nearby **Walton Heath**, which has played host to the Ryder Cup, Walker Cup, and other top championships, is equally challenging with its old and new courses vying for distinction as the best inland courses in England.

Royal Birkdale in Southport, Lancashire, England, is designed in the traditional links style. Home to the British Open, Royal Birkdale awes spectators and players with its expansive sand dunes and majestic natural beauty. Like so many of the most exciting links courses, Birkdale provides golfers with the traditional challenges of nature and the elements. Golf purists should love these courses.

Some of the many other noteworthy courses in England include **Cleeve Hill**, sitting some 1,000 feet above sea level, and the beautiful parkland **Ullenwood Course**. The **Oxfordshire Golf Course**, in Thames, has hosted some of the games' top tournaments. This Rees Jones gem, opened in 1993, has the sprawling British feel, with plenty of mounds and tucked-away traps to challenge all levels of golfers.

Ballybunion, in the Republic of Ireland, features two of the most highly rated courses

THE LEGENDARY ST. ANDREWS AND YOU

So, you want to play the Old Course at St. Andrews? The legendary St. Andrews, the one in Scotland, the one that has chapters and entire books devoted to its lure, is now home to five 18-hole courses and one 9-hole course. If you're visiting Scotland and you play golf, it is your duty to at least make a wholehearted effort to play one of these courses.

All courses require that you reserve well in advance of travel. There are no reservations taken for Saturday play. Four courses, the New, the Jubilee, the Eden, and the Strathyrum are delightful, scenic, and challenging. The Old Course, however, is a walk through golfing history. The Old Course will accept applications for the following year's play as of the prior October 1st, and you should not delay. If you do get onto the Old Course, dress appropriately, speak softly, and mind your manners. Applications will be read and playing times allocated in early to mid-January, so wait by the phone for that all-important call.

If you send an application to play the Old Course, you must apply to play one of the other courses as well. This assures that you are indeed serious about the game, and it gives the folks at St. Andrews a chance to check you out and make sure you are Old Course material. You must also send proof of your current handicap. This is tricky since no one believes you most of the time anyway. To apply, contact: The Reservations Manager, St. Andrews Links Management Committee, St. Andrews, Fife KY16 9SF, Scotland, U.K.; Tel: 011 44 1334 475 757; Fax: 011 44 1334 477 036.

Applications are registered, and a provisional reservation form is issued indicating the reservation, greens fees, and the latest date for payment. This provisional reservation will be held until that date. Reservations will be confirmed upon receipt of payment by pound sterling check or credit card.

If you do not get an Old Course ballot, do not despair. There is an Old Course lottery. You can apply in person at 1:45 p.m. the day prior to the day on which you wish to play and enter a lottery held at 2 p.m. Results are posted at 4 p.m. for the following day. You can apply for the lottery by calling 011 44 1334 473 393 from the U.S.A. or 01334 473 393 within Great Britain.

If you'd like to pay for a complete tour including a chance at the Old Course, you can contact The Pensus Group, which offers the "Old Course Experience" excursion to Scotland. The package includes play on one of the other courses as well. Call them in Arizona at (602) 230-9000.

Handicaps required to play the Old Course are: men, below 12; women, below 14. Men up to 18 and women up to 22 inquire as well!

in the world. These historic, scenic seaside links have hosted the Irish Amateur Championship and many other great golfing events. **Killarney Golf and Fishing Club** has been home to the Irish Open, and the two marvelous courses are ranked not only among Ireland's finest, but among the best in all of Europe and perhaps the world.

Other courses throughout Ireland include the championship links course at **Waterville** in the southwest, and Arnold Palmer's seaside links design, **Tralee**. In the north, the historic **Royal Dublin Golf Club** and nearby **Portmarnock Golf Club** are both musts for those passing through Dublin. **Royal Country Down** and the **Portsteart** seaside links are also among the most challenging in the northeast part of Ireland. Northwest, you might want to check out **Rosses Point** in County Slige, or the difficult **Enniscrone Golf Club** in Clifden.

Considered to be the premier golfing resort in Wales, the **St. Pierre and Country Club** is a lavish, old, elegant venue sitting on some 400 acres of beautiful parkland. Home of the 1996 Solheim Cup, the two championship courses flank a fourteenth-century manorhouse.

SPAIN, PORTUGAL, AND MOROCCO

On the Mediterranean Sea, covering some seventy miles of arid, hilly terrain, sits the popular vacation spot of Costa Del Sol. The lavish beauty of the area is sprinkled with over forty golf courses, including the world famous Valderrama, home of the 1997 Ryder Cup. No other area, outside of U.S. golf meccas like Florida or California, has such a large concentration of first-rate golf courses in one place. The variety is astounding and includes seaside layouts, parkland courses, and mountainous terrain.

Among the premier courses in the area include **Valderrama**, labeled the Augusta of Europe. This Robert Trent Jones course tests golfers' accuracy and ability to navigate around trees and through cork oaks on hilly ground. It is a true championship course in an extremely scenic setting.

The **Aloha Golf Course** is also among the finest in the area, featuring tight, tough fairways, large greens, and marvelous scenery. Nearby sits **Sotogrande**, a course from the mid-'60s that remains one of the favorites in Costa Del Sol and overlooks Gibraltar and the Mediterranean Sea. The course is ranked among the top 100 in the world. **Las Brisas** is another favorite along this scenic stretch of land that has seen its share of European tournaments.

Beyond Costa Del Sol, the region of Andalucia is home to courses in and around Sevilla, Huelva, Malaga, and Cordoba. **Las Brisas, Los Arqueros**, and **Mira Flores** in Malaga; **San Roque Club** and **Novo Sancti Petri** in Cadiz; **Granada Golf** and **Los Moriscos** in Granada; and **Bozoblanco** in Cordoba are among the many intriguing courses.

Golf has been popular in Spain for many years, but players like Seve Ballesteros from Pedrena and Jose Maria Olazabal of Fuenterrabia, with great play and charisma, have elevated the popularity of the game to new heights over the past ten to fifteen years. What was once a game for the monarchy and the wealthy has become a game for everyone. The influx of resorts and heightened tourist business has also helped the game grow in Spain to where it is now very much a part of the lifestyle.

Portugal has also grown into a major golfing country. **Estoril** is a scenic old course dating back to 1929 at the Hotel Palacio. **Penina**, built in 1966, featuring an 18-hole course and two nine holers; **Vilamoura** from 1969; and the more recent **Vila Sol** are highly rated. The Robert Trent Jones Jr. courses, **Penha Longa, Quinta da Marinha**, and **Troia**, are also considered among the finest in the country.

Morocco is home to several interesting courses. American golf architect Cabell Robinson has been instrumental in building courses in Morocco, as well as in Spain and Portugal. Robinson, who spends a great deal of time working in these areas, notes Morocco as one of the burgeoning sites for courses. **Royal Golf d'El Jadida** is one of the most scenic, well-designed layouts, sporting eucalyptus covered dunes along the ocean on this 7,000-yard gem. A colorful course in Marrakech called **Amelkis** is home to a new 7,200

yarder in what will soon be a resort development. It is a top-level course that is already very photogenic.

Agadir is home to some enjoyable courses as well, including Club Med's **Les Dunes**, a Robinson-designed course with deep fairway bunkers, plenty of water, and some nice elevation changes. Other courses in Morocco include **Royal Golf de Anfa** in Casablanca, **Royal Golf de Tanger** in Tanger,. **Golf de El Palmeral** in El Palmeral, and **Royal Golf de Agadir** in Adagir.

ELSEWHERE IN EUROPE

France has long been a popular golfing destination, featuring nearly 500 courses. The outskirts of Paris boast private golf clubs that are majestic and historic. The **Golf de Chantilly** is a stone's throw from the city and is a testimony to golf's tranquility. This 1909 course still meets the challenges of today's golfers. **St. Germain** is within an hour of downtown Paris and sits aside an exquisite clubhouse. Chiseled from what was once a hunting forest, this course is scenic, quiet, and difficult. Both of these courses, and several others in the Paris area including the **Golf Club de Feucherolles**, are semi-private and generally available to the public on weekdays. **Morfontaine**, also not far from Paris, offers another fine, challenging course that has been billed as one of the most attractive courses in France, or Europe for that matter.

Outside of Paris are some spectacular courses along the French countryside, including the courses at Biarritz. Other gems in France include the **Makila Country Club**, the **Real Golf Club de San Sebastian**, and the **Royal Club Evian**, a world-renowned resort and spa in Evian-les-Bains.

Switzerland, meanwhile, offers more than just skiing. If you like mountainous courses, the Alps have resort courses tucked away, that feature breathtaking views. The Lindner Golf Hotel is one of the most highly recommended resorts in Switzerland because it sits near the famed **Plan Barmois Golf Course**, and within a long tee shot of the **Super Crans** and **Sierre** courses designed by Jack Nicklaus.

CANADA

Canada is home to some 2,000 golf courses, with more on the way as the game continues to grow in popularity. In fact, Canada has the highest number of players per capita of any country in the world, nearly 20 percent. Second only to ice hockey, golf has been a long-time favorite in America's neighbor to the north, and possibly because of ice hockey, Canada has the most left-handed golfers of any country in the world.

Perhaps the biggest concern to Canada's golfing community are the harsh winters. In recent years, the problem has been

addressed. Domed golf facilities have sprung up in most major Canadian cities. Up to 150 yards long with double-tiered tee decks, practice bunkers, and putting greens, these are popular alternatives to braving the conditions and playing winter rules.

Golf is far from new to Canada. The Royal Montreal Golf Club, still going strong and having hosted the 1975 and 1980 Canadian Opens, was originally built in 1873, the first golf club in North America. Other clubs formed by the turn of the century, and the game grew rapidly. The most prominent area for golf emerged in Ontario, which is now home to nearly one-third of the country's courses. Ladies golf has long been a staple on the Canadian golf scene. A new organization, the National Women's Golf Network, has been established to acclimate new female golfers to the game and provide competitive opportunities. Toronto is home to an all-women's golf club, simply known as the Toronto Women's Golf Club.

Some of the most significant courses in Canada include:

Banff Springs Golf Course in Banff, Alberta, is a public course dating back to the 1920s, and it sits among the spectacular Canadian Rockies. The Bow and Spray rivers flank the majestic course. At 5,000 feet high, you may think you can drive like John Daly, but don't be fooled: the 6,700-yard course is no walk in the park. Tough as it is to play, you'll survive if you forget to bring a particular club, but do not forget to bring your camera.

Kananaskis Country Golf Club, just about an hour from Calgary, was called by

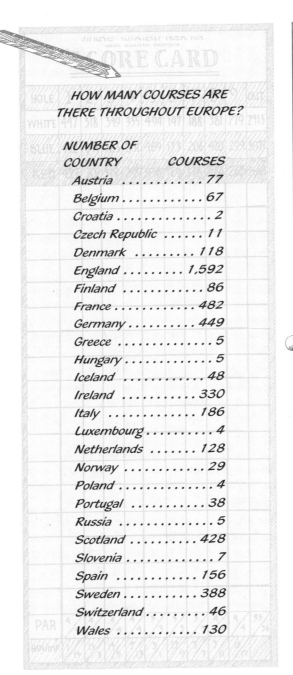

HOW MANY COURSES ARE THERE THROUGHOUT EUROPE?

NUMBER OF COUNTRY	COURSES
Austria	77
Belgium	67
Croatia	2
Czech Republic	11
Denmark	118
England	1,592
Finland	86
France	482
Germany	449
Greece	5
Hungary	5
Iceland	48
Ireland	330
Italy	186
Luxembourg	4
Netherlands	128
Norway	29
Poland	4
Portugal	38
Russia	5
Scotland	428
Slovenia	7
Spain	156
Sweden	388
Switzerland	46
Wales	130

Robert Trent Jones "The finest location I have ever seen for a public golf course." Actually there are two incredible courses in a setting you'll never forget.

Chateau Whistler Golf Club in British Columbia is a fabulous, scenic, mountainous course just north of Vancouver. Those who've played it rave.

Crown Isle Golf Club in Courtenay, British Columbia, is a highly rated new public course, and is both scenic and inexpensive.

Gallagher's Canyon Golf and Country Club, in Kelowana, British Columbia, has hosted the Canadian Amateur Championships. It's a good, challenging course for all levels of players.

Riverside Country Club, in New Brunswick, overlooks the Kennebecasis River and is a top-level course that has hosted many championships in its sixty-plus years.

The Highland Links Golf Course, Nova Scotia, has been called the Cypress Point of Canada. Overlooking the Atlantic Ocean on the remote Cape Breton Island, this public course is a fabulous golfing experience, both scenic and challenging.

Belleview Golf Course, in Woodslee, Ontario, is a 27-hole layout, with an 18-hole and neighboring 9-hole executive course. The Belle River winds its way through the course, waiting to soak up off-target shots. Ponds and some hills add to the challenge.

Eagle Creek Golf Club in Dunrobin, Ontario, is a relatively new Ken Venturi design in a wooded setting. This tough, target course is a good test for any golfer.

The Glen Abbey Golf Course, in Oakville, Ontario, home to the Bell Canadian Open and the offices of the Royal Canadian Golf Association, is a championship course. This public course, the first designed by Jack Nicklaus on his own, is a marvelous test for golfers at all handicap levels.

The **Osprey Valley Heathlands Golf Course** sits just northwest of Toronto, but golfers swear it's a piece of Scotland. It's a highly rated Doug Carrick links course that shouldn't be missed if you're in Ontario.

The Devil's Pulpet Golf Association offers two of the premier courses in Ontario: **Devil's Pulpet** and **Devil's Paintbrush**. These Mike Hurdzan gems play host to tournaments and feature some spectacular holes, including the first on Devil's Pulpet with its spectacular view of the surrounding city.

Brudnell River Provincial Golf Course on Prince Edwards Island is one of a few challenging public courses run by the province. This one is set in the woodlands and, for a reasonable price, tests golfers' entire game.

The Links at Crowbush Cove, also on Prince Edwards Island, is a top-rated, relatively new links course with incredible, breathtaking views.

There are many other highly rated courses throughout Canada offering everything from woodlands to links to mountainous golf. *Score*, Canada's leading golf magazine, rates and reviews most of the country's courses. Two books, *The Great Golf Courses of Canada*, volumes one and two (by John Gordon), also sum up most of the significant courses throughout the country. Like the United States, there are many private clubs and resort courses, but there is also an increase in public and daily-fee golf courses as the demand grows.

JAPAN

Another of the most prominent golfing nations in the world today is Japan. Golf firmly established itself in Japan with the Kobe Club, built in 1903. However, it was not until 1935 that Japan was recognized for its golfing prowess by the rest of the world. It was that year that six Japanese professional golfers played an exhibition tour in the United States. Playing a competition against an American team that included Sam Snead and Bobby Jones, the Japanese team won 60 percent of the games. These pros returned to great enthusiasm in Japan and devoted themselves to teaching their excellent techniques to their successors. This series of events helped facilitate the popularity of golf in Japan and spurred the construction of many new courses.

After World War II, the U.S. Occupation Force initiated the restoration of many of the golf courses in Japan. By 1953, many of the seized clubs were returned to their original owners and the number of Japanese players, once again, started to increase.

In the mid-1950s, Japan was invited to enter the Canada Cup, which later became the World Cup. In 1957, Japan won both team and individual honors. Minokichi Nakamura became a major hero with his individual victory in the '57 cup matches. This was another major step in the status of golf in Japan, from hobby of the wealthy to sport for the masses.

Today, the number of courses in Japan is over 2,200, with many more being built. There are over 10 million golfers playing and a Japanese PGA tour for the pros. One of the stars of the Japanese tour, Isao Aoki, helped generate great interest in the game. International stars like Seve Ballesteros were also instrumental in bringing the game to the forefront in Japan.

Course building in Japan is not easy, as most of the available lands are mountainous. Mike Poellot, the principal owner of J. Michael Poellot Golf Design in Saratoga, California, a firm that has designed numerous top-rated courses throughout Japan and Asia, explains the land situation in the country: "Japan presents many unique scenarios." Courses are frequently tucked in between farms, on steep mountain slopes surrounded by wetlands. Due to the scarcity of land available for golf-course development, we've had to work in comparatively small spaces. Besides working in tight spaces, there are strict environmental restrictions. Courses have to be constructed in harmony with their surroundings." Despite the obstacles presented, Poellot and his team have designed over twenty courses in Japan.

Some interesting notes on golf in Japan include:

Professional Female Caddies: After World War II, the golf boom was so great in Japan that it caused a scarcity of labor in most of the Japanese golf clubs. Young girls in the towns and villages were hired to work as caddies. They were housed in dormitories and paid a salary. There are still professional female caddies in Japan. However, they are housewives who caddy as a part-time job.

Lunch Break: The custom in Japan has been to take a lunch break after the first nine holes.

Cleats Anywhere: Most of the Japanese clubhouses are designed so that you don't need to remove your cleats to walk around. This may be in conjunction with the above-mentioned idea of having lunch before finishing the course.

Double Greens: Because of the variance in climate, many Japanese courses feature two greens per hole: one of bent grass and the other of korai, a strain of grass designed to withstand the strong summer heat. New strains of grass have eliminated the two-green concept on many of Japan's newer or remodeled courses, but many courses still continue the two-green tradition.

Among the most significant courses in Japan are the **Tokyo Golf Club** and the **Kasumigaseki Country Club** in the eastern part of the country. Kasumigaskei, in Tokyo, is where the Japanese team won the 1957 World Cup, shocking the golf world. There are two challenging 18-hole courses on the site designed originally by Kinya Fujita and refurbished by British architect Charles Allison.

The **Hirono** and **Naruo** golf clubs in the western part of the country are also significant courses because they are excellent championship-level courses and they have great history. Newer gems in Japan include the **Caledonian Golf Club** in Chiba Prefecture. This lavish Poellot layout opened

FIVE OF THE WORLD'S MOST UNIQUE HOLES!

The Devil's Paintbrush course at the Devil's Pulpet Golf Association in Ontario, Canada. The 574-yard seventeenth hole is constructed around a barn and a neighboring house, which splits the fairway in three. You can play around them, between them, or if the windows are open, perhaps right on through. And if this real-life miniature-golf obstacle isn't enough of a challenge, the hole also features a fifteen-foot-high sod wall bunker, said to be the biggest of its kind in the world.

The Royal Westmoreland course in Barbados. The 320-meter sixth hole plays into a magnificent limestone quarry. When the hole was constructed, a hermit was discovered living in the quarry, hence the hole is known as the Hermit Hole. The hermit has since moved, but the hole still has neighborhood inhabitants—the green monkeys—so watch your ball carefully, as they may get to it before you do.

Cypress Point Golf Course in Barbados. The sixteenth is only 233 yards but is considered one of the toughest in the world. The one little catch, however, is that the green sits on a peninsula across the Atlantic Ocean. Yes, you can bail out and take the long way around, or do your Lindbergh impression and solo across the ocean.

The Seddiner See Golf Course in Potsdamn Germany. The 420-meter par four eighteenth at the New Course leads to a huge double green shared by the ninth hole. A lake separates the two fairways until they finally come together at a dramatic double green built to symbolize the reunification of East and West Germany.

One last hole that is no longer in use once had the distinction of being the longest golf hole in the world. The hole was built on a course on Koolan Island in Australia, to be played by miners who were working the island. The mining expedition ended in late 1995, and the island was returned to its original natural manner, which meant scrapping the golf course that had been constructed. The course, during its short lifespan, was home to a par-seven, 860-yard sixth hole. Besides being the longest hole, it included one of the world's most unparalleled hazards—airplanes. The hole sat on land occupied by the local airport, and played across a landing strip. Striking an incoming flight was a penalty stroke, and finding the ball afterward was a miracle.

in 1990 and blends Scottish architecture and contemporary technology to create an innovative, dramatic, and scenic course. Also of note among the many exciting new courses in Japan is the **Golden Palm Country Club** Course, a spectacular, somewhat flat course that opened in Kagoshima in 1994.

CHINA AND ASIA

Along with the phenomenal golf boom in Japan, The People's Republic of China, Taiwan, Malaysia, Indonesia, Thailand, and the Philippines are all caught up in the mystique of golf.

Much of the golf boom in these nations stems from the Japanese tourist and business travelers, who over the last fifteen to twenty years have promoted the growth of the game by financing courses. The Hong Kong region is a popular area, with the local population acquiring a major interest in the game. China has a tremendous amount of land offering a variety of settings and course layouts. Most courses are private clubs selling memberships, but they are affiliated with hotels and resorts and are actually semi-private. Business transactions today are often discussed while on the golf course.

Golf is not new to China; in fact, century-old art books depict drawings of Chinese men playing a game that resembled golf long before the game was discovered in Scotland or anywhere else. It was officially introduced, however, in the later half of the nineteenth century when the British had settlements primarily in and around Hong Kong.

During the cultural and political changes in China, most of the early courses were obliterated and golf was swept away. Moratoriums were put on playing golf and using the land. Some of these restrictions are still in effect today. Capitalism and golf, a leisure activity, have been slow at making their appeal to a strict Chinese government. However, as the climate began to change in the early 1980s, golf once again saw the light of day and reemerged in China. In recent years, builders have been busy with new courses opening in Beijing, Shanghai, and the Shandong Province.

Customarily, the Japanese businessmen have had some influence on golf in China, while the British have also added their influences and love of the game. American course builders have put their stamp on the game, while Chinese customs and architecture have also played a part in the development of courses. This creates a very mixed bag of courses. Large clubhouses, female caddies, Jack Nicklaus–designed courses, and Feng Shui are all part of the resulting mixture of influences. From it all, there are some first-rate courses throughout China. Some of the marvelous courses in The People's Republic of China include the **Beijing Golf Club** in Beijing, the **Long Island Golf and Country Club** in Chang-An, and the **Zhuhai International Circuit Lakewood Golf and Country Club** in Zhuhai.

Taiwan's golf boom has coincided with the popularity of golf in Japan. There isn't, however, a great deal of land for courses and much of the available land is extremely mountainous and hard to build on. Naturally the land is needed for growth and food production and therefore too valuable to build on. Still, there are some courses and much interest in the game, a lot which emanated originally from Japan. Taiwan's new courses include the **Royal Kuan-Hsi Golf Club** in Kuan Hsi City and the **Mintai International Golf Club** in Mintai.

Today the Southeast Asia market is largely driven by their own resources. Clubhouses in Southeast Asia are often spectacular, including bowling alleys, theaters, hair salons, and more! In Thailand, where labor is very abundant, players often have as many as three caddies: one for the clubs, one for a cooler, and one for an umbrella.

Indonesia sports several old courses from the early Dutch influences and other courses from the military occupation. Most recently, lavish resort courses such as **Bukit Pelangi Resort**, a relatively new 27-hole course in Bogar, and the brand new **Royal Sumatra Golf and Country Club** in Medan, have drawn attention to the game.

In the Philippines, courses are quite varied and include mountainous courses, flat courses, and other variations on the theme. Many large tracts of land are owned by wealthy families, making it easier to secure land than in other countries where smaller tracts of land are owned by many individuals or the government. Resort courses are now trying to bring in the tourist trade. Hotels such as the new **Mount Alarayat Resort**, featuring twenty-seven holes in Lipa City, or the **Cebu Golf Resort**, are being built on Cebu Island.

ELSEWHERE!

There may not be a wealth of courses to choose from in many countries around the world, and daily-fee courses are not prominent in every town and city, but top-level championship courses exist everywhere. In Africa, for example, the **Durban Country Club** is a meticulously well-kept course in the American tradition, with several links-style holes comparable to those of Scotland. The challenging course has typical golf hazards, plus monkeys ready to scoop up your ball if you don't get to it first.

Australia, which has its own pro tour, has produced some top names in golf including Wayne Grady, Greg Norman, and Karrie Webb. Alister MacKenzie started building classic courses in the land down under in the 1920s, and many of these gems are still attracting foursomes today. From major cities such as Melbourne and Sydney to Queensland, also known as the Gold Coast, golf is prominent. The **South Wales Club** and the **Kingston Heath** courses both hail from the 1920s and from MacKenzie, as does the **Royal Melbourne** in Victoria. One of several courses in the Melbourne area, the Royal Melbourne sports two courses in the links style of Britain. Australia, like Europe, has tour packages that often include nearby New Zealand.

In Brazil, the **Gavea Golf and Country Club** in Rio de Janeiro sits between the fabulous beaches that line the Atlantic Ocean and the majestic mountains, making it an incredible place for a course. This challenging course has been home to the Brazil Open and has seen the top golfers in the world pay a visit on several occasions.

Royal Calcutta, in West Bengal, India, is one of the premier courses in the world and also one of the oldest. The club was formed in 1829 and chartered in 1911. The dhoob grass, endemic to India, is carefully maintained and this wide-open course is sprinkled with beautifully colored trees and many water hazards.

Israel saw golf first appear in 1961 in Tel Aviv, while North Korea didn't have courses until Japanese contractors built one just outside of the capital, Pyongyang, in 1987. Singapore, Indonesia, the Philippines, Zambia, and Zimbabwe have all gotten into the swing of the great game. Tunisia has even staged a European Tour Event.

Much closer to American soil, Bermuda is home to spectacular resort courses. **Cambridge Beaches** resort, along with six or seven lavish beaches, sits out on a twenty-five-mile peninsula that has room for a marvelous

golf course. **Port Royal Golf Course** in Southampton is a fabulous public course and a favorite among vacationers, as is the resort course at **Castle Harbour** on Hamilton Parish. Since 1930, this hilly resort course has been offering great golf and breathtaking views.

Mexico has a wide array of golf courses, with several new resort courses sporting spectacular views at several popular vacation spots. It's advisable to consider a lot of sunblock while playing on any of the Mexican golf courses. The **Acapulco Princess Club de Golf** features an excellent short course that is open to nonguests of the resort. In nearby Ixtapa, the **Marina Ixtapa Golf Club** is a rather new top-rated course, as is **El Cid** in Mazatlan. The **Westin Regina Resort** in Cancun features a lavish Robert Trent Jones layout, while other Cancun resorts like the **Presidente Inter-Continental** and the **Melia Cancun** also offer golf.

From the **Harstad Golf Club** in Norway, just 1,474 miles from the North Pole, the northernmost course in the world, to the **Puntas Arenas Golf Club** in Chile, the southernmost course, featuring blistering winds along a serious water hazard, the Straight of Magellan, golf is the universal game.

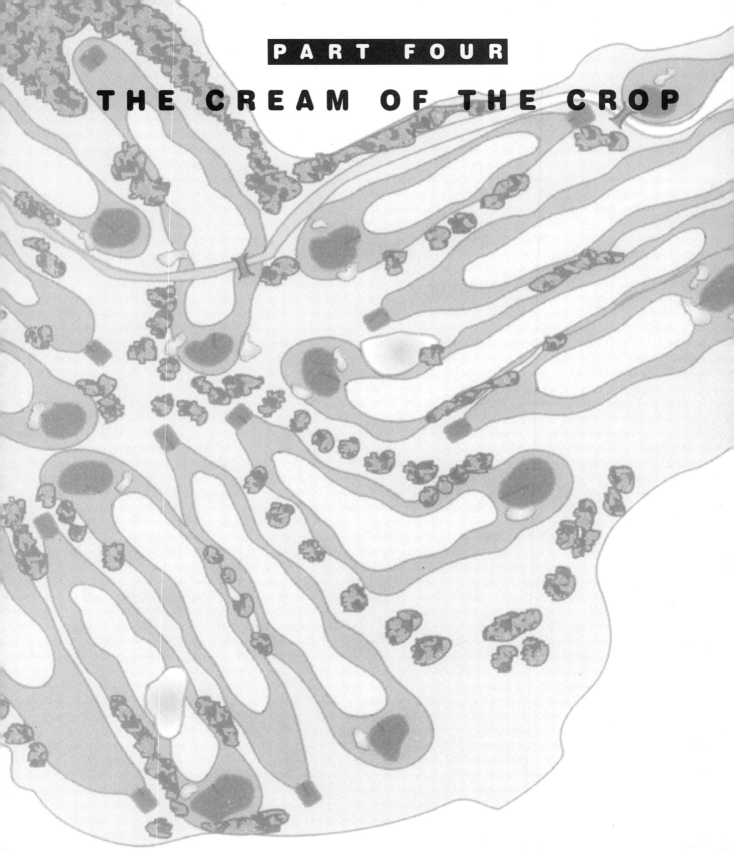

PART FOUR
THE CREAM OF THE CROP

TOURS AND TOURNAMENTS

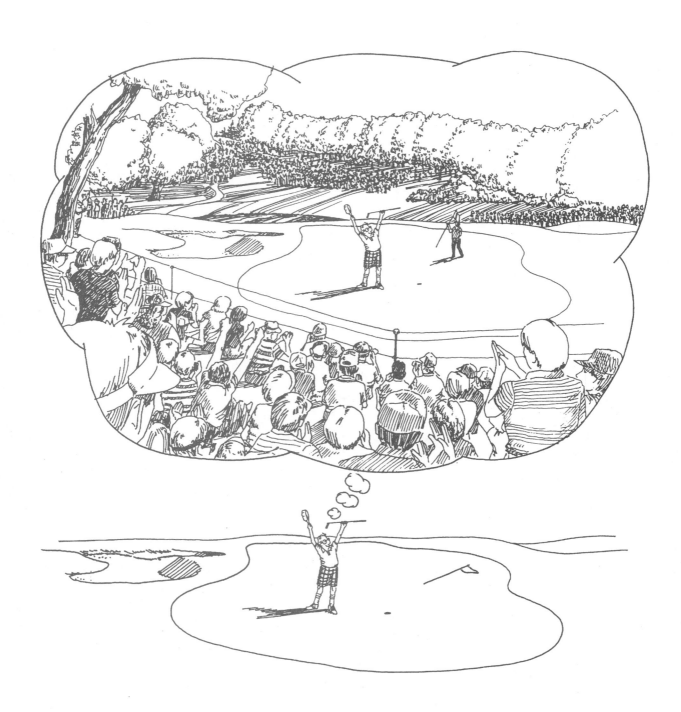

Golf has become the fastest-growing televised spectator sport in America. Thanks to ESPN and the major networks golf has become a staple of weekend programming. A new twenty-four-hour golf channel also provides added information, as does the Worldwide Web with golf sites.

In this section we look at the top tours and tournaments from the PGA, LPGA, and PGA Senior Tours, as well as the college golf scene, the Nike Tour, and other tours and tournaments in the United States and abroad. Also included is a brief section on watching a tournament and some important information on running one, should you be interested in putting on such an event.

Coast to coast and around the world on any given weekend there are thousands of tournaments going on offering cash prizes, trophies, or any number of gift prizes that corporate sponsors or companies can throw in to make it interesting. At almost any level, a player can find a tournament to enter.

Below are some of golf's most significant tours, starting at the top.

THE PGA TOUR

Below is the PGA schedule as of 1997. A tournament or two may come and go each year, and some will change sponsorship, but for the most part, these are ongoing events that mark the annual PGA calendar.

Check your television listings; most of these will be seen either on network or on a cable sports channel such as ESPN. If you just so happen to be planning to be in the neighborhood when one of these is taking place, you might want to get out your cap and comfortable shoes and be on-hand to watch the game as only the pros can play it. If you would like to attend one of the majors, such as the Masters, order your tickets well in advance.

JANUARY
Mercedes Championship
Bob Hope Chrysler Classic
Phoenix Open
AT&T Pebble Beach Pro-Am: Until about a decade ago this was the Bing Crosby Tournament. The Crosby family asked to have their name removed when the corporate sponsors moved in. Nonetheless, the tourney, which pits celebrities against pros in the most majestic golf setting in the country, Pebble Beach, is very popular. It doesn't necessarily feature the best golf on the tour, but the celebrity/pro pairings make it interesting. The tournament usually takes place at the end of January and is held at the Pebble Beach Golf Links, Poppy Hills Golf Course, and Spyglass Hills Golf Course on the Monterey Peninsula.

FEBRUARY
Buick Invitational
United Airlines Hawaiian Open
Tucson Open

The Los Angeles Nissan Open: This tournament has been going strong for over seventy years. Known as The Los Angeles until Glen Campbell added his name in 1971, Nissan took over sponsorship in 1987. Ben Hogan, Sam Snead, and Arnold Palmer have all won this one. The Riviera Country Club on the Pacific Palisades makes for a marvelous place to watch a tournament and enjoy the beauty of nature.

MARCH
Doral Ryder Open
The Honda Classic
Bay Hill Invitational
The Player's Championship

APRIL
Freeport-McDermott Classic
The Master's Tournament
The MCI Classic: The course, the Harbour Town Golf Links on Hilton Head Island in South Carolina, is considered by many golf pros and writers as one of the finest in the nation. Designed by Pete Dye with his wife and a little help from Jack Nicklaus, the course has been host to most of the premier names in the game, including Arnold Palmer, Tom Watson, and Greg Norman, all of whom have won the tournament since its 1969 debut on the tour as the Heritage Classic.
Greater Greensboro Open

MAY
Shell Houston Open
BellSouth Classic
GTE Byron Nelson Classic
MasterCard Colonial

JUNE
The Memorial: Hosted by Jack Nicklaus, this nonmajor draws some of the best on the pro tour and is always popular among the spectator set, so much so that there is a waiting list to get tickets. Played on a Nicklaus-designed course, this holiday tournament has been moved to shortly after the actual holiday for television purposes, which also allows for less chance of bad weather as June begins. If you want to get on the waiting list, call Muirfield Village in Dublin, Ohio, not far from Columbus.
Kemper Open
 U.S. Open
  Buick Classic
  FedEx St. Jude Classic

JULY
 Motorola Western Open
 Quad City Classic
 British Open
 Deposit Guaranty Golf Classic
 Canon Greater Hartford Open
Sprint International

AUGUST
Buick Open
 PGA Championship
NEC World Series of Golf
Greater Vancouver Open
Greater Milwaukee Open

SEPTEMBER
Bell Canadian Open
CVS Charity Classic
LaCantera Texas Open
B.C. Open
Ryder Cup

OCTOBER
Buick Challenge
Michelob Championship
Walt Disney World/Oldsmobile Classic:
For players it's a chance to escape the change of seasons. For onlookers it's an opportunity to take a family vacation and watch a tournament as well. This Disney tournament usually draws some top players, along with some well-known Disney characters. It's played on several of the marvelous Disney courses and ticket prices are reasonable.
Las Vegas Invitational
The Tour Championship

NOVEMBER
Lincoln-Mercury Kapalua
International: Lincoln-Mercury joined the tour in recent years, sponsoring this event, which has been going strong since 1983. A lot of top names play in this one because they like the Ben Crenshaw course and because it takes place in Maui. Onlookers enjoy this one because it's free. Complete with some fun-filled tournament parties, with guest performers like Charly Pride or the Gatlin Brothers, this nonmajor is great.

SCORE CARD

PGA MEN OF THE WORLD

Fulton Allem, Ernie Els, and David Frost of SOUTH AFRICA

Stuart Appleby, Ian Baker-Finch, Steve Elkington, Wayne Grady, Greg Norman, Brett Ogle, Craig Parry, and Peter Senior of AUSTRALIA

Bernhard Langer of GERMANY

Nick Faldo, David Gilford, Mark James, Barry Lane, Sandy Lyle, and Sam Torrance of ENGLAND

Colin Montgomerie of SCOTLAND

Andrew Magee of FRANCE

Joe Ozaki and Masashi Ozaki of JAPAN

Jesper Parnevik of SWEDEN

Vijay Singh of FIJI

Nick Price, Mark McNulty, and Dennis Watson of ZIMBABWE

Robert Allenby, Michael Campbell, and Frank Nobilo of NEW ZEALAND

Seve Ballesteros, Miguel Angel Jimenez, and Jose Maria Olazabal of SPAIN

Costantino Rocca of ITALY

Ian Woosnam of WALES

MasterCard PGA Grand Slam of Golf:
This $1 million get together in Hawaii pits
the winners of the year's majors against
each other in a post-season all-star game.
Franklin Templeton Shark Shootout
The World Cup of Golf
The Skins Game

DECEMBER
JC Penney Classic
Diners Club Matches
Wendy's Three-Tour Challenge
Anderson Consulting WCOG: With $1
million at stake in a match-play shoot-out
between some of the world's best, this
tournament wraps up the golf season in
grand style.

LPGA TOURNAMENTS

The LPGA tour spans not only the United
States, but Great Britain and Japan. The tournaments listed below run from January
through December. While only the first two
are in January, the schedule picks up
quickly, and, with the exception of
November, there are generally at least three
tournaments per month, usually four.

JANUARY
Chrysler-Plymouth Tournament of
Champions: This event early in the year
at Grand Cypress Resort is a new entry
to the world of women's professional
golf, around only since 1994.
Healthsouth Inaugural

FEBRUARY
Diet Dr. Pepper National Pro-Am
Los Angeles Women's Championship
Cup o' Noodles Hawaiian Ladies Open:
Ko Olina Golf Course has been home to
this event since 1990 and since '89 the
annual purse has risen by $50,000 a year
from $350,000 to $600,000, making 2004
the year this one should hit the $1 mil-
lion mark. The Hawaii Ladies Open also
has the distinction of having changed
names six times in the eleven years since
its inception, so it may be called something else by the time you read this.

MARCH
Welch's/Circle K Championship
Standard Register Ping
Nabisco Dinah Shore: Since 1972 this is
the only LPGA tournament sporting a
female celebrity name. Formerly sponsored by Colgate, this event, held annually in the Mission Hills Country Club in
Rancho Mirage, California, was designated
a major in 1983. The purse has risen
from $110,000 to nearly $1 million. Nancy
Lopez and Sally Little still hold the tournament record, each with a 64 for eighteen holes.

APRIL
Longs Drugs Challenge
Myrtle Beach LPGA Classic
Chick-Fil-A Charity Championship: This
tournament has the distinction of having
seen the prize money drop since its 1992
debut as the SEGA Women's
Championship. The tourney has been

played at Eagles's Landing in Atlanta, and was known as the Atlanta Women's Championship in 1993 and '94.

MAY

Sprint Titleholders Championship

Sara Lee Classic: Nobody doesn't like this early season event, which since its 1988 inception has seen prize money rise from $335,000 to $675,000.

McDonald's LPGA Championship

LPGA Corning Classic

JC Penney/LPGA Skins Game

Michelob Lite Classic

JUNE

Oldsmobile Classic

The Edina Realty LPGA Classic
   (Sponsored by First Bank)

Rochester International

ShopRite LPGA Classic

JULY

Jamie Farr Kroger Classic: Perhaps actor Jamie Farr's apparel on M*A*S*H prompted the popularity of this LPGA event. Nonetheless, this Toledo classic has been going strong since 1984. Purse money has grown rapidly from the initial $175,000. Highland Meadows Golf Club is home to this one.

U.S. Women's Open

JAL Big Apple Classic

Giant Eagle LPGA Classic

du Maurier Classic: One of the highest purses for an LPGA event, this Canadian major was once known as La Canadienne, then became the Peter Jackson Classic

SCORE CARD

LPGA WOMEN OF THE WORLD

The current international crop includes:

Estefania Knuth, Marta Figueras-Dotti, and Tania Abitbol of SPAIN

Carin Hj Kock, Eva Dahllof, Helen Alfredsson, Liselotte Neumann, Annika Sorenstam, and Catrin Nilsmark of SWEDEN

Hiromi Kobayashi, Ayako Okamoto, and Mayumi Hirase of JAPAN

Liz Earley and Luciana Bemvenuti of BRAZIL

Karin Mundinger, Tina Tombs, Nancy White-Brophy, Tara Fleming, Laura Witvoet, Jennifer Wyatt, Deborah Lee, Judy Sams, and Barb Bunkowsky-Scherbak of CANADA

Alison Munt, Wendy Doolan, Corinne Dibnah, Jan Stephenson, Jane Crafter, Shani Waugh, Karrie Webb, and Karen and Mardi Lunn of AUSTRALIA

Stefania Croce of ITALY

Karen Davies of WALES

Helen Dobson, Suzanne Peta Strudwick, Caroline Pierce, Alison Nicholas, Laura Davies, and Stephanie Maynor of ENGLAND

Florence Descampe of BELGIUM

Jenny Lidback and Alicia Dibos of PERU

Nicky Le Roux and Sally Little of South AFRICA

Pamela Wright, Dale Reid, Kathryn Marshall, and Catriona Matthew of SCOTLAND

Anne-Marie Palli of FRANCE

Chela Quintana of VENEZUELA

Pearl Sinn of SOUTH KOREA

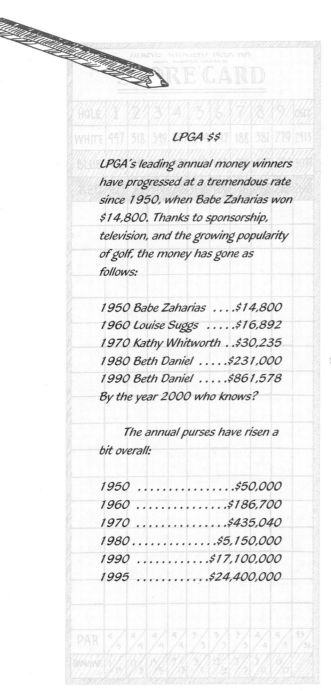

LPGA $$

LPGA's leading annual money winners have progressed at a tremendous rate since 1950, when Babe Zaharias won $14,800. Thanks to sponsorship, television, and the growing popularity of golf, the money has gone as follows:

1950 Babe Zaharias $14,800
1960 Louise Suggs $16,892
1970 Kathy Whitworth . . $30,235
1980 Beth Daniel $231,000
1990 Beth Daniel $861,578
By the year 2000 who knows?

The annual purses have risen a bit overall:

1950 . . . . $50,000
1960 . . . . $186,700
1970 . . . . $435,040
1980 . . . . $5,150,000
1990 . . . . $17,100,000
1995 . . . . $24,400,000

from 1974 through 1982. The annual event has moved around from Montreal to Toronto to Ontario to Vancouver.

AUGUST
Friendly's Classic
Weetbix Women's British Open
Star Bank LPGA Classic
State Farm Rail Classic

SEPTEMBER
The Safeway LPGA Golf Championship
SAFECO Classic
Ping Welch's Championship

OCTOBER
Fieldcrest Cannon Classic
CoreStates Betsy King Classic
Samsung World Championship of Women's Golf
Nichirei International: This United States versus Japan team championship has been dominated heavily by the United States. In eighteen years, Japan has won only twice. Known as the Pioneer Cup until 1982, and as the Sports Nippon Team Match thereafter in the '80s, this individual competition became strictly team competition after 1989. The tournament has seen several homes throughout Japan while giving LPGAers an opportunity to visit Japan.

NOVEMBER
Toray Japan Queens Cup: The Japanese women golfers have done very well in this event, which began in 1973 as the

LPGA Japan Classic. First prize has gone from only $7,500 to over $100,000 in just twenty years. The tournament has been held in Musashigaoka, Hanayashiki, Horyuju, Sagamihara, and Ibaraki Kukusai, providing some hard-to-pronounce travel stickers for LPGAers.

ITT LPGA Tour Championship

DECEMBER

JC Penney Classic: The equivalent of mixed doubles in tennis, this annual event has paired men and women since 1976, when JoAnn Washam and Chi Chi Rodriguez took the honors in what was then known as the Pepsi-Cola Mixed Team Championships.

Diners Club Matches

Wendy's Three-Tour Challenge

The Solheim Cup: The women's version of the Ryder Cup, this biennial competition pits women from the United States LPGA against members of the Women's Professional European Tour. Founded in 1990, the tournament trophy is designed by the world-famous Waterford Crystal company, and is named for Karsten Solheim, the founder of Ping clubs. Solheim signed a twenty-year contract for ten matches, the next of which will be in Muirfield Village in the fall of 1998. So far the cup has been played in Orlando, Florida; Edinburgh, Scotland; White Sulphur Springs, West Virginia; and St. Pierre, Wales. Qualifying for the teams is based on a point system that combines scores from 1997 and 1998.

The LPGA also features Teaching and Club Professional Championships, seminars, a senior challenge, and other events throughout the year. The LPGA Teaching and Club Professional Division (T & CP) was founded in 1959. The large membership of women golf professionals includes golf directors, head professionals, owners of golf schools and driving ranges, high school and college coaches, and golf administrators. One-day clinics, golf seminars, classes, club-fitting workshops, junior golf programs, and even a women's golf summit are part of the LPGA's T & CP division.

THE SENIOR PGA TOUR

Many golfers age like fine wine, and the PGA Senior Tour is a marvelous tour to watch and a very successful one as well. No other sport has had the success with senior players as golf, thanks in part to the no-need-to-run requirement of the game. While senior baseball was a bust in the late '80s and senior tennis, despite Jimmy Connor's promotions, teeters on the edge, senior golf is a mainstay on television.

The Senior PGA Tour kicked off in 1980 with two tournaments. The one in Atlantic City was won by Don January, while the other, in Florida, was won by Charlie Sifford. By 1983 there were eighteen events, and prize money on the circuit exceeded $3 million!

By 1987 there were seventy-two players on the tour, and by '88 there were thirty-seven tournaments, and tour champion, left-hander Bob Charles, raked in over $530,000. Then in 1990 the tour struck gold, as four members of golf's elite circle were together competing again. Arnold Palmer, Jack Nicklaus, Lee Trevino, and Gary Player were all on the senior circuit, with Trevino becoming the first million-dollar winner on it.

From that point forward, the senior circuit was big-time, big-money golf, and the TV cameras were out covering each event. By 1996 the tour was awarding over $35 million in prize money. Wow!

Because many of the Senior Tour players have already made their fame and fortune, the attitude, while still extremely competitive, has a flavor of sportsmanship, and the players have a good time. Below are the tournaments, with comments to reflect the fun spirit of the very popular tour.

The Senior Skins Game.

The Royal Caribbean Classic in sunny Key Biscayne in January.

The FHP Healthcare Classic in Ojai, California.

The Senior Slam, since 1994 and in Mexico.

The Liberty Mutual Legends of Golf, which has an over-sixty category and an over-seventy category, and we're not talking about the scores here. It moved from Austin, Texas, to La Quinta, California, in 1995, and features pairs.

NICE SHOT, MOM.

The Dominion Seniors, which changes sponsors more often than you change your grip, but remains in San Antonio, Texas.

The Tradition, which is traditionally in Scottsdale, Arizona.

The PGA Seniors' Championship, which has been going strong since 1937 and in Florida since 1940.

The Las Vegas Senior Classic, which left the Desert Inn after '93 for the TPC in Summerlin.

The Paine Weber Invitational, in North Carolina.

The Cadillac NFL Golf Classic in Clifton New Jersey, featuring Senior PGAers and pro football players like Al Del Grecco, whose shot has a lot of "kick" to it.

The BellSouth Senior Classic, which has attracted a large field to country-music land in Nashville, Tennessee.

The U.S. Senior Open, which has made the rounds over the years from New York to Nevada to Chicago, since its 1980 inception.

The Northville Long Island Classic in Jericho, New York.

The Brickyard Crossing Championship, on a non-race day, in the infield at the Brickyard (motor speedway) in Indianapolis.

The Bank One Classic in Lexington, Kentucky, which was once known as The Vantage Presents Bank One Senior Golf Classic.

The Transamerica in Napa, California, in the fall.

Raley's Senior Gold Rush, right nearby in California, usually a week or two after the Transamerica.

Ralph's Senior Classic, in Los Angeles, paying tribute to the great golf played by Ralph Kramden.

The Hyatt Regency Maui Kaanaoali Classic in Hawaii.

The Energizer Senior Tour Championship in Myrtle Beach, which has changed sponsors five times since 1990 but now keeps on going and going. . . .

The Diners Club Matches with PGA, LPGA, and Senior PGA tour players all getting together to play golf shortly before Christmas.

The Lexus Challenge, which pits celebrities with seniors, such as Jim Colbert and William Devane, Jack Nicklaus and Alan Thicke, or Bob Murphy with Clint Eastwood.

Despite having fun with a few of the tournament names, these are indeed among the best events to watch because they feature some of the legends you have seen and read about over the years. The PGA Senior Tour is a highly competitive tribute to the over-fifty generation.

THE NIKE TOUR

Originally sponsored by the Ben Hogan Company in 1990, Nike took over sponsorship in 1993. Today this is considered by many to be the premier tour for future PGAers. Through 1996, fourteen Nike Tour players had moved on to win on the PGA

OTHER USGA TOURNAMENTS
Other USGA tournaments include:

	Handicap Index Limit	Age Limit
U.S. Women's Amateur Championship	*5.4*	*—*
U.S. Mid-Amateur	*5.4*	*25+*
U.S. Women's Mid-Amateur Championship	*9.4*	*25+*
USGA Senior Amateur Championship	*8.4*	*55+*
USGA Senior Women's Amateur	*12.4*	*50+*
Women's State Team Championship		
Men's State Team Championship		
The Walker Cup (Biennial international team event)		
The Curtis Cup (Biennial international team event)		

tour. Under the auspices of the PGA, the Nike Tour is designed to teach players to compete at the top level. Another major success of the Nike Tour is its over $8.5 million in charitable contributions since its inception in 1990.

Nike Tour event highlights include: the Nike San Jose Open in San Jose, California; The Nike Inland Empire Open in Moreno Valley, California; the Nike Monterey Open in Monterey, Mexico; the Nike Louisiana in Broussard, Louisiana; as well as opens or "classics" in South Carolina, Tallahassee, Alabama, Shreveport, Mississippi, North Carolina, Greenville, Virginia, Cleveland, Knoxville, Springfield, South Dakota, Buffalo, Philadelphia, Miami Valley, Wichita, Utah, Boise, Olympia, Odessa, The Tri-Cities Open in Richland (Washington), and the Gateway Classic in Montana. There is also a season-ending Nike Tour Championship. As the competition heats up and the demand for events grows, more events are being planned.

MINI TOURS

There are mini tours all over the United States. These regional tours have been billed as golf's boot camp, giving non-card carrying PGA players, top collegiate golfers, up-and-coming players, top amateurs, and those honing their skills for the senior circuit a chance to play constantly. Some thirty to thirty-five such tours are usually making their way around sections of the country between April and October. The National Mini-tour Association (402) 484-8687, can fill you in on tours in your area, entrance fees, handicap requirements, and other qualifying information.

One such mini tour is the North Atlantic Tour, which is still going strong in New England and parts of New York after nearly a decade. The tour features twenty-five events between May and September, with purses in the area of $15,000. It is one of the more significant minis by virtue of its longevity. Most events feature forty to sixty players in two-day competitions.

For women there is the Future's Tour, which like the Nike Tour, is a national training ground for future LPGAers and other top female golfers. The Future's has grown in stature in recent years and is highly regarded in the women's golf market and by the LPGA.

Among the top women's regional mini tours is the Player's West Tour. The twenty-four-event tour has been going strong since the late '80s and has placed about twenty-five top female golfers in the LPGA. The development tour, as it's often referred to, plays throughout the scenic courses of California, Nevada, Arizona, and Oregon between March and October. Events are three-day 54-hole competitions.

USGA TOURNAMENTS

Besides being the governing body of golf in the United States, the USGA sponsors many of the most significant tournaments in the country.

Below is a listing of the events of the USGA, with a background history in brief for some and qualifying information for most. You can contact the USGA for entry forms and dates for the upcoming year's events at the Golf House in New Jersey at (908) 234-2300.

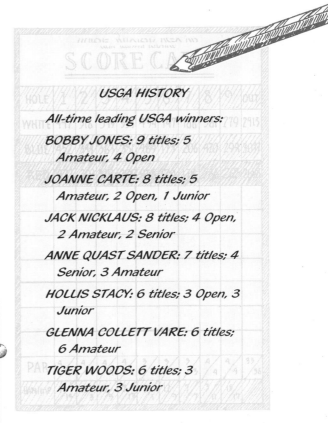

USGA HISTORY

All-time leading USGA winners:

BOBBY JONES: 9 titles; 5 Amateur, 4 Open

JOANNE CARTE: 8 titles; 5 Amateur, 2 Open, 1 Junior

JACK NICKLAUS: 8 titles; 4 Open, 2 Amateur, 2 Senior

ANNE QUAST SANDER: 7 titles; 4 Senior, 3 Amateur

HOLLIS STACY: 6 titles; 3 Open, 3 Junior

GLENNA COLLETT VARE: 6 titles; 6 Amateur

TIGER WOODS: 6 titles; 3 Amateur, 3 Junior

THE U.S. OPEN CHAMPIONSHIP

It started in 1895 and featured mostly immigrants from England and Scotland. The tournament grew in stature very quickly and by 1922 tickets were being sold to an enthusiastic audience. In 1954, the open hit television from Baltusrol Golf Club in New Jersey. By 1959 the number of entries had reached nearly 2,500, which meant the qualifying stages now had to be divided, with local and sectional requirements. The tournament, which consists of four 18-hole rounds (since 1965) requires a handicap index of 2.4 or lower.

THE U.S. WOMEN'S OPEN CHAMPIONSHIP

Originally an event of the now defunct Women's Professional Golf Association, the U.S. Women's Open has been going strong since 1953. By 1965 the event had reached television. From its original thirty-seven participants, the Women's Open has grown to the need for qualifying rounds to ensure a manageable starting field. The Women's Open requires a handicap index at or below 4.4.

THE U.S. SENIOR OPEN CHAMPIONSHIP

As the popularity of golf increased among the over-fifty set, the Senior Open was established in 1980. The first tournament, at Winged Foot, attracted 631 entries. The tournament, which has been won by such seniors as Arnold Palmer, Miller Barber, and Tom Weiskopf, awards the Francis D. Ouimet Trophy to the winner. You need a 5.4 index handicap or better to qualify.

THE U.S. AMATEUR PUBLIC LINKS CHAMPIONSHIP

Termed "America's blue-collar championship," the Amateur Public Links Championship has been a huge success since the 1920s. In 1922, 140 entries were received. Today a field of 156 participants is narrowed down from over 6,000 entries received by the USGA. This is truly America's championship of golf, with players coming from all walks of life trying to take home a trophy before returning to their daily jobs. There are qualifying rounds, and they are yours for the trying.

WOMEN'S AMATEUR PUBLIC LINKS CHAMPIONSHIP

It started in 1977 with twenty-seven qualifying sites and a concern that there would not be enough interest from women across the country. Pretty soon there were nearly 700 entries. By the 1990s there were thousands of women golfers vying for a chance to win this tournament.

THE U.S. JUNIOR AMATEUR CHAMPIONSHIP

This tournament was initiated in 1948 and has been a showcase for great golfers of the future. The first U.S. Junior Amateur drew nearly 500 entries, and that was back in '48. Today the event draws thousands of applicants. One such applicant, Tiger Woods, recently became the first to win the event three times. The event is open to boys under 18 with a handicap index of 9.4 or under.

THE U.S. GIRLS JUNIOR CHAMPIONSHIP

One year after the boys got started in 1948, the girls began. The initial event drew twenty-eight girls from seventeen states and was won by fifteen-year-

MEN'S AMATEUR CHAMPIONS: A BRIEF HISTORY

The British Amateur began in 1885 with All MacFie winning his first, last, and only title. It would soon be dominated to some extent by John Ball, who would win eight times over the next twenty-five years. The first American, Walter Travis, would win the British Amateur in 1904, and the first Brit, Harold Hilton, would win the U.S. Amateur in 1911. Hilton was the first player to win both Amateurs in one year. Neither Hilton nor any other British golfer would dominate in the U.S. Amateur again. Jerome Travers was the main force before the war, winning four U.S. Amateur titles between 1907 and 1913.

After World War I came Bobby Jones. Jones would post five U.S. Amateur titles and a British Amateur title in his grand slam year of 1930. The amazing Jones would retire after "achieving all there was to achieve in the game" by the age of 28! Following Jones was the double "L," Lawson Little, who would proceed to take both titles in 1934 and 1935 by wide margins, making people compare him to the legendary Jones.

From Little's two Amateur Championships in Great Britain forward, the Americans dominated the British Amateur Championship, winning ten times in sixteen years. Ireland's Joe Carr and Australia's Doug Bachli won back-to-back titles in 1953 and '54, the first for their respective countries.

Meanwhile, the U.S. Amateur Championships saw only one non-American win between 1911 and 1966, Canada's Ross Somerville. No one took a strong hold on the Amateur Championships, as players opted to turn pro quickly.

Nonetheless, the titles have gone to a few familiar names over the past thirty years, including Arnold Palmer, Jack Nicklaus (who won twice), Lanny Wadkins, Hal Sutton, and most recently, Tiger Woods. Woods set a record winning the U.S. Amateur three years in a row, something that even Bobby Jones did not do.

old Marlene Bauer of Los Angeles. Today there are thousands of girls playing golf, and those under eighteen with a handicap of 18.4 or under can enter and start on their way to the pros. Nancy Lopez won in 1972 and '74.

U.S. AMATEUR CHAMPIONSHIP

Partially responsible for the founding of the USGA, this tournament dates back to 1894 and has been a staple of American golf ever since. From Bobby Jones to Tiger Woods, some great amateur champions have taken home the trophy. This is open to the top amateur players in the country with a 3.4 handicap index or lower.

COLLEGIATE GOLF: THE ROLEX COLLEGIATE TOUR

The College Golf Foundation, founded with the corporate sponsorship of Rolex Watch, U.S.A., is a nonprofit organization dedicated to the growth and promotion of collegiate golf programs for both men and women. Initiated in 1995, the Rolex Collegiate Tour offers some 150 events on both a national and regional level. The tour was so successful in its maiden year that by the second year the number of events had grown to 200, including 110 men's and 90 women's events.

Golfstat began assisting in calculating and tracking the statistics from the tournaments that now receive media attention on the new Golf Channel. Much in the same manner as NCAA basketball and football teams are ranked, the top fifty collegiate teams are now ranked throughout the season, along with the top 100 individual players.

The Jack Nicklaus College Player of the Year Award, presented by Rolex, is given to the top men's player for the year. One recent recipient was none other than Tiger Woods, in his sophomore year at Stanford. The women's best collegiate golfer is awarded the Elenore Dudley award, presented by Jack Nicklaus Equipment. Elenore Dudley was the first women's college champion in 1941. University of Arizona freshman Marisa Baena won the award on the tour's inaugural season.

Among the many featured tournaments are the **Rolex Fall Preview** for the women, the **Ping/***Golfweek* **Preview** for the men, the **Golf World Palmetto Dunes Intercollegiate**, and **The Rolex National Intercollegiate Match Play Championship**.

INTERNATIONALLY

IN BRITAIN

England, Scotland, Wales, and Northern Ireland are home to a host of significant tournaments. Many such events have a long and rich golf history. From mid-May to late October, the calendar is full of annual golf championships at a variety of levels. Included are:

The Benson and Hedges International
    Open
The British Amateur Championships
The Ladies' British Amateur
    Championships
The North of Ireland Amateur Open
    Golf Championship
The Scottish Open
The English Amateur Championship
Prince's Famous Open Amateur Golf
    Week, open to both men and women
    players
Boys Amateur Golf Championship
Scarborough Open Golf Week
The British Masters featuring top golfers
    from throughout Europe
West of England Open Amateur
    Championship
The Alfred Dunhill Cup Final, an
    international teams competition. This
    tournament, played on the legendary
    St. Andrews Old Course, features the
    world's biggest names in one of the
    most prestigious of the European
    tour events.

THE EUROPEAN PGA TOUR

Professional golf in Europe has grown by leaps and bounds over the past twenty years. However, there has been organized professional golf in Europe since the turn of the century, when the PGA of Europe was formed in 1901. The PGA was initially formed as a trade union for the professional golfers at each club. For a long time, the job of the pro golfers was to serve and teach the members the game.

LATE BLOOMERS

If you are over the age of thirty-five you may be too old to be Rookie of the Year in Major League Baseball, or have much of a chance to compete in tennis, but in politics and golf, you're still very much in the running. In fact, below is a list of golfers who won their first major title after the age of thirty-five.

Age	
45	Jerry Barber, the 1961 PGA Championship
44	Roberto de Vicenzo, the 1967 British Open
42	Tom Kite, the 1992 U.S. Open
39	Kel Nagle, the 1960 British Open
37	Jay Hebert, the 1960 PGA Championship
37	Don January, the 1967 PGA Championship
37	Steve Jones, the 1996 U.S. Open
37	Tom Lehman, the 1996 British Open
36	Tommy Aaron, the 1973 Masters
35	Gay Brewer, Jr., the 1967 Masters
35	Orville Moody, the 1969 U.S. Open
35	Nick Price, the 1992 PGA Championship
35	Corey Pavin, the 1995 U.S. Open
35	Mark Brooks, the 1996 PGA Championship

By the 1970s, however, things had changed dramatically and the club professionals were playing the tours, representing their clubs and countries. Thanks to increased sponsorship, the money was growing by leaps and bounds and by the mid '70s the Tournament Professionals broke away from the main body of the European PGA and formed the PGA European Tour.

Players from around the world flocked to Europe to take part in top tournaments throughout the continent. At the start of the '80s, the PGA European Tour consisted of twenty-two events, with prize money nearing $2 million. Thanks to television exposure, public relations, top-name players from all over the globe, and sponsorship by Volvo, the 1997 tour had thirty-seven events, with prize money over $16 million.

IN CANADA

One of the premier tours for developing talent is the Canadian Professional Golf Tour. Many up-and-coming stars have graduated to bigger success on the PGA Tours of Europe, Japan, and the United States. In the late 1980s the Canadian Golf Tour unified various tournaments throughout the country. By 1989 the tour had twelve events, with total prize money of more than $1.2 million. The events were highly competitive, with an average of two-over par needed to qualify and nearly thirteen-under par needed to win. By 1996 the money exceeded $1.5 million and the Canadian Golf Tour was firmly established as the best professional golf in Canada.

As of 1997, nearly 100 players have graduated from the Canadian tour to the U.S., European, or Japanese PGA tours. Some of the ongoing events on the Canadian tour include these tournaments:

The Payless Open
The BC Tel Pacific Open
Morningstar Classic
Henry Singer Alberta Open
ED TEL Planet Open
Xerox Manitoba Open
Infiniti Championship
Canadian Masters
Export "A" Ontario Open
Montclair Quebec Open
Montclair PEI Classic
CPGA Championship

Top prize money is usually either $100,000 or $125,000, with the Canadian Masters offering $250,000.

SOME OFF-BEAT TOURNAMENTS

Golf is so universal that it's safe to assume that any kind of tournament exists with any theme imaginable.

For example, the **Oakwood Hospital Open-Heart Open**, established in 1987 in Dearborn, Michigan, is the only golf tournament of its kind, featuring a field of participants who have had open-heart surgery, plus doctors and anesthesiologists. From a player who has had open-heart surgery when she was four years old to a couple of heart transplant players, this is a tournament with a lot of heart.

The **Eskimo Open** in Chicago is played in the coldest days of January. In Alaska the Bering Sea Ice Golf Classic is played annually as a fundraiser. The tournament is played with orange golf balls on a 6-hole course on the frozen Bering Sea in March. Par is forty-one and players shoot at flagged coffee cans placed on the ice.

There are, or have been, left-handers' tournaments; a beer drinkers' tournament in Virginia, sponsored by a national brewery with beer on tap from hole to hole; a tournament in Kansas City called the **Jim Smith Open**, for people named Jim Smith (at least they don't have to engrave the trophy); and a topless tournament in Atlanta, with topless female caddies.

HOW TO WATCH A TOURNAMENT

There are several ways to watch a golf tournament. Some enjoy following a favorite player from hole to hole, while others enjoy parking themselves at a particular vantage point, such as the first or last hole, and watching each player pass by. If you choose to follow a player or foursome, be careful to stay on designated paths, follow the instructions of those working the tournament, and don't distract players on other holes.

Besides being careful not to distract players, it's important not to get creamed by a shot. Should Gerald Ford be playing, or if you are attending a tournament where the holes are tightly placed with not a great deal of space for the gallery in between, you must be aware and awake at all times. Watching as various players hit from the tee area or land on a challenging green and putt their way to a possible title is a marvelous way to witness a variety of swings and styles. It's a great way to learn. Take note of players' approaches to the ball, how they line up their shots, and how they read the greens.

As for personal comfort, if you're heading out to take in a tournament, you should check the weather forecast in advance and be prepared for bugs and rain or wind. Even though it's not the beach and there may be plenty of trees around, you can get quite a sunburn on the course. Sunscreen, visors, and other such items are recommended. If you are allergic to grass or have hay fever, know how much you can take without putting your health in jeopardy.

Also, wear comfortable and appropriate attire. Despite the name "skins game," golf is still somewhat conservative in its approach to attire. Yes, badly coordinated color schemes have been known to appeal to some players, but as a general rule many clubs do not prefer shorts, cutoffs, and halters. Wear comfortable shoes since you'll be standing or walking a lot.

While following your favorite player from hole to hole, you might quietly and discreetly opt for a photo. As a general rule, don't take photos unless you are using a camera that does not make a sound. The best places to take shots are the tournament grandstands, the clubhouse (with a telephoto lens), or videotape a tournament on TV.

If you like autographs, you should get them after the tournament is over. If a player is hanging around the clubhouse or accessible off the course, you might ask for their John Hancock, or Tiger Woods, as the case may be. But don't be a nuisance. If a player is eating, resting, or simply worn out from a demanding round, don't be a pest.

And finally, try not to make the course your own personal picnic ground, outdoor cafe, or restroom. Eating and other activities are accounted for in specific locations.

Here are five ways to watch a tournament:

1. Stand by one tee area and watch players tee off.
2. Follow a player you like around the course.
3. Park yourself by a green and watch them chip on up.
4. Sit in the stadium seats at one of the seventeen TPC courses, relax, and quietly stuff your face.
5. Sit home, watch on television, and yell and scream all you like.

SO, YOU WANT TO HOLD A TOURNAMENT

Tournaments serve as fundraisers, morale builders, social occasions, membership builders, or strictly as a means of friendly competition for fun.

Whatever the purpose, tournaments are an ideal way to bring people together for any particular reason you have in mind. There are numerous ways in which you can present and hold a tournament. Below we offer ways to hold a tournament, as well as ways to organize one.

There are several key elements in making a tournament work for your club, group, organization, or company, and each area needs to be carefully thought out prior to publicizing the event.

In planning such a tournament you must consider:

1. **Your budget**.
   Do you have one?
2. **Why a tournament?**
   Plan, based on your goals. Are you trying to promote your business? Put your name before the public? Are you raising money for a charity? Promoting corporate team building?
3. **Where?**
   Pick a course that is challenging as well as accessible and available for your particular group. It's recommended to scout out several courses and to try to book a club at least eight months in advance. Aim for a Monday or another quiet day when the club is not open to members.
4. **When?**
   If you're planning a tournament in Maine, your seasonal limitations are certainly going to be different from those of a tournament planner in Florida who can plan a Christmas tournament if desired. Naturally, you will want to find a time that will get the biggest turnout. However, you must keep in mind that the larger the group, the greater the impossibility of pleasing everyone, so set the date and hope for the best. Give plenty of advance notice so that the junior

executives can take a crash course and not totally embarrass themselves.

5. **Prizes and trophies**.
   If you're going to stir them up about a tournament, you'll have to provide a reason for them to play. If you're not dealing with sponsorship or a wealthy philanthropist, then be clever.
6. **Choose a format.**
   The USGA lists thirty-six formats that you can select from to play a tournament. Planners and outing managers have added to that list by using variations on those themes. Get feedback from your membership on what they are familiar with.

   John Marshall, a corporate tournament planning specialist and consultant suggests a shotgun start so that everybody starts and finishes at the same time. He recommends a scramble, because handicaps vary so much. "You can have a scratch golfer and a bunch of 30 handicaps. That's why you do a scramble, so everybody can make a contribution with a good drive or good putt somewhere along the way. It's usually a more enjoyable way to run a tournament, and it includes everyone."

   It's also a good idea to handicap your players so that everyone has a fair opportunity.
7. **Everything else:**
   Booking rooms for out of town guests. Getting invitations, flyers, and other

printed matter prepared and mailed. Hiring a photographer and videographer. Arranging for equipment needs like carts and even clubs or bags. Gift items. Publicity. A pre- and/or post-tournament dinner, banquet, or party. Decide who will present the trophy, and where and when. Spectators welcome or not? Families? How about having a pro on-hand, or a special guest? Do you have a rain date? Does the club know about it?

In planning a tournament make sure you have paid close attention to every detail, or book a club that will handle the details for you. A good tournament gives players a feeling of competition and camaraderie, and accomplishes the goals you set at the start.

TOP TIPS FROM A CORPORATE GOLF PLANNER

John Marshall has planned numerous golf tournaments for companies of all sizes. He offers the following words of wisdom.

1. **Invitations.** "Try to keep your invitation list to such a point where you don't get so many people that it's bad for the enjoyment of the people. Plan on a 3:1 ratio, meaning if you're looking for 50 people to take part, spread the word to 150."

2. **Having a Pro Make an Appearance.** "If you want to attract the top CEOs, and have some money to invest, get a top tour player to attend the event and spend the day there mingling with the folks. It costs a bit more, but will be very effective if you are looking to impress your clients. Hal Sutton, Fred Couples, or someone of that caliber can attract a more prestigious crowd."

3. **Advance Planning.** "Start planning well in advance and know your prime season. In New York, for example, you can schedule comfortably between May and September. In Atlanta, Georgia, however, you would aim for April/May or September/October, and probably avoid the months in between when it's too hot. It's a good idea to book the course eight to twelve months in advance. Also check their policy regarding getting rained out. Most clubs have a situation where if nobody plays golf, they won't charge you; the only expense is for food and beverages. If, however, you play three or four holes, they'll charge you for the whole thing. There are even companies that sell rain insurance for such golf outings."

4. **Prizes.** "Merchandise is your best prize for corporate events. Trophies are not as practical. An individual entering a local tournament may take pride in a trophy, but at the corporate level, prizes are your best bet—

and not cash, which can immediately put someone's amateur standing in jeopardy (not to mention their tax return). When you book some clubs, they will include a minimum purchase in their golf shop of perhaps $500 to $1,000, or $10 per player, so you can get clubs or shirts or other items as prizes. A major prize or perhaps a trip is always a way to attract players."

5. **Parties.** "This is the biggest variable, which can range from a sit-down buffet lunch to a box lunch on the carts. After the tournament you can offer anything, from hot and cold hors d'oeuvres to a five-course sit-down banquet. It all depends on what you want to spend and whom you are trying to impress."

6. **Costs.** "Most clubs require an opening fee, X number of dollars to open the club and staff it. Don't forget, they have to get people in who would otherwise have a day off. Club fee, cart fee, food and beverage, plus gratuity (usually 15 percent) are the primary costs. Corporate tournaments generally range anywhere from $15,000 to $25,000. They are a great source of revenue for private clubs, some of which may do as many as fifteen to twenty-five a year."

GREATS OF THE GAME

There are too many great golfers world-wide to mention them all. In this section, however, we look at a few of the numerous greats of the game, many of whom have truly secured themselves as sports legends while helping to promote the popularity of golf. Many are still going strong on the PGA, LPGA, Senior, or European circuits.

Paul Azinger

It took Azinger three trips to qualifying school and several years before finally winning a PGA event in 1987. Zinger, as he is known, honed his game on the Florida circuit, and has raked in over $7 million as a pro. From 1987 through 1993, Azinger won eleven tournaments and finished in the top three thirty-eight times. Azinger was then sidelined with lymphoma and has been battling back ever since. He is truly inspirational. He returned to the PGA tour in 1995 and made over $180,000. He has since written a book about his ordeal and hosts a tournament for lymphoma research.

Severiano Ballesteros

Spain's answer to Arnold Palmer, Seve put golf on the map in Spain and did wonders for the European PGA, not to mention golf in Japan and around the world. He grew up next to the seaside course of Pedrena, where his uncle was the course pro. From caddying as a boy to turning pro at age sixteen, golf was always a part of Seve's life. A marvelous golfer to watch, a fierce competitor, and a crowd favorite, Ballesteros is one of golf's international legends. He has posted over sixty worldwide victories, including the British Open, French Open, German Open, Irish Open, Japanese Open, Kenya Open, the Madrid and Spanish Opens, and the Masters in the United States in 1980 at the age of just twenty-three. For some golfers there are many new places to conquer; Seve is running short on new locales.

Pat Bradley

One of the greats of women's golf, Bradley became only the second player ever to top the $5 million earnings mark. An amateur champion in New England in the early '70s, she became a standout on the LPGA tour after her graduation from Florida International University in 1974. The Rolex Player of the Year in 1986 and leading LPGA money winner, Bradley battled and overcame Graves' disease in 1988, and by 1991 was once again the leading money winner atop the LPGA circuit. In 1991 she won the Golf Writer's Association's Ben Hogan Award as a tribute to her remarkable comeback. There's even a Pat Bradley Invitational Tournament!

Fred Couples

Couples is a low-key, easygoing, big-money winner from the University of Houston who sailed through Q-School in 1980. Couples won a host of tournaments throughout the '80s, starting with the 1983 Kemper Open, but 1992 was his year. In 1992 he earned over $1.3 million and led the PGA Tour. It was his second consecutive year as PGA Player of the Year, and he won the Masters in the process.

In 1995 Couples had the honor of being part of the World Cup Championship team in Shenzhen, China. A Seattle native, Couples, nicknamed "Boom Boom," has earned more than $7 million in his seventeen years on the tour, which has helped him to enhance his collection of vintage cars.

Ben Crenshaw

A PGA pro since the early '70s, Crenshaw is not only a tour veteran but an avid golf historian. The 1984 and 1995 Master's winner, Crenshaw finished as high as second place on the tour in 1976. Prior to his professional success, the popular Crenshaw won three consecutive NCAA championships in the early '70s, winning the Fred Haskins Award as the nation's outstanding college golfer each of those years. Very interested in golf architecture, Crenshaw has worked with architects in course planning and will continue in that direction, along with playing golf and studying its history.

Beth Daniel

A fairly recent inductee into the Golf Hall of Fame, Daniel has been one of the most consistent stars of the tour since her emergence in 1979 as LPGA Rookie of the Year. Following two U.S. Amateur victories at ages nineteen and twenty-one, Daniel has spent most of her nearly twenty years as a pro ranked among the top ten LPGA money winners.

The 1990 United Press International Female Athlete of the Year, and three-time Rolex Player of the Year award winner, Daniel, now in her early forties, has surpassed $5 million in tour earnings and shows no signs of letting up.

Laura Davies

A member of the British Empire, as named by Queen Elizabeth in 1988, Davies is now also a member of the golfing elite. After six successful years on the LPGA tour, the British native leaped to the top of the circuit in 1994 and has been a major force since posting nine tour victories in a three-year span. Consistency has become the trademark of the hard-hitting Davies, who in 1995 finished in the top ten in twelve of the seventeen tournaments she entered. Some call her the female John Daly because of her powerful drives and no-holding-back style of play. Her natural ability and go-for-broke attitude have made Davies one of the most exciting players in golf today and a crowd favorite.

Nick Faldo

The man with the near-perfect swing, known for his pinpoint precision and accuracy, Nick Faldo has won big in his native Britain, on the U.S. tour, and around the world. He took up golf at age fourteen and within four years was winning titles.

Following his British Youths Amateur and English Amateur Championships at the age of eighteen, he turned pro in 1976 and began a tremendous string of victories on the European PGA tour. At Royal Laytham in 1977, he was part of the winning Ryder Cup team, defeating Tom Watson in a singles match. His five major titles include three British Opens and back-to-back Master's Tournaments in 1989 and 1990. Faldo is one of the most recognizable golfers worldwide, with a stroke many try to emulate but simply cannot.

Ray Floyd

A devoted Cubs fan, Floyd opted for a professional golf career over one in professional baseball. It has paid off, as he continues to shine after some thirty-four years in tournament play. Floyd, now a star on the Senior PGA circuit, has amassed some $10 million between the PGA and PGA Senior tours. Floyd has won a laundry list of top events since his 1963 victory in the St. Petersburg Open at the age of twenty-one. His last PGA title came twenty-eight years later at the age of forty-nine. A tenacious player, Floyd won the Masters in 1976, the Tournament Players Championship in 1981, the U.S. Open in 1986, and the 1988 Skins Game. Floyd is one of only two PGAers (along with Sam Snead) to win PGA Tour events in four decades. He has also been a member of the Ryder Cup Team in four decades!

Ben Hogan

A bona fide golf legend now in his seventies, Hogan was inducted into the World Golf Hall of Fame in 1974. It was one of countless honors bestowed upon him. The man in the trademark white cap, Hogan posted over sixty tour victories in a career interrupted by the Second World War and a near-fatal car accident. Hogan does not accredit his amazing success to natural talent. "Practice through unrelenting labor" is what he attributes his success to. He was *the* golfer of the '40s and '50s, following in the footsteps of Bobby Jones. Perhaps his most amazing of many tour feats was thirteen victories in one year (1946). Only Byron Nelson could claim more in a single season. One of the true legends of the game, Hogan rode down Broadway in a tickertape parade. Today there are tournaments named for him and an award for overcoming a great handicap.

Hale Irwin

Following an NCAA golf championship in 1967, Irwin turned pro in 1968. Interestingly enough, he was also a top defensive back in college football. He chose, however, the more lasting career, and after thirty years has no regrets about his decision. A three-time U.S. Open champion, Irwin finished among the top ten money winners from 1972 through 1978, and three times subsequently. A true world champion of golf, Hale has won the Australian and South African PGA Championships, the Brazilian Open, the Bahamas Classic, and other national titles. Irwin, now on the senior circuit, has won over $7 million in his stellar career.

Bobby Jones

Golf's legendary superstar of the 1920s, Jones redefined golf in America as a game to watch. The public was inspired by him as he took over the amateur ranks and became a household name. He would win on both sides of the Atlantic, taking the U.S. Open four times and the British Open three times. Jones had popularity comparable to Arnold Palmer and Tiger Woods in a time when there was no television to spread your name and accomplishments. In 1930 Jones set a new precedent by winning all four major events in one year: the U.S. Open, British Open, U.S. Amateur, and British Amateur. After the amazing feat, with nothing left to conquer, Jones called it quits at the age of twenty-eight. He would later start a little tournament in Augusta Georgia called the Masters. Jones won twenty-three tournaments in thirteen years, had a tickertape parade down Broadway in New York City, and is still considered by many today as the greatest of them all.

Betsy King

King is the queen of the LPGA, the all-time leading money winner, and one of the most renowned female athletes ever. A slow starter, King spent seven years on the tour before finally winning an event. After nearly 200 tour events, she won the 1984 Women's Kemper Open. She took to winning so well that she went on to become the Rolex Player of the Year in 1984 as the top LPGA money winner. From that point on she was consistently ranked among the top ten year after year, accumulating numerous titles, awards, and trophies. Her volunteer and humanitarian efforts have ranked as equally impressive, including organizing Habitat house-building

projects in Phoenix and Charlotte, and helping the orphans of Rumania.

Tom Kite

The prototype of consistency, Tom Kite posted fourteen consecutive seasons with $200,000 or more in prize money on the tour. Kite, a native of Austin, Texas, took up the game at the age of six, and by age eleven had won his first championship. He's still winning them today. Not a long hitter, Kite simply does everything else with expert precision. From his first tour title in 1976 at the IVC-Bicentennial Golf Classic to the 1983 Bing Crosby Open to the '92 U.S. Open, Kite has won his share of tour events, posting over 200 top-ten finishes. His biggest year came in 1989 when he earned over $1.3 million of his nearly $10 million in all-time earnings. Captain of the 1997 U.S. Ryder Cup team, Kite is nearing the move to the senior circuit while still going strong on the PGA Tour.

Nancy Lopez

One of the most popular stars of the LPGA, Lopez rose to prominence at a young age. At age twelve she won the New Mexico Women's Amateur, and shortly thereafter won the USGA Junior Girls Championship, twice. In 1977 she turned pro and by 1978 was topping the LPGA list of money winners. Part of a rare two-professional-athlete marriage, Nancy married major-league baseball player Ray Knight in 1982. Whereas Ray ended his pro career, Nancy's has just kept on going, and by 1994 she topped the $4 million career earnings mark. For her success between 1978 and 1987, Nancy was named Golfer of the Decade by *Golf Magazine*, for whom she became a contributing writer. She has since added numerous trophies and honors to a long list of credits, and although she enters less events, she is always a major drawing card at any tournament.

Byron Nelson

Nelson, like Ben Hogan, picked a bad time to become the most prominent golfer in the world, the late 1930s into the 1940s. Nonetheless, Nelson became a legend of the game, winning twenty-six of his fifty-two tour victories in 1944 and an amazing eleven wins in a row in 1945. He continued to post victories throughout the '40s and into the '50s. As a tribute to his outstanding career, the PGA Byron Nelson Award was established in 1995 to honor the tour's scoring leader.

Jack Nicklaus

Considered by many to be the greatest in golf history, Nicklaus was named Golfer of the Century in 1988, following his Athlete of the Decade honors for the 1970s. Perhaps he will be up for and award for his architectural work for the '90s. Besides being in the Golf Hall of Fame, Nicklaus was named PGA Player of the Year five times, won some seventy tour events, and became the first tour player to reach $2, $3, $4, and then $5 million in career earnings. Had he reached his heyday in the 1990s instead of the '70s, he might have made five times his

career earnings, which exceeded $5.5 million on the PGA Tour.

Nicklaus is one of the prime reasons for the growth of the game. A household name along with Arnold Palmer, he symbolized golf to the growing TV audience of the 1960s and '70s. He set numerous scoring records and has continued his reign onto the senior circuit some thirty-five years after turning pro. His instinct was always to win major tournaments, and that is exactly what he did. Nicklaus is also one of the leading course designers in the world, working with his own company Golden Bear International.

Greg Norman

Norman has won everything his native homeland Australia had to offer, as well as the Hong Kong Open, Scandinavian Open, Taiheyo Masters in Japan, and a string of PGA titles. In fact, Norman had won tournaments in thirteen countries by 1996. Ranked as the PGA top money winner in 1986, '90, and '95, Greg was able to amass some $10 million in prize money on the PGA Tour, most of it in the 1990s. In 1995, despite missing several weeks with back problems, he posted three tour victories and took in over $1.6 million in earnings.

"The Shark," as he's known, is one of the world's finest and has quietly garnered legendary status since turning pro in 1976. He has a tremendous presence on the course and leaves players and spectators in awe. He says he owes much of his ongoing success to early Jack Nicklaus instructional golf books and the self-help book *Zen and the Martial Arts*. Norman is one of the most charismatic and spectacular golfers to watch on the course, helping him to become one of the most sought-after for endorsements, as well as by his many fans and followers.

Ayako Okamoto

Japan's most prominent female athlete, Okamoto joined the LPGA at the age of thirty after playing on the Japanese circuit and enjoying a successful career as a softball pitcher. By 1987 she was ranked number one on the LPGA Tour, and with four tournament victories, she won the Rolex Player of the Year. In Japan she won the Prime Minister's award for being a tremendous inspiration to Japanese athletes.

Jose Maria Olazabal

Just as Seve Ballesteros grew up with golf, so did Jose Maria Olazabal. Also from Spain, Olazabal's family included greenskeepers and other golfers, and he learned the game at an early age. By the age of twenty he had won the Amateur Triple Crown: taking the three top events in Britain. From

his first professional years in the late '80s on, he has continued to win throughout Europe. One of the game's most renowned putters, Olazabal is known for having a smooth swing and great determination to win. In 1994 he made his biggest splash in the United States by capturing the Masters at Augusta.

Arnold Palmer

Palmer *is* golf in America. He played a significant role in the transformation of golf into the multimillion-dollar business it is today. His PGA career spanned a remarkable six decades. The first player to reach the $1 million mark in career earnings, Palmer won at least one event in each of seventeen consecutive years, including seven majors, a record tied only by Nicklaus. Palmer's victories, eighty-nine worldwide, plus his numerous honors and awards, including Associated Press Sportsman of the Decade in the 1960s, could go on for pages. So, instead let's note that he's a grandfather of six, has a course-design company, is involved in club making, has his own golf club, and is chairman of the board of the Golf Channel. Oh, yes, he's also a pilot, with a number of aviation records.

Corey Pavin

A basketball enthusiast, at 5'9" Corey Pavin knew golf was more likely in his future. He graduated Q-School in 1983 and by 1991 was ranked number one on the PGA Tour. One of the most consistent on the tour, Pavin finally won a major in 1995, taking the U.S

Open on his way to his first million-dollar winning season. Pavin is now one of the top names on the money board consistently.

Gary Player

Holder of numerous golf titles, awards, and frequent-flier miles, Player is one of the most traveled athletes in history. Truly an international legend of golf, Player has won more than 140 tournaments around the world, including 21 on the PGA Tour, 7 Australian Opens, 4 South African Opens, and 3 British Opens. He is one of only four to win all four majors. From Johannesburg, South Africa, Player is the consummate professional, keeping himself in marvelous physical shape well into his sixties. And when not on a course some-where in the world, Player has been found at the track watching one of the several race horses he owns.

Nick Price

At eighteen years of age, Price was playing on the South African and European tours as an amateur. A native of Rhodesia, now Zimbabwe, Price is in excellent physical condition and keeps fit with water sports, such as water skiing, which he enjoys almost as much as golf. Price joined the PGA Tour in 1983, winning one event that year. But it wasn't until 1991 when his career took off. With two victories that year, plus the PGA Championship in 1992, he was on his way. In a span of four years, Price would win eleven PGA events and place in the top ten in thirty-eight, winning a significant amount of his now $8 million-plus tour earnings.

Betsy Rawls

During the war years of the mid-'40s, a teenage Betsy Rawls took up golf. Within a few years she was winning amateur events in Texas, and by 1951 was winning on the LPGA Tour. In the span of twenty-four years she amassed some fifty-five tour victories while winning only just over $300,000 in a stellar career that ended before the big-money days of golf began. From her stardom on the course, she moved into the front office as the LPGA's Tournament Director for six years. From that point on Rawls's resume is that of major positions in the world of golf, including becoming the first woman to sit on the rules committee for the men's U.S. Open. In 1995 she won the Sprint Lifetime Achievement Award.

Patty Sheehan

For five straight years in the late '70s, Pat Sheehan won state amateur titles in Nevada and California. The former top-rated junior skier then went on to a college career that put her in the Collegiate Golf Hall of Fame. Therefore it was not a big surprise that she would go on to the LPGA Hall of Fame. She emerged on the professional scene in 1980, won her first tour event in 1981, the Mazda Japan Classic, and kept on winning right on into the '90s. Some $5 million in career earnings later, she is playing editor for *Golf for Women* magazine while emerging as a golf-course-design consultant.

Sam Snead

His forty-two-year PGA total of $620,000 could be matched with a couple major victories in the modern era. Yet, Snead posted eighty-one career PGA victories. Slammin' Sam was known for having one of the most graceful swings the game has ever seen. From the age of twenty-five through the age of fifty-two Snead won everything in sight, except the U.S. Open. But while the Open eluded him, the legendary Snead was the epitome of golf from the '30s through the war years of the '40s, and right up into the '50s and '60s.

Payne Stewart

Stewart, in vivid colors, is hard to miss on any course. Turning pro back in 1979, Stewart honed his skills for two years on the Asian circuit, winning the Indonesian Open. Stewart then hit the PGA Tour in 1981, but kept falling short of the mark in the big events. Finally, after utilizing the services of a sports psychologist, he hit his stride and took the PGA Championship in 1989 and the U.S. Open in 1991. Throughout the '90s Stewart's career has had its ups and downs, but the always flamboyant Stewart remains a top competitor and big money winner. He ranks among the top ten all-time PGA money winners.

Curtis Strange

A top competitor and PGA pro for over twenty years, Strange was an amateur champion in 1973 and won individual honors on the NCAA circuit in 1974. Accuracy and devotion to honing his skills have made Strange a big winner on the tour, topping the PGA in earnings three times in the late '80s and taking back-to-back U.S. Open titles in 1988 and 1989. Curtis Strange had the dis-

tinction of being the first American to pull in $1 million in earnings in one year by winning four titles. But perhaps his biggest distinction may have been setting a record with a 62, ten under par, at the legendary Old Course at St. Andrews.

Lee Trevino

His quote, "You don't know what pressure is until you play for five bucks when you have only two in your pocket" exemplifies the type of colorful and gritty player that is Lee Trevino. A self-made golfer, Trevino dropped out of school at the age of fourteen and worked on a driving range. After a stint in the military he went home to Texas to work on his game, and the rest is history. Trevino was the Tour Rookie of the Year in 1967 and in '68 won the U.S. Open at Oak Hill. In 1971 he took the U.S. Open again and went on to win back-to-back British Open titles in the early '70s.

Despite being struck by lightning at the Western Open in 1976, Trevino never let his love for the game fade. A fun-loving, comical character, with numerous golf quotes to his credits, Trevino is now a consistent top winner on the senior circuit, having pulled in over $10 million on the PGA and Senior tours combined.

Tom Watson

In 1971 Watson graduated from Stanford University and turned pro, taking a postgraduate degree in Q-School and passing with flying golf balls. By 1974 he ranked in the top ten, and by the late '70s, topped the charts for four consecutive years, leading the

PGA Tour in earnings and winning twenty tour events in that span. Watson has won over $7 million in a career that from the mid-'70s into the early '80s was nothing short of sensational.

Karrie Webb

Billed as the female Tiger Woods, Karrie took the golf scene by storm in her rookie 1996 season. Winner of the Rolex Rookie of the Year Award, the Queensland, Australia, native posted nearly $1 million in earnings over her first twenty-five events. Webb took up golf at the age of eight, and by the time she reached age twenty she had represented Australia in six international competitions before qualifying for the LPGA at the end of 1995. Webb is someone to watch closely as her career takes off.

Kathy Whitworth

Kathy posted eighty-eight victories in a spectacular LPGA career that ran from 1959 through 1991. Tutored by Harvey Penick, Whitworth took up golf at the age of fifteen and turned pro by age nineteen. She was the LPGA leading money winner eight times and winner of the Player of the Year honors seven times. A member of the LPGA Hall of Fame, she has won numerous honors, including the Associate Press Athlete of the year on two occasions. She and Mickey Wright teamed up to make history by competing in the PGA-sanctioned Legends of Golf as the first women's team. Now a member of

the President's Campaign Against Drug Abuse, Whitworth has set a stellar example in women's athletics for four decades on and off the course.

Tiger Woods

Tiger-mania has kicked in, and the young star is certainly living up to the onslaught of cover stories and comparisons to the game's all-time best. Woods, who in his sophomore year at Stanford took College Player of the Year honors, became one of an elite few to capture six USGA Amateur titles, including three U.S. Junior Amateur and three U.S. Amateur titles. In 1994 he became the youngest player to win the U.S. Amateur Championship. But Woods didn't stop as one of the legendary amateurs. Turning pro, Woods proceeded to $1 million in earnings faster than anyone else, hitting the mark in only nine events. His record-shattering performance at the 1997 Masters made him a star not only to the golf world, but to the general public as well. Tiger has come of age in a big way, and it's a big boost for a sport that has been without a media hero in recent years.

Ian Woosnam

At only 5'4", Woosnam is small in height but big in stature as one of the games premier international players. He is a big swinger with tremendous determination. After three trips to qualifying school, he qualified at the pro level but struggled for his first several years before finally capturing two titles in 1982, including the Swiss Open. He won his first major in 1991 at the Masters in Augusta. After twenty years as a pro, he has amassed some thirty European titles. The year 1987 was *the* year for this Wales native, as he captured eight titles and was heralded as the best player in the world. Despite lower-back problems, Woosnam has continued to be a world-class golfer.

Mickey Wright

Mickey took up golf at age twelve, and by seventeen she was the U.S. Girls Junior title holder. At twenty she turned pro, and by twenty-six was ranked the number one money winner on the LPGA Tour. In 1961 she posted three victories in the four LPGA majors. Eighty-two tour victories later, Wright retired, having won more than $40,000 in a single season in her outstanding career. Considered one of the greatest female golfers of all time, Wright is a member of the LPGA Hall of Fame.

Fuzzy Zoeller

Other golfers have won more money, more majors, and more titles, but no one else is named Fuzzy. Frank Urban dons his trademark sunglasses and pleases the crowd with his style. In 1994 he topped $1 million in earnings without winning a tour event, but the following year his earnings fell off dramatically due to back problems.

Nonetheless, he's a favorite on the tour, and like many of the touring pros, Fuzzy is now turning some of his attention to course design.

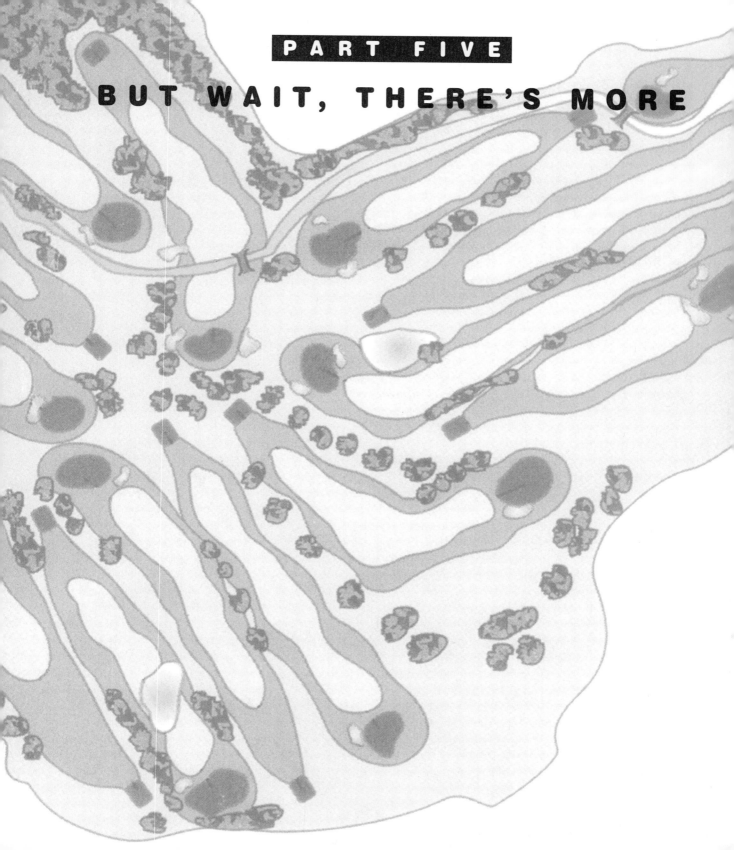

ANECDOTES, QUOTES, JOKES, AND TRIVIA

ANECDOTES

There's a story of a guest at the famed Augusta National golf course complaining to a caddie about all the gnats. "What are these things?" he asked the caddie. "They're Jackass flies," replied the caddie, "They're always found around jackasses." The angry guest quickly responded, "Are you calling me a jackass?" "No," replied the caddie "but apparently the flies can't seem to tell the difference."

Tommy Bolt, not pleased with his caddie of the day, once asked a tour official for a ruling. "I know you can get fined for throwing a club," said Bolt, "but can you get fined for throwing a caddie?"

Tommy Armour, a former champion, once asked a caddie in Scotland where he should play a blind shot to the green. The caddie told him to aim for a mast off in the distance on a ship. Armour, not the fastest player on the tour, did as the caddie suggested, then complained when his shot fell well to the side of the putting green. "I thought you said to aim for the mast?" he asked the caddie. "I did," replied the caddie, "but by the time you hit it, the ship had sailed."

Bob Hope once got a present of ninety golf balls with the words "Happy Birthday Bob" engraved on them. Said Hope, "Now when I hit a ball into the water, the fish will know who it belonged to."

Former Detroit Lions football star Alex Karras once hit a ball through a plate-glass window and into a dining room at a club where he was playing. Karras calmly walked over to a groundskeeper of the course and asked, "Is this room out of bounds?"

Ben Hogan once commented to the club president of Seminole that on that particular day the greens seemed slower than usual. The club president quipped back, "Well, if you didn't take so long to putt, the grass wouldn't have a chance to grow so long."

One year Bing Crosby, tired of the unpredictable weather at Pebble Beach, asked a friend of his who was a priest if he could put in a good word with the guy upstairs for some better weather. The priest replied, "Sorry, Bing. I'm in sales, not management."

Also at Pebble Beach, in the 1965 Bing Crosby Tournament, an amateur named Matt Palacio hooked a drive on the eighteenth hole. As it headed toward the water he said, "Well, looks like only God can save that one." Just as he said it, the tide receded and the ball hit a rock and landed on the fairway. Palacio looked up and said, "Thank you."

There are those who are waiting for the ex-champion brat of tennis to take up golf someday. Apparently John McEnroe was quoted as saying, "Golf is artistic expression like ballet, except you can be a fat slob and still play golf." It will be interesting to see how easy it is for John to play through.

⛳ ⛳ ⛳

King Hassan II of Morocco loved the game of golf and had his own private course built. The 9-hole course had forty-three bunkers and the king could never seem to avoid landing in most of them. He called in golf pros who were experts at sand play to help him improve his game. After this failed, he did what any king would do and ordered the course changed and all forty-three bunkers filed-in with sod, proving once again, it's good to be the king.

⛳ ⛳ ⛳

President Grant supposedly took to the course with a friend because he heard golf was good exercise. After watching his friend struggle a bit on the course, he agreed that the game looked very much like it was good exercise. He then asked, "But what's that little white ball for?"

⛳ ⛳ ⛳

Jay Morrish, a top golf architect, recalls getting a phone call from a guy from Fort Lauderdale who said he wanted to build the greatest

course that had ever been built in the state of Florida and that money was no object. "He said, 'I want this thing to be done properly.' We were excited and told him we were ready to do that. We asked him how many acres he had for us to build on. Apparently not knowing much about the space needed to build a course, he replied, 'About twenty-seven.'"

⛳ ⛳ ⛳

The mayor of Tallahassee, Florida, thought that because he was the mayor he could stroll onto the city-owned Hiliman Golf Course and play after the course was closed for the day. His off-hour practicing disturbed some, but he kept up his activity of practicing during the off hours. Finally, one evening, a maintenance worker asked the mayor to leave, and when he refused, he did what any good golf maintenance worker should do . . . he turned on the sprinklers. The mayor had the worker suspended, but the voters, outraged, backed the maintenance worker and eventually the mayor (and the employee) both apologized. The mayor promised his constituency he would not practice after hours again, and the maintenance worker returned to work and got his full pay.

LOST 3 BALLS, GOT A TRIPLE BOGEY, WHAT ELSE COULD GO WRONG

QUOTES

"You don't know what pressure is until you play for five bucks and you only have two in your pocket."

— *Lee Trevino*

Ian Baker-Finch commented on the incredible driving skill of John Daly. Said Finch, "I don't even drive that far on my holidays.d like to make a living playing golf, but it wouldn't pay the bills."

— *Mark Rypien, former NFL quarterback*

"Building a golf course is like a tailor cutting a cloth. The routing is the cut of the cloth. If the routing is done well, the suit will fit. There may be some changes when you gain or lose some weight, but adjustments can be made if the original cut is done properly."

— *Rees Jones on building and rebuilding courses.*

"Golf is a good walk spoiled."
— *Mark Twain*

"Some worship in churches, some in synagogues, some on golf courses."
— *Adlai Stephenson*

DIARY OF A SINGLE GOLFING GODDESS

"Today I learned it's difficult to follow through on a swing when you are wearing a Wonder Bra," writes stand-up comic, writer, and journalist Cynthia Daddona of Westport, Connecticut.

Cynthia, who fancies herself a single female goddess, chronicled her first golf lessons with two friends. "Our mission was to successfully hit a golf ball without getting injured or injuring anyone else." Cynthia clearly explained her goals to the instructor, Bob Dugan, "I'd like to learn two things, how to put the golf cart in reverse and how to spend less time searching for my ball in the duck pond."

The lesson was a success and Cynthia joined the ranks of golfers everywhere, and yes, she's now meeting single male golfing "gods" who are giving her all kinds of pointers. Adds Cynthia, "We're only taking tips from our golf pro to avoid confusion, sorry guys." But she's not saying she doesn't enjoy the attention.

Describing his game: "I'd say I'm one under. One under a tree, one under a rock, one under a bush . . ."
— *former NHL goalie Gerry Cheevers*

Comparing golf to baseball: "In golf, when we hit a foul ball, we've got to go out there and play it."
— *Sam Snead*

"Golf is a game in which you yell fore, shoot six, and write down five."
— *unknown golfer . . . but a very profound one!*

"Golf isn't a sport, it's men in bad pants walking."
— *Rosie O'Donnell*

"Golf is a game in which one endeavors to control a ball with implements ill-adapted for the purposes."
— *Woodrow Wilson*

A golfer playing in Scotland once asked his caddie how long the hole was. The caddie replied, "It will take you three fine shots to get there in two."

"Golf is the most fun you can have without taking your clothes off."
— *Chi Chi Rodriguez*

"Isn't it fun to go out on the course and lie in the sun?"
— *Bob Hope*

"If you are going to throw a club, it's important to throw it ahead of you, down the fairway, so you don't have to go back and pick it up."
— *Tommy Bolt, professional golfer*

"Golf is like a puzzle without an answer."
— *Gary Player*

"It is reasonable to assume that in the last five years Americans have lost, collectively, one billion golf balls. No other sporting endeavor can match that kind of dogged perseverance in the face of such manifest futility."
— *Peter Andrews*

"I've seen courses built on landfills, and they've ruined a perfectly good garbage dump."

— *Jay Moorish, golf architect*

GOLF HUMOR—OPTIMIST VS. PESSIMIST: A QUIZ

Are you an optimist or a pessimist? Golf can easily help you to determine that personality trait.

1. A 200-yard drive on a 400-yard hole has you
   A. halfway to the green.
   B. halfway from the tee area.
   C. in the parking lot taking a chip shot from the hood of an '89 Camaro.

2. When you leave the course
   A. you feel that your game is improving.
   B. you seriously consider switching to tennis.
   C. the back nine is declared a federal disaster area.

3. The ball is sixty yards from the green, in thick rough, down a hill. You picture:
   A. the ball sailing onto the green.
   B. the ball rolling farther down the hill into an abyss.
   C. General Custer at his last stand.

4. There is a ravine in front of you.
   A. You are confident that you can clear it.
   B. You are packing up to head home.
   C. You consider throwing your club, bag, and partner in it.

5. If you play golf often, you look forward to someday:
   A. having a low handicap.
   B. having high blood pressure.
   C. having your head examined.

If you answered "A" to all of the above, you are the true golf optimist and despite your level of skill, you will always dream about playing at St. Andrews.

If you answered "B" to all of the above, you are the typical golf pessimist, but will keep on playing in hopes of that one great round.

If you answered "C" to all of the above, you might seriously consider tagging you golf clubs at your next garage sale.

PRESIDENTS ON THE COURSE

A book called <u>Presidential Lies</u> (Macmillan, 1996) detailed the history of the presidents of the United States on the golf course. According to authors Shephed Campbell and Peter Landau, who did the marvelous (and tiring) research, these presidents were considered the top ten. In making their assessments, the writers took into consideration the differences in skill and equipment—and they appropriately ignored policy and party.

1. John F. Kennedy—Handicap: 7–10. Good short iron game; started playing in college.

2. Gerald Ford—Handicap: 12. Powerful long tee shots, but dangerous to the spectators.

3. Dwight D. Eisenhower—Handicap: 14–18. Practiced often and had a good short iron game, but was an impatient putter.

4. Franklin D. Roosevelt—Handicap: 14–18. Great strength produced long drives and made him proficient at getting out of deep rough, but he wasn't known for direction.

5. George Bush—Handicap: 11 (prior to his days in the White House). Hit woods and longer iron shots accurately but didn't have the short game or the putting game down.

6. Ronald Reagan—Handicap: 12. Drives and recovery shots from the rough were his strengths.

7. Richard Nixon—Handicap: 12 at his best (primarily pre-White House years). Had a decent short game and putted well, but drives were short.

8. Bill Clinton—Handicap: 14–20. Good long drives are his strength, but his game has been known to be inconsistent and slow.

9. William H. Taft—Handicap: unknown. Good putter, but because he gripped the club like a baseball bat he had a short choppy swing.

10. Warren G. Harding—Handicap: unknown. Good putting and on short pitches to the green, but had a weak follow-through, rushed his swing, and was, overall, mediocre.

"If you hold a golfer close to your ear and listen like you would to a seashell, you'll hear an alibi."

— *Fred Beck*

"Most people play a fair game of golf . . . if you watch them."

— *Joey Adams*

"I must say, my pal Charley (Pride) hit some good woods . . . most of them were trees."

— *Glen Campbell*

"It's good sportsmanship not to pick up loose golf balls while they're still rolling."

— *Mark Twain*

"The Lord answers my prayers everywhere except on the golf course."

— *Reverend Billy Graham*

"Golf is a game of expletives not deleted."

— *Dr. Irving Gladstone*

"Golf is like love. One day you think you're too old, the next day you want to do it again."

— *Robert Di Vicenzo*

"I've done as much for golf as Truman Capote has done for Sumo wrestling."

— *Bob Hope*

JOKES

Golf jokes have been popular since the first tee shot sailed through a nearby clubhouse window and someone had to break the tension. Bob Hope, Milton Berle, and a host of comics have done routines, and Johnny Carson even ended his nightly *Tonight Show* monologue with his patented air tee shot. Many of these golf jokes have been around for a long time; others are new. The bottom line is they make sport of the world's greatest sport.

A golf lover near Augusta stood outside his parked car en route to see the Masters tournament. A passing motorist stopped at a light and the golf lover asked, "Can you tell me how to get to the Masters?" Replied the passing motorist, "Practice, practice, practice."

TEEING OFF IN SOME STRANGE PLACES

Below are a few of the oddest places from which a golf shot was taken.

1. *The Moon: Alan Shepard used a makeshift 6-iron to hit what could have been the longest iron shot ever (considering the gravity or lack thereof on the moon). However, he didn't hit the ball well, and it traveled only about 200 yards. Not bad for a mis-hit, nonetheless.*

2. *Wrigley Field in Chicago: As part of a publicity stunt, Sam Snead teed off from home plate and bounced balls off and over the scoreboard. The Cubs immediately wanted to sign him up.*

3. *The Eiffel Tower: In 1976 Arnold Palmer hit a drive off the Eiffel Tower. Talk about playing through on the French Open.*

4. *An Airport Runway in Denver, Colorado: Not as exotic as the Eiffel Tower, John Daly hit a shot down the runway over 850 yards, thanks to the mile-high air of Colorado. The runway, of course, was a par twelve.*

The duffer swung and then said to his partner, "I'd move heaven and earth just to break a hundred." His partner replied, "You'd better work on heaven; you've already moved enough earth."

Two golfers were on the seventeenth green when one stopped for several moments to watch a funeral procession go by. "Why the interest in the procession?" asked one golfer. "She was the best wife I ever had," replied the other.

How can you tell an employee from the boss on a golf course? The employee is the one congratulating the other player on a 10. The employee is also the only player who can get a hole-in-one and say "Oops."

The golfer asked his friend if he had yet broken 100. Replied the friend, "Not yet, but I'm sure bending the hell out of 110."

After hitting three balls into the water, the furious golfer flung the club into the water and screamed, "Damn caddie!"

"What did he do?" asked his partner.

"He gave me the wrong club," replied the irate golfer.

"What club was that?" inquired his partner.

The now more complacent golfer turned to his partner and replied, "Yours."

A man was cured of deafness when a golf ball struck him in the head. He was thrilled and told friends, "That's two things I was cured of in one day." What was the other? asked his friend. "Hanging around golf courses," replied the man.

One player complained to his friend, "The way I slice and lose balls in the bushes, I should not only address the ball, I should put a return address on it as well."

The golfer asked his caddie, "Am I the worst golfer you've ever seen?" "I don't know yet," said the caddie. "This is my first day, but if you continue at this pace, I may never get to caddie again."

You can always tell the golfers in church: they pray with an interlocking grip.

"Why are you so upset about your day on the course?"

"I kept my head down all day."

"Isn't that how you're supposed to play?"

"Sure, but while my head was down someone swiped my cart."

One golfer said to the other after watching a duffer digging up the course, "Should we swipe the ball for a joke?" "What joke?" said the other. "The way he plays he'll never know it's gone."

Said one golfer to his partner, "My wife left me because I told her I spent the whole day with a hooker."

I just missed a hole in one . . . by eight strokes.

The golfer asked his friend, "What should I give as a tip for the caddy?" Replied his pal, "Tell him to take up tennis."

How can you play thirty-six holes in a day without leaving your house? Buy a harmonica.

The blushing bride rushed up to the first tee in her gown. The groom-to-be turned to her and said, "I told you, only if it rained."

"You love golf so much you probably don't even remember our wedding day," said the wife. "Sure I do," replied her husband. "It was the day after I birdied a 550-yard par five."

A group of players were just putting the pin back in the cup and leaving the green as a ball sailed onto the green. One of the golfers nudged the ball into the cup. Moments later a golfer came up and asked them if any of them had seen his ball. They told him it went right into the cup. Excited, the golfer yelled to his friends, "Hey guys, I shot a 12!"

The golf pro told the duffer, "You should go through the motion of the swing without

hitting the ball." Replied the duffer, "I do that all the time; that's why I came to you for $100 a lesson!"

Two older women had just taken up the game. On the first tee, one of them hit a ball that sliced to the right, hit a tree, ricocheted off the roof of the clubhouse, bounced off a branch, careened off a rock, and rolled down a large hill onto the green and right into the cup. The second woman turned to her and said, "Why didn't you tell me you've been practicing?"

WOW, THAT WAS SOME SLICE

"You made one nice drive this afternoon."
"Which one?"
"The one in your car that got us to the course."

"How come your caddie keeps checking his watch?"
"What watch? The way I've been playing, I bought him a compass."

The golfer took a series of giant steps as he made his way to the green. "What's that all about," asked his partner? "Well," replied the golfer, "my wife told me that if I want to play tomorrow, it'll be over her dead body, so I'm practicing."

You know your game isn't improving when the course pro sets you up for a lesson . . . with the tennis instructor.

St. Peter and Moses were playing a game of golf. On the third tee St. Peter hit a shot that sliced way off course. Suddenly an angel swooped in, caught the ball, and flew it over to the hole, where she deposited the ball on the green. Moses turned to St. Peter and said, "C'mon Pete, not when we're playing for money."

The golfer swung and swung in the sand trap. Finally he yelled out, "I hit it." One of his foursome responded, "You hit it? I didn't see the ball." "What ball?" said the golfer from the trap. "I hit oil."

"I had a terrible round today," said the golfer. "I hit three birdies." "That sounds like a good round," replied his friend. "Not when you consider the three birdies were in a pet store window," responded the aggravated golfer.

GOLF TRIVIA

DID YOU KNOW:

That only 17 percent of adult golfers maintain a handicap?

That the minimum depth in inches for a golf hole is four?

That the first miniature golf course was opened in Pinehurst, North Carolina, in 1916?

That in 1895 the USGA banned the pool cue as a putter?

That the founder of the Walker Cup in 1922 was the grandfather of former President George Bush?

That in 1930 a fellow named Bobby Cruickshank bet on amateur Bobby Jones to win the grand slam and pulled in (at odds of 120 to 1) an astounding $60,000?

That only four pros have ever won the grand slam? Bobby Jones, Jack Nicklaus, Gary Player, and Gene Sarazen.

THE GOLFER'S PERSONALITY INDEX

ANALYZE YOURSELF (AND OTHERS) THROUGH GOLF

More than a game, golf is a way of life. It is an obsession to some and an addiction to others. It is a true test of what a person is made of, expressing their attributes, their disposition, and their personality traits and characteristics.

Much like the Minnesota Multiphasic Personality Inventory is used to try to determine an individual's personality, the Golfer's Personality Index will do just that, based on nothing but the game, the courses, and the simple logic of illogic.

The system has been carefully devised by three weekend golfers who spent long hours doing painstaking research while watching a lopsided Sunday-night NFL game at a hotel resort bar on the outskirts of Trenton, New Jersey. Its accuracy is therefore unmatched by any other golf psychological personality profile known today.

GOLFER'S PERSONALITY PROFILE

Indicate your answer by circling one of the following:

1   Doesn't describe me at all
2   Describes me somewhat
3   Describes me very much
4   Describes me to a tee

1. When I slice my tee shot, I hear people laughing at me and making jokes.	1	2	3	4
2. I suggest carrying our own clubs as a sign of bravado, but I really want to use an electric cart.	1	2	3	4
3. After $500 worth of lessons my game is worse than it was before.	1	2	3	4
4. I tell people who don't play with me that my drives go 250 yards, when at best they reach 200.	1	2	3	4

THE GOLFER'S PERSONALITY INDEX

5. I like playing new courses because they give me a host of opportunities to use new and innovative excuses.   1   2   3   4

6A. (For men) I feel my putter is an extension of myself.   1   2   3   4

6B. (For women) Whenever I'm on the course I always meet some jerk who thinks his putter is an extension of himself.   1   2   3   4

7. I'm convinced my 3-iron is getting shorter.   1   2   3   4

8. I tell dirty jokes while walking down the fairway to relieve tension and take others' minds off the fact that my short game stinks.   1   2   3   4

9. I find the fact that my father-in-law has a membership in a country club with a championship course to be his only redeeming feature.   1   2   3   4

10. The overlapping grip makes me hit like a trained chimp with a club in its hands.   1   2   3   4

If you scored between 10 and 15 points, you have no real idea of who you are on the course. You probably think St. Andrews is the patron saint of golf.

If you scored 16 to 25, you are getting familiar with the game. You recognize that the only thing a double green means to you is that you have two targets to miss.

If you scored between 26 and 35, welcome to the club. You are a lying, cheating, somewhat paranoid, typical golfer, who wasted money on lessons and would sell his or her in-laws for a shot at playing the Augusta National.

If you scored 36 to 40, you're trying to show off again!

**YOU KNOW YOU'RE PLAYING
TOO MUCH GOLF WHEN...**

*You try to read the break in
your new area rug.*

*You hold your fishing rod with
an overlapping grip.*

*You refer to a flood in your
basement as casual water.*

*At the bank you let the person
farthest from the teller window
go first.*

*You rarely ever wear clothes
that match.*

*Your pets are named Fuzzy and
Tiger.*

*You have to ask if you can putt
out so you can make your
daughter's wedding.*

*Your speed dialer includes the
USGA, the local pro shop, and a
dozen of your favorite courses.*

*You take your sand wedge for a
day at the beach.*

That a man by the name of Dr. Joseph Boydstone, in 1962, recorded eleven aces in one calendar year, three in one round?

That a man named Ollie Bowers, from South Carolina, played a record 9,756 holes of golf in one year (542 rounds)? Needless to say, his wife didn't see him often.

That Simon Chandler caddied at Augusta for over forty years?

That Byron Nelson captured his nineteenth victory of 1945 at Glen Garden, on the Fort Worth course, where he caddied as a boy?

That early America golfers wore tricorner and wide-brimmed hats on the course until the commissioner's office determined that these hats were being used as target sites? They were ruled illegal for play on the links.

That a golfer named Gary Wright, obviously in a hurry, played eighteen holes in just over twenty-eight minutes in Australia in 1980? Perhaps there were no bathrooms available.

That a golfer named Lori Garbacz, apparently fed up with slow play, staged a protest by ordering a pizza between holes at the 1988 U.S. Open?

That at the 1989 U.S. Open in Oak Hill, four golfers hit aces on the same par-three hole in one day?

That two men, Simon Clough and Boris Janic, played 18-hole rounds of golf in five different countries in Europe in one day? "If it's the 2:30, we must be teeing off in Belgium."

That you can buy Grateful Dead golf products, including golf bags with dancing neon skeletons and head covers with the famed skull-and-roses design?

That in 1945 Byron Nelson scored an amazing eighteen PGA victories in one year? Ben Hogan made a run at that record the following year but fell five short at thirteen.

That in 1992 a six-year-old girl scored a hole-in-one at the Jimmy Clay Golf Course in Austin, Texas, on the eighty-five-yard par-three second hole?

That Ladies Softball superstar Joan Joyce has been on the professional golf circuit since 1977? Her unbelievable professional softball accomplishments include throwing 150 no-hitters, 50 perfect games, and striking out Ted Williams in an exhibition.

That the first men-only clubs in the United States were nicknamed "Eveless Edens"?

That the Masters began in 1934 as a gathering of Bobby Jones's friends?

That there are two women golfers in the PGA Hall of Fame? They are Babe Zaharias and Patty Berg.

That Christmas Day is the easiest day to get a good tee-off time at Pebble Beach?

That Calamity Jane was the name of Bobby Jones's putter?

That the oldest clubhouse in America is at Shinnecock?

That golf is a $30 billion-a-year industry?

That 200 million golf balls are lost every year?

That if you play the third hole at Kittansett during low tide you can walk along the beach to the green? During high tide, however, good luck finding your ball.

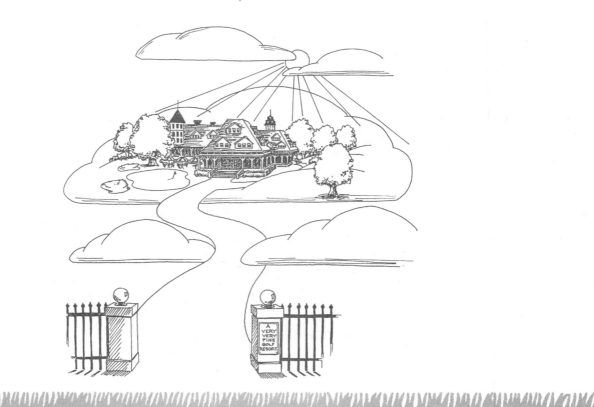

GOLF BOOKS, VIDEOS, CD·ROMS, MOVIES, AND MAGAZINES

GOLF CATALOGS

Golfsmart—(800) 673-3557

This catalog is filled with selections of golf books, videos, audio tapes, and CD-ROM items. Their service and attitude are great, and the materials and information are easily accessible. Many of the items listed in the audio, video, and CD-ROM section of this chapter are available through this catalog.

GolfSmith—(800) 456-3344

Catalog 1: Contained within is quality golf equipment, clothing, and memorabilia. You'll find golf clubs, golf bags, practice devices, shoes, hats, and even some silly, kitschy things. Their service is available twenty-four hours a day, seven days a week.

Catalog 2: Due to the growing interest of creating and repairing one's own clubs, GolfSmith puts out a second catalog called

"Components and Repair." Sprinkled among the shafts, hosels, and grips are odd quotes in English and Japanese. Go figure.

Jack Nicklaus Golf Collection—
(800) 544-2327

No slouch in the golf business, the Golden Bear smartly capitalizes here on his reputation. You can get high-end merchandise featuring Jack's Golden Bear logo, newspaper reprints of Nicklaus's championship accomplishments, and some great clothing for the course. Be prepared to pay, however; this is primo stuff.

Las Vegas Discount Golf and Tennis—
(800) 933-7777

A discount house stocking clubs, equipment, and kitsch. You can get anything from top-of-the-line clubs to golf paraphernalia and gadgets.

The USGA Members Guide and Catalogue—(800) 755-0293

A class act. Top-quality merchandise featuring clothing, books, and memorabilia. Because the USGA sponsors the U.S. Open, U.S. Open merchandise is only available here, and it's good stuff. Members of the USGA receive very good discounts. It's worth it to join the USGA just to save on the items listed in the catalog.

CATALOGS THAT CONTAIN SOME INTERESTING GOLF ITEMS

Garnet Hill—(800) 622-6216

Golf percale sheets. This wonderful, simple, vintage artwork of trees, a hole with a flagstick, and a golfer with a club in hand and a bag on the shoulder, was recently unearthed and printed on a smooth, 220-thread-count white cotton percale. Sheets are manufactured in all sizes. Comforter covers and tailored pillow shams are available as well.

The Mind's Eye—(800) 949-3333

A hip flask and funnel crafted from fine polished pewter commemorating St. Andrews—The Old Course. The flask features an incised map and history of the course on the front, and distances and pars for all eighteen holes on the back. Included are the years of St. Andrews' British Opens.

Herrington—(800) 622-5221

This catalog is known as a catalog for fine golf, skiing, motoring, travel, fitness photography, audio, and video. You can purchase a variety of clubs here as well as golf memorabilia. A sample of some of the things offered are a genuine walnut collector's cabinet to display balls from every course you've conquered, golf clothing, a Swiss Army knife made specifically for golf, and even quirky NFL head covers for your metalwoods. There are also practical items here like traveling covers for your golf bag.

Early Winters—(800) 458-4438

Basically for skiing, the clothes provided here can also be used for golf. There are garments that you can use in the rain that allow your body to breathe as well as thermals and underwear that wick away moisture and keep you warm for those of you who are out there during the winter.

Brookstone—(800) 926-7000

A sampling of items include a handy golf-club cleaner, an electronic golf-score keeper/bag tag, a golf-range viewfinder (not USGA approved), and a golf-club beverage cooler and dispenser. There's also a handy little gadget called an electronic golf meter that you can keep score on and track your walking mileage with a pedometer.

Tiffany & Co.—(800) 526-0649

This high-class, high-end, richly designed, and colorful catalog offers a unique golf gift or two. Along with the Swiss Army knife in sterling silver with 18K gold emblem and the 14K gold heart locket, you'll find a sterling silver golf-ball key ring ($55), a golf ball and tee pen made of sterling silver for $75, and a golf ball paperweight in full-lead crystal at 2¼" in diameter ($50).

Godiva Chocolates—(800) 946-3482

This famous chocolatier offers the following items: foil-wrapped dark-chocolate golf balls filled with hazelnut praline, caramel, and walnuts ($13); a nine-piece assortment of Godiva's finest chocolates containing milk, dark, and ivory favorites; plus a collection of solid milk chocolates. The chocolates are wrapped in green foil with Godiva's exclusive golfing motif. It's a great, simple gift for clients and fellow golfers ($12).

Art & Tapestry—(212) 722-3222

Although this store specializes in personalized children's gifts, it carries an incredibly crafted golf chess set made in England from grounded marble. Here's the description from the manufacturer: "This specially commissioned set by Peter Calvesvert is a whimsical portrayal of old golfers against new. Although no particular characters are represented, we have used St. Andrews as the castle for the old site and Turnbury Lighthouse for the new. The pawns are represented by old and new golf bags. The remaining characters can be distinguished by their form of dress. The old side in their plus fours and tweeds and the new with bright colors and baseball hats ($750).

The following list of books, videos, and CD-ROMs is a smattering of interesting, popular, and bestselling golf-related items.

AUDIO TAPES

A Good Walk Spoiled by John Feinstein,
Here's the bestseller about what it's like to be inside the PGA Tour.

"And Then Jack Said to Arnie…" by Don Wade
A collection of great golf stories read by Arte Johnson of *Laugh-In* fame.

"And Then Arnie Told Chi Chi…" by Don Wade
More great golf stories read by Laugh-In's Arte Johnson.

Golf Is Not a Game of Perfect by Bob Rotella
Instruction and inspiration from the bestselling book

Golf in the Kingdom by Michael Murphy
Life and links. Here's the book as read by Mitchell Ryan that is soon to be a movie.

Harvey Penick's Little Red Book by Harvey Penick
The bestseller narrated by Jack Whitaker.

For All Who Love the Game by Harvey Penick
Lessons and teachings for women.

Zinger
Paul Azinger tells his story about his triumph over cancer. Wonderfully inspiring.

CD-ROMS

GolfAmerica Golf Guide
A popular CD-ROM that contains details on over 14,500 golf courses. This information includes pars, yardages, course descriptions, addresses and telephone numbers. You also get a resort directory and travel and tournament information. The setup is menu driven, making it easy to access all of the pertinent information. State maps are here too, so you can pinpoint where you want to hit a few.
Windows and Macintosh

Fundamentals of a Model Swing, Deluxe Edition
Dr. Ralph Mann, Olympic medalist, and PGA pro Fred Griffin show you fifteen drills to improve your swing. You get step-by-step instructions on how to master the perfect swings with over 8½ hours of drills and instruction.
Windows

Golf Digest Scorecard 3.0

Find out what your strengths and weaknesses are to help save strokes and improve your game. Twenty-nine detailed reports and graphs analyze your game.

Windows

Golf's Greatest Collection

The eight titles included in this package are: The Masters; ESPN Golf: Tom Kite's Shotmaking; Links: The Challenge of Golf; Links: Dorado Course Disk; Jack Nicklaus Signature Edition; Jack Nicklaus Tour Volume; Infamous Golf Holes; and GolfAmerica. This great value contains over $300 in software. There's even a cool screen saver.

Windows

From Golf Tips *magazine and David Leadbetter.*

Each package comes with three Wilson TC2 golf balls and includes over twenty hours of instruction.

Golf Tips: Breaking 90

Learn the subtle techniques and strategies on how to link swing components and bending the ball. For advanced golfers.

Windows and Macintosh

Golf Tips: Breaking 100

Learn basic techniques on judging dis-

tance, proper grip, and more. For beginning and intermediate golfers.

Greg Norman's Ultimate Golf Challenge

In this CD-ROM, forty-four programmable player characteristics provide true golf simulation. You can play in the simulation mode or with an arcade-style swing meter. Play as the Shark, or play against him.

Windows

Links LS

Recently redesigned, this new golf engine (meaning you need this CD-ROM to run other available peripheral CD-ROMs from the same manufacturer) has been enhanced to let you explore each shot from four different camera angles. This package features Kapalua Resort in Maui, allowing you to play the Plantation or the Village courses. You can play stroke, match, best ball, or skins. You can even play against Arnold Palmer at the Latrobe Country Club, or you can play as Palmer.

Windows 95 with 16 MB of RAM

Links Pro CD (Originally titled LINKS 386 CD-ROM)

The non-Windows version of Links LS, this comes bundled with the world-class golf courses, Harbor Town Golf Links and Banff Springs. Below are the other courses you can purchase to add to your enjoyment. Keep in mind, though, that you need this CD-ROM to run them.

IBM MS DOS (will not run on Windows) and Macintosh

Volume 1, Mauna Keo, Firestone, Innisbrook, Prairie Dunes, and Bighorn
Volume 2, Banff Springs, Troon North, Cog Hill, Devil's Island, and The Belfry
Volume 3, Pinehurst, Riviera, Harbor Town, Bountiful, and Barton Creek
Volume 4, Pebble Beach

You Don't Know Jack about Sports
An interactive CD-ROM game with trivia questions about all kinds of sports including golf. How many questions we're not quite sure, but it is a lot of fun.
Windows 95 and 3.1 and Macintosh

BOOKS ABOUT THE GAME

Sports Illustrated: Tiger Woods
This ninety-six-page book chronicles the life of the young Tiger Woods, *Sports Illustrated*'s Sportsman of the Year in 1996. Includes forty-eight color photos.

Tiger Woods: The Making of a Champion by Tim Rosaforte
This 224-page biography from the author of *Heartbreak Hill* profiles the excitement of Tiger Woods's life from the time he was four to his first PGA win.

The Six Inch Swing or "One Between the Ears" by Marty Trachtenberg

Trachtenberg, director of the Alternative Golf Workshop Inc., fleshes out his theories and practical knowledge of the golf swing in this easy-to-read and enjoyable book. See the interview with him in the "Learning to Play" chapter of this book and learn why he's lightyears ahead of conventional golf wisdom.

This publication is available directly from The Alternative Golf Workshop Inc. at (310) 453-1552 or by Web site: www.altgolf.com.

Secrets of the Master: The Best of Bobby Jones by Sidney Matthew
Learn the game from Jones, perhaps the best golfer ever to grace the greens, from his own personal writings of the 1920s and 1930s. Jones discusses his secrets of a good golf swing and how to improve every aspect of your game with humorous anecdotes and refreshingly candid views.

The ABC's of Golf by Susan Greene
Here's a great way for parents to introduce their children to golf and teach them the ABC's at the same time. The book is filled with playful illustrations of golf clubs, golf balls, tees, and golf shoes, with educational rhymes to go with them.

Four Cornerstones of Winning Golf by Claude "Butch" Harmon Jr. and John Andrisani
From the "hottest instructor in golf" learn the same secrets Harmon learned from his legendary instructor-father. Harmon's clients include Greg Norman, Davis Love III, and Tiger Woods. The book covers the

swing, the short game, and the mental game, as well as staying in physical shape.

Golf Is Not a Game of Perfect by Dr. Bob Rotella
The bestselling mental guru of golf discusses how to master and enjoy the game.

Golf Is a Game of Confidence by Dr. Bob Rotella and Bob Cullen
A second book from golf's mental-game guru, this one is filled with inspirational instructions and stories of the game's legendary players.

Hogan Five Lessons—Fundamentals by Ben Hogan
This all-time classic book covers Hogan's fundamentals of the game.

Harvey Penick's Little Red Book
Lessons and teachings from a lifetime of golf.

Harvey Penick's Little Green Book
More lessons and teachings.

For All Who Love the Game
Lessons and teachings for women.

Putt Like the Pros by Dave Pelz
The short-game master gives you scientific ways to improve your putting stroke.

Golf Etiquette by Puett & Apfelbaum
If all golfers practiced proper etiquette on the course, then slow play would be nonexistent. Here, Puett and Apfelbaum have

written a lively and informative reference guide about the protocol of the game. The authors even give you a way to contact them with your questions.

A Good Walk Spoiled: Days and Nights on the PGA Tour by John Feinstein
This bestselling book is filled with stories of what it's like to be on the inside of the most popular sport on the planet.

Golf Games by R.M. Ussak
A pocket-sized guide to 110 betting games for golf.

Golf in the Kingdom by Michael Murphy
The inspirational, fantastical story of a man who learns the lessons of life as he plays golf. Slated to be a major motion picture.

Golf for Women by Whitworth & Glenn
An enjoyable guide to golf from the women's point of view written by women.

Around the World in 18 Holes by Tom Callahan & Dave Kindred
For sixty-nine days Tom Callahan, contributing editor to *Golf Digest*, and close friend Dave Kindred, writer for *Sporting News* and *Golf Digest*, set out to play the best holes in golf. It's a fun read as the boys take you to exotic places like Kathmandu, Singapore, and Beijing, as well as the famous holes at Augusta, Pebble Beach, and St. Andrews. It's one of life's great journeys into the often wild world of golf.

The Unofficial Golfer's Handbook by Richard Mintzer

Before Richard Mintzer co-authored *The Everything Golf Book*, he took a humorous look at the game. Included here are a collection of jokes, lists, trivia, and quizzes about golf, along with wonderful anecdotes and answers to the wackiest questions you would never dare ask about the game. This book is available only by e-mail at RSMZ@aol.com.

GOLF VIDEOS

How I Played Golf

In 1931 Bobby Jones made a series of movie shorts that featured cameos from Hollywood stars. The tapes were recently discovered in storage and transferred onto video. As you're watching, remember that Jones did not have the benefit of today's technology and editing capabilities. He executes perfect shots one right after the other, live.

Ben Hogan in Pursuit of Perfection

Recently unearthed footage taken by a fan of Mr. Hogan perfecting his game, this rare inside view of instruction is fast becoming a collector's item.

Tiger Triumphs

Celebrate Tiger Woods's three amateur victories ('94, '95, and '96) through video highlights of his games. He's the only golfer in his-tory to win the Amateur Championship three years in a row.

Dave Pelz's Amazing Truth about Putting

David Leadbetter's Practice Makes Perfect David Leadbetter's Simple Solutions for Great Golf

Twenty-five quick and simple solutions to assist players at every level.

Johnny Miller's Golf Tips Great tips to help golfers play better.

Kathy Whitworth's Breaking 100

Ms. Whitworth gives five steps to lower your score. Great for golfers of all abilities.

There's also a bonus segment here entitled How to Practice on a Driving Range.

Lessons with Leadbetter
The Full Golf Swing
The Short Game
Take your own personal lessons here with one of the great golf gurus.

Little Green Video
Penick's second instructional video with Ben Crenshaw and Tom Kite.

Little Red Video
Highlights from Penick's *Little Red Book.*

Moe Norman: Golf's Journey
Through the use of stop-action and slow motion, you get to see one of the most effective and responsible swings on the planet.

Nice Shot!
Chuck Hogan steps away from conventional wisdom and breaks down the mental part of game, covering exercises, instruction, and forming good habits. If you're looking for something different and effective, this is it.

Nick Faldo's Fixes
Faldo shares long-term solutions for golfers' most common difficulties.

Nick Faldo's Tips and Drills
Faldo gives his personally developed regime of drills and prac-

tice tips, many of which you can use on a daily basis.

Ray Floyd's Cutting Strokes
Ray focuses on the short game, with creative secrets on pitching, bunker shots, and putting.

Rick Smith's Range Tips, Volume 15
Basic elements of a great golf swing.

Rick Smith's Swing Equation, Volume 2
For golfers of all levels, Smith gives the elements of an efficient and repeatable golf swing.

Sixty Yards In
Floyd focuses on what clubs to select for the short game. Includes instruction on sand play and putting.

Beginning Golf for Women
Essentially two videos covering the long game and the short game. Available separately or together as a unit.

Women's Golf 2-Pack
Peggy Kirk Bell and Dede Owens give instruction on the full swing and how to approach the game.

Women's Golf Guide
Though it says "women" in the title, this is for male golfers too. This very informa-

tive video delves into the crucial parts of the game: etiquette, rules, and customs.

Bad Golf Made Easier

Leslie Nielsen—from *Airplane!* and the *Police Academy* movies—takes on golf. Lots of funny bits, but the behind-the-scenes look at the making of the video appears as if they ran out of stuff to do, so it's been added on. Nonetheless, it's a big seller.

Bad Golf My Way

It seems that Mr. Nielsen didn't get enough of terrorizing the links in his first video, so he's made a sequel—and it might be better than the first one. Check out Nielsen's tongue-placed-firmly-in-cheek take on PBS's *Masterpiece Theatre* as he outsmarts a betting lout on the course. Great stuff about all those silly games within the game.

Dorf on Golf

Slapstick schtick from Tim Conway, one of television's favorite personalities.

Golf's Goof-ups and Miraculous Moments

Hosted by Robert Wuhl (*Bull Durham*, *Batman* and star of HBO's comedy series *Arliss* about a sports agent) this fun video, produced by *Sports Illustrated*, will have you yelling things like "Ohhh!" "Incredible!" and "Unbelievable!" for close to an hour. Wuhl is a devotee of the game and makes the video a pleasure.

Peter's Party

Celebrities and pros exhibit their talents at Peter Jacobsen's Fred Meyer Challenge.

GOLF MOVIES

When it's too rainy for the course, it's time for a movie—a golf movie! We are generally an impatient lot and when we're watching a movie, especially about sports, the story's got to keep moving or the movie theater will quickly empty. Naturally, when people hear that a movie about golf has come into town, they're a bit wary. "How do you make an interesting story about golf?" is often asked. The answer is don't make a story about golf. Let it be the vehicle to tell the story. As is the case with most movies, some make the cut and some don't. Here's your guide to getting through the hazards.

The Caddy

Starring Dean Martin and Jerry Lewis

Even though the great Ben Hogan makes an appearance in this picture, you take your life into your hands if you suddenly hit the wrong button while fast forwarding to his role. Why? Because you might hear Jerry Lewis singing with that voice just north of the stratosphere. You'd think he must have had a canister of helium hanging around right off the set and sucked it down between takes to get that insufferable pitch. No doubt you're wondering, what the heck does this have to do with golf? Well, in the setup Jerry and Dean's ever-popular road show takes a nose dive and the boys find themselves flat broke. How are they going to regain their fortune? Golf! It turns out that Lewis's father was a tournament pro who won many a match. Lewis himself is good, but, alas, he's got a slight handicap: he can't play in front of people. Dean to the rescue! He seems to have some talent in the golf department too, so Lewis teaches him the game and becomes his caddy. Off they go in pursuit of the big bucks in Santa Barbara, where Dean hooks up with Donna Reed. Hogan and Reed are the only saving graces of this picture. Just remember, we warned you.

Caddyshack

Starring Bill Murray, Ted Knight, Rodney Dangerfield, and Chevy Chase.

Pitting the clichéd uptight rich against the clichéd classless nouveau-riche works well in this movie that takes place at a country club. Good stories thrive on conflict, and the best conflict often comes when two extremes clash and that's what happens here in one of the funniest movies ever produced. Ted Knight, who wears his wealthy inheritance like he deserves it, battles with Rodney Dangerfield, who in this movie could care less about respect. He just wants to stick it to snooty Ted, who represents those chosen few who feel golf is only for them and the sleek, blue-blazer crowd.

Meanwhile, Bill Murray plays the ultimate disturbed groundskeeper who hunts down the bane of his existence—gophers. Scene after scene with Murray is hilarious as he strug-

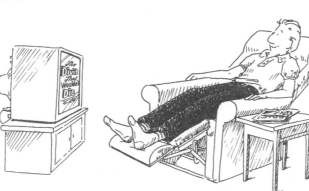

gles with what's left of his brain to fulfill his mission. Look for Chevy Chase also (whom Murray replaced in *Saturday Night Live*) as a high-flying leech who doesn't even have to lift a finger to be with Knight's ever-so-seductive daughter. Don't miss this one, even if you don't golf.

Caddyshack II

To even consider giving this picture a paragraph would be in violation of the "What were they thinking when they made this movie?" act.

Follow the Sun

Starring Glenn Ford, Anne Baxter, and other golfing greats

Here's a movie for golfers and nongolfers alike. Glenn Ford stars as Ben Hogan, one of the greatest golfers in modern history. In this truly inspiring biography we're taken from Hogan's days as a caddy in Texas to his championships on the pro tour. Things are going great for Hogan when he suddenly has a near-fatal automobile accident. Told by his doctors that he would never walk again, much less play golf, we see Hogan go on to play at the L.A. Open where he battles Sam Snead (who plays himself, as do golfing greats Cary

Middlecoff and James Demaret) for the ultimate comeback. Hogan doesn't go the trip alone, however. His devoted wife Valerie (played by Anne Baxter) is the key to his recovery and success. A great golf and love story.

Goldfinger
Starring Sean Connery

"Do you expect me to talk, Goldfinger?" "No, Mr. Bond, I expect you to die." But before that, let's shoot a round. In one of golf's most memorable scenes on the big screen, Bond, James Bond, shoots less than a 007 handicap in his game with the terrifying megalomaniac, Goldfinger. That's no small accomplishment with Goldfinger's caddy, Odd Job, standing just feet away. You see, Odd Job, the world's most surly, intimidating caddy, has a hat rim that can decapitate stone statues, not to mention he can carry a full staff bag as if it's a student's knapsack. High marks for snappy dressers Bond and Goldfinger.

Happy Gilmore
Starring Adam Sandler and Bob Barker

This picture lights up the moronic sides of our personas and sometimes that's not such a bad thing. Adam Sandler, the *Saturday Night Live* alumnus (what's with these guys and golf movies?) plays a failed hockey player who takes on golf and works his way into the pro circuit. Naturally, Sandler brings his hockey attitude with him and there's often hell to pay. Some of the gags are a bit overused, and there's a lot of yelling and screaming. Bob Barker, host of

the game show *The Price Is Right*, plays a stuffy sort and Sandler checks, rather, decks him, getting a great laugh. So, if you're a Sandler fan, grab a beer, figure out how to work the VCR, and enjoy.

Pat and Mike

Golf is the theme here in this classic Tracy and Hepburn picture. Spencer Tracy plays the ethically challenged Mike, a sports promoter/manager who wants to sign the talented golfing pro Pat (Katherine Hepburn). He sees cash in her as well as her waggle, and doesn't easily admit to the latter. Once Pat and Mike hook up, Pat reveals that she is also great at tennis. With this, Mike feels he's landed a gold mine. Mike's love for Pat is realized when the mob wants Pat to throw a match. Mike refuses. Fisticuffs soon occur, but Hepburn, being the athlete that she is, decks the boys and helps save Mike, who she's now in love with. Look for Charles Bronson.

Three Little Beers

Through divine intervention or some other miracle, Larry, Moe, and Curly have made a golf movie and it's very funny. The premise is that the boys make a beer delivery to a tournament. The Three Stooges and beer. Can you think of a scarier combination? The fact is, though, that the boys don't even need to drink it to cause mayhem. Check it out.

(Note: This movie short can be found in volume four of a Three Stooges box set that contains thirteen volumes.)

Tin Cup

In one of the best golf movies ever made, Ron Shelton, the man who gave us *Bull Durham*, gives us the same star, Kevin Costner, this time playing a down-and-out golf pro who runs a marginal driving range. Broken in spirit (many a golfer can relate to that), he's a talented pro who has the potential to be one of the greats. Accompanying him on his journey to a shot at the U.S. Open is his great friend and caddy, played by Cheech Marin, whose antics give this picture a lot of flavor.

How does Costner take the first step to the stars? How does he begin to scratch his potential? Two words: Rene Russo. Ms. Russo plays a psychologist who wants to improve her game, and Costner is only too happy to show her how. Unfortunately, she's dating the ultimate Mr. Smooth, Don Johnson, a touring pro who also happens to be Costner's arch-nemesis. Johnson often wins many a tournament by playing it safe and chides Costner for taking too many chances on the course. But now Costner is driven to accomplish two things: seize Russo's heart and defeat Johnson in the U.S. Open.

On the road to the U.S. Open, Costner encounters the shanks and loss of his trusted caddy and can't seem to lock in Russo. There's a great scene where Costner, desperately in need of dollars, challenges a good player, saying he can beat him by using garden tools against the golfer's clubs. The picture cli-maxes at the U.S. Open, where Costner's character takes the biggest risk in his career, and like his character Crash Davis in *Bull Durham*, Shelton has him win and lose at the same time. Look for Gary McCord as a commentator, as well as many pros from the circuit who play themselves.

CABLE

For those of us who can't get enough golf coverage from the major networks, golf coverage can also be found on ESPN, TBS, and CSN—the Classic Sports Network. CSN shows things like classic matches, including opens, Ryders, and other incredible golf highlights.

The Golf Channel

Yes! This is true! For those of us who shoot the links, all those nods to the gods have been answered. The Golf Channel, launched on January 17, 1995, was first conceived by Arnold Palmer, who is co-chairman of the operation. The channel gives viewers live coverage of PGA, LPGA, Senior, Nike, and European tour events. The Golf Channel covers the hottest news and players; talks with tournament winners; shows tournament highlights; and has a weekly viewer call-in show that puts viewers in touch with the pros and celebrity guests. You also get profiles and interviews with your favorite players, instruction and tips from the best in the business. The Golf Channel, which has also expanded into Japan and has reports in both Japanese and English, is scheduled to expand into Taiwan, the Philippines, and Australia.

The Golf Channel is carried by your local cable company and on satellite-dish feeds. For the satellite feeds, chances are it's already available without having to pay an extra fee. To get the Golf Channel carried by your local cable company, you've got to keep calling them to request it. Channels are always opening up on cable systems, and if the cable company feels there's enough demand for the Golf Channel, they'll put it on their system.

Another way to get the Golf Channel carried on your local cable system is to phone/fax/write/e-mail the Golf Channel directly to inform them that they should market their product to your cable system. You can also get a group of fellow golfers from your local club or public course to sign a petition stating that there is great enthusiasm for the channel. This works. Here's the pertinent info:

The Golf Channel
7580 Commerce Center Drive
Orlando, FL 32819
Tel: (800) 363-4650
Fax: (407) 363-7976
Web site: http//www.thegolfchannel.com

GOLF MAGAZINES

Following are periodicals relating to golf, covering a wide spectrum of playing techniques, equipment tests, and even more tips from the pros. In some instances, the publication will send you a free sample of their magazine for you to peruse and decide if you'd like to subscribe.

Many states and regions, such as southern California, have their own separate golf magazines. Their advantage is that they focus on your home turf. Some of the better ones are listed below with a brief profile so that you can get an idea of what they're generally like. The national golf magazines are followed by a few of the top regional ones.

Golf Digest
Circulation: 1.5 million
Written for: Beginning to advanced golfers
Published: Monthly
Web site: www.golf.com
Subscription rate: $27.94 one year, $41.94 two years, $55.88 three years
To subscribe: Call (800) PAR-GOLF

This is not only a magazine, but an entire golf industry. The company owns and operates a network of over 375 golf schools across the nation. The instructors at these schools are top professionals and contribute to the instructional part of the magazine. In fact, a whole section every month is devoted to instruction. Departments have names like Mind on Golf, The Advisor, Travel Information Service, and Instant Lesson. Although the magazine's readership is 94 percent male, there are special sections devoted to women. More and more women, especially in the business world, are playing golf and

Golf Digest recognizes this. Profiles of great golfers, as well as top-100 course rankings, and top-75 public course rankings are an enjoyable and valuable tool. The magazine is immersed deeply in the golf world and is both dedicated and devoted to it.

Golf

Circulation: 1.3 million
Published: Monthly
Web site: www.golfonline.com
Subscription rate: $19.94 one year,
$29.94 two years, $39.88 three years
To subscribe: Call (800) 876-7726

Like *Golf Digest*, these folks are an entire industry unto themselves and are known in the business as *Golf* Magazine Properties. How involved in the industry are they? Well, for openers, they own the Golf Channel. The layout of this magazine reads like an 18-hole course. Each "chapter" is noted with a number resembling a hole. This is actually a good idea, as it helps the reader and the magazine focus on each issue it addresses. For instance, the first hole is called "Within the Rules." Hole four is the "Short Game." Hole fourteen is "Health," and so on. It's very well put together and covers a lot of ground.

The Golfer

Circulation: 250,000
Written for: Beginners to professional enthusiasts
Published: Six times per year
Subscription rate: $24 per year
To subscribe: Call (212) 696-2484

The Golfer is a fun, lush magazine that focuses on an individual subject in each issue. For instance, three recent magazines focused on travel, performance, and champions. What's really great and exclusive about this magazine is the photography. It captures the essence of the game, often from a point of view we seldom get to see. Frozen in time is the top of a ball just below the cup line, a nanosecond before it makes every golfer's favorite sound in the world, plopping into the bottom of the tin. Other features include things like "Cures for the Most Common Golfing Problems." The photographs accompanying an article on putters really brings you up-close and personal. The lush pictures of golf courses bring the fairways and the greens right under your toes. You can practically smell the fresh air. The writing is enjoyable and concise.

Golf Tips

Circulation: 275,000
Written for: Beginners, amateurs, and professionals
Published: Monthly, except bimonthly in Jan./Feb., Sept./Oct., and Nov./Dec.
Subscription rate: $17.94 per year
To subscribe: Call (800) 283-4640

Known as the "Game's Most In-depth Instruction & Equipment Magazine," *Golf Tips*'s goal is to educate devoted golfers. The magazine's growth rate was over 19 percent in 1996. That says a lot in the very competitive golf-readership market. There are tips on instruction, equipment, and travel. Along with featured articles on instruction, there are the monthly departments, some of which include "New and Notable," a column that focuses on the latest and greatest equipment and apparel; "Fore Women," thoughts about the game from the woman's perspective; "12 Tips from 12 Pros," a column from America's top teachers offering advice on common swing flaws; and seven more departments. Each issue devotes an in-depth article to a golf school.

Golf Week

Circulation: 75,000
Published: Weekly
Written for: Amateur and professional devotees
Subscription rate: $59.95 per year
To subscribe: Call (800) 996-4653

Do you enjoy the game so much that monthly publications aren't quite enough for you? Luckily, there's *Golf Week*. This magazine is similar to a newspaper, providing up-to-the-minute information on who's playing where, standings, and when new equipment is coming onto the marketplace. A column called "The Forecaddie" gives cutting-edge news about the game. Then there's the weekly behind-the-scenes look at how television covers the game, as well as schedules for upcoming events on television. *Golf Week* covers amateur and international news too, and lists all of the tours' scoreboards. And last but not least, there are pages highlighting business and travel. *Golf Week* is enjoyable and easy to read. And if you want to get into the golf business, *Golf Week* publishes a biweekly industry report for golf retailers and operators.

Golf for Women

Circulation: 330,000
Published: Monthly
Written for: Women, from beginners to professionals
E-mail: golfwomen@aol.com
Subscription rate: $16.97 per year. If you renew, it's $8.49 per year afterwards.
To subscribe: Call (800) 374-7941

Here's an oasis for women in the middle of a male-dominated market. Like other golf magazines, there are articles and departments on instruction, equipment, and travel, but with a warmer tone. Fashion is focused on more here than in other golf magazines, and that's wonderful. Women's health is also different from men's, and *Golf for Women* addresses this. For women who love golf, their prayers have been answered. This is a place to come home to.

Petersen's Golfing

Circulation: 175,000
Published: Monthly
Written for: All golf enthusiasts
Subscription rate: $19.94 per year
To subscribe: Call (800) 866-5184

Petersen's Golfing is big on testing and evaluating golf products, including the latest equipment, gadgets, and travel packages. They even evaluate golf apparel. Also included are instruction tips on how to lower your scores, interviews with pros, reviews of videos for the average golfer, and previews of major tournaments including the LPGA. Departments include "Ask Doctor Know," a column in which the good doctor invites readers to ask nagging questions about equipment; "Trends," a column about the latest in equipment and gadgets; and a fun "Golf Quiz."

Golf Illustrated

Circulation: 250,000
Published: Bimonthly
Written for: Amateurs and professionals
E-mail: 73172.2054@compuserve.com
Subscription rate: $29.95 per year
To subscribe: Call (800) 554-1999

Revamped for the '90s, *Golf Illustrated* has one of the longest-running track records in the magazine arena. Sports psychologists contribute their views on the mental side of the game in practically every issue. There's advice here too on the best resort and general public-access courses to play. Departments include "Fit for Golf," which focuses on the physical mechanics of the game; "Stroke Shaver," which gives golfers tips on various parts of the golf swing; and just to show you that they're not always serious, there's a fun, silly column called "Golf Astrology," which takes the attributes of each sun sign and applies them to the game. Cool.

Golf Journal (Published by the USGA)

Circulation: 525,000
Published: nine times a year
Written for: All golfers
Web site: www.usga.com
Subscription rate: $25 per year
To subscribe: Free with membership in the USGA. Call (800) 345-USGA.

The *Golf Journal* is very informative without being slick. It features articles on golf-course design, golf clubs, history, new equipment, and the USGA championships. One thing the *Golf Journal* has that many publications don't have is information on handicapping.

The Senior Golfer

Circulation: 150,000
Published: Bimonthly
Subscription rate: $18 per year
To subscribe: Call (203) 459-5190

This publication focuses on the senior market and its issues, covering equipment innovations, travel and leisure, fashion, and course designs. Instructional tips, along with profiles of senior players, are also included.

Golf World

Circulation: 150,000
Written for: Golfers interested in national and international golf
Published: Weekly, except for three times in November and once in December.
Subscription rate: $49 per year
To subscribe: Call (800) 627-4438

Published by *Golf Digest, Golf World* covers amateur, collegiate, professional, and international tournaments. Every month there is an in-depth article on golf architecture. Also included are profiles of national and international pros on the various tours.

PGA Magazine

Circulation: 36,000
Published: Monthly

Subscription rate: $19.97 per year
To subscribe: Call (810) 362-7400

This is more of a professional publication, with articles on merchandising and the general business of golf, as well as news from the PGA. The publication also discusses emerging golf trends and economic and environmental issues that affect courses around the country. As with many of the other publications, you'll find golf instruction here.

Score (Canada's golf magazine)
Circulation: 120,000
Focus: Canada
Published: Five times per year
Subscription rate: $18 per year
To subscribe: Call (416) 928-2909

For the Canadian golfer with a Canadian viewpoint on the game, this magazine offers instruction, reviews on new equipment, general golf news, and reviews on courses. Travel profiles are also included.

REGIONAL MAGAZINES

Chicagoland Golf
Circulation: 40,000
Published: Fifteen times per year
Subscription rate: $14 per year
To subscribe: Call (708) 719-1000

This magazine covers golf news in and around the Chicago area. There are articles analyzing both public and private courses, as well as new product reviews and tips to improve your game.

Golf News
Circulation: 55,000
Focus: Southern California
Published: Eleven times per year
E-mail: golfnews@aol.com
Subscription rate: $18 (12 issues) one year, $32 (24 issues) two years
To subscribe: Call (619) 836-3700 (in Orange County: (714) 833-3703)

The really good thing about regional magazines is that they are customized for golfers in a particular area and they're very genuine because in most cases the publisher's life is golf. And so it is with Dan and Joan Poppers at *Golf News*. Articles focus on local personalities as well as national ones. A favorite is a humor column by Gordon Mitchell, who manages to pull in things not seemingly relative to golf and somehow equate them with his game. For instance, Mitchell, inspired by Hillary Clinton's reported talks with Eleanor Roosevelt, tried to improve his game by contacting Harvey Penick. *Golf News* includes a column on the status of area courses whether they're public, semi-private, or private; par; what kind of shape they're in; and phone numbers to make reservations.

The Met Golfer

Circulation: 100,000
Focus: New York metropolitan area including the surrounding areas of New Jersey and Connecticut
Published: Six times a year
Written for: All golfers
Subscription rate: N/A

This magazine is available at golf centers in the New York metropolitan area.

Met Golf has several things going for it. The best probably is that along with its dedicated crew the publication is infused with articles from the staff of *Golf* magazine. *Met Golf* also reports on results of local tournaments, gives tips from pros, and has a calendar listing upcoming events.

Long Island Golfer

Circulation: 75,000
Focus: Long Island and the New York metropolitan area
Published: Five times a year
Written for: All golfers
Subscription rate: $8.95
To subscribe: Call (516) 822-LIGM

This down-to-earth regional magazine features columns on golf shows, golf psychology, environmental issues, and local golf manufacturers. There are also profiles of golf clubs, as well as in-depth discussions with golf instructors. You'll also find reviews on the latest videos and books, as well as a calendar of events.

IMPORTANT GOLF TERMS

ace. A hole-in-one.

address. The stance taken by a player in preparing to hit the ball.

albatross. Score for a hole made in three strokes under par, also known as a double eagle.

all square. A tied match.

approach. A shot played to the putting green or pin.

Arnie. Scoring a par from the rough.

apron. The grassy area surrounding the putting surface, also known as the fringe.

away. The ball that is the greatest distance from the hole when more than one golfer is playing. Also known as "out."

back door. A ball that drops in the rear of the hole after appearing to have no chance to go in.

back nine. The second nine holes of an 18-hole course.

backspin. A reverse spin placed on the ball to make it stop short on the putting surface.

backswing. The first part of the swing, starting from the ground and going back over the head.

ball holed. A ball is holed when it is at rest entirely below the level of the lip of the hole.

ball in play. A ball is in play as soon as the player has made a stroke from the teeing area. It remains in play until it is holed out, except when it is out of bounds, lost, or lifted, or when another ball is substituted in accordance with the rules.

ball marker. A token or a small coin used to spot the position of the ball on the green.

banana ball. A shot that curves sharply to the right.

barkie. Scoring a par off a tree.

beach. A sand hazard on the course.

bend one. To hook or slice the ball.

bent grass. Type of grass seen for the most part on northern courses.

Bermuda. Type of grass seen mostly on southern courses.

best ball. A match in which one player plays against the better of two balls or the best ball of three players.

birdie. One stroke under par for a hole.

bisk. Handicap stroke that can be claimed at any hole during a match.

bite. To land a ball with backspin on the green.

blade. A type of putter, also sometimes the clubhead of an iron.

blast. A shot that takes a large amount of sand with it when hitting out of a sand trap, also known as an explosion shot.

blind bogey. A type of competition in which each player tries to come the closest to a score that has been drawn out of a hat.

blind hole. A green that cannot be seen by a player from the fairway.

bogey. One stroke over par for a particular hole.

bold. A firmly played approach to a well-protected pin. Also, too strong or long a shot.

borrow. To play to one side of the hole or the other in order to compensate for the slope of the green.

bounce. The degree to which the club-head's flange lies below its leading edge.

bowker. A shot that appears to be horrible and then hits a tree, a rock, a spectator, etc. and bounces back into play. Sample usage: "I would have bogied the fourth hole but I got a bowker."

bunker. A natural or artificial depression on a fairway or around the green. This depression is usually filled with sand, but can be made of earth or grass.

bunt. To hit an intentionally short shot.

burn. The Scottish term for a creek or stream.

bye. A term used in tournaments. The player who draws a "bye" is allowed to advance to the next round without playing an opponent.

caddie or **caddy.** Someone who carries a player's clubs during play and offers him or her assistance in accordance with the rules. This name came into existence during the reign of Mary, Queen of Scots.

Calloway. Handicapping system in which a player's score is determined by his worst holes.

can. To hole a putt.

cap. The top end of a club grip and shaft.

carry. The length of travel by the ball once it is hit until it first hits the ground; also to successfully clear a hazard.

casual water. Any temporary accumulations of water that are visible before or after a player takes his or her stance. This does not include a hazard or water hazard. A player may lift his or her ball from casual water without penalty.

cavity-backed clubs. Golf clubs that have the weight removed from the back and distributed to the perimeter, creating a greater sweet spot.

chip shot. A short approach shot from near the green. Usually a hit incorporating overspin or bite.

choke. To hit the ball with a hacking motion.

closed stance. When the front foot extends over the line of flight, also known as a hook stance.

clubhead. The hitting area of the club.

clubhouse lawyer. A self-appointed caller or arbiter of the rules.

comebacker. A putt that returns after a ball has skirted or run past the hole.

concede. When a putt, hole, or match is surrendered.

control shot. A shot that is played with less than full power.

course. The playing area, usually made up of nine or eighteen holes, with each hole having a tee-off area, fairway, and green.

course rating. A course comparison expressed in strokes or decimal fractions of strokes. The yardage of the course and the ability of a scratch golfer are the basis for determination.

cut. A shot played with a slightly open clubface that results in the ball's stopping almost immediately on the green without a roll.

dead ball. A ball that will be sunk on the next shot.

deuce. A score of two strokes.

dimples. The scientifically designed and often round indentations on the cover of the golf ball that enable it to make a steady, true flight.

divot. A piece of turf removed with a shot. It should always be replaced and stamped down.

dogleg. A left or right bend in the fairway.

dog license. Slang for a seven and six result in a match-play contest. Derived from seven shillings and six pence, once the cost of a dog license.

dormy or **dormie.** Situation in match play where a player leads by the same number of holes as there are left to play and therefore cannot be beaten.

double bogey. A score of two over par for a single hole.

double eagle. A score of three under par for a single hole. Same as albatross.

draw. A shot that turns gradually from right to left in flight, not to be confused with a hook. Also the pairing of golfers for a match-play tournament.

drive. To hit a ball from a tee.

driver. The 1-wood. Used when a golfer needs maximum distance and usually used off the tee.

dub. A missed or badly hit shot.

duck hook. Shot that hooks sharply to the left of the target line.

duffer. An unskilled golfer. Also called a hacker.

dunk. To hit your ball into a water hazard.

eagle. Two strokes under par for a single hole.

enough club. The appropriate club for the given yardage.

equipment. Anything that is used by a player or is carried or worn (not including a ball in play).

explosion shot. A shot that takes large quantities of sand out of a sand trap.

fable spooned. A wood (or metal-wood) that was allegedly used to shoot a hole-in-one.

face. The hitting area or surface of the clubhead.

fade. A shot that turns gradually from left to right in flight; not to be confused with a slice.

fairway. The area of the course between the tee and the green that is well maintained and allows a good lie for the ball.

fan. To miss the ball completely. Also known as a whiff.

fat. When the club hits the ground behind the ball and takes too much turf.

feathery or **featherie.** A ball that replaced the original wooden ball, with a leather cover stuffed with boiled feathers and used until about 1848. It is now a valuable collector's item.

fib stick. A club that was allegedly used for a hole-in-one. See also fable spooned.

field. The players in a tournament.

flagstick. A movable marker that shows the location of the hole.

flange. The surface on the back of the clubhead that protrudes at the sole, usually noted on sand, lob (third), and pitching wedges.

flat swing. A swing in which the clubhead is carried back in a less upright manner.

flier. A ball hit without spin; it goes for a greater distance than normal.

flight. The division of players of equal ability in tournament play.

flub. A poorly hit shot, usually caused by hitting the ground before the ball. Also known as a fluff or a whiff.

follow-through. The continuation of the swing after the ball has been hit.

fore. The accepted expression used to warn anyone in danger of being struck by a ball.

forecaddie. Someone employed by the course or tournament committee to mark the position of a player's ball.

four ball. A match in which the better ball of two players is played against the better ball of their opponents.

foursome. Four players playing together. Also a match in which two players play against another two players, with each side playing one ball.

fried-egg lie. A ball half buried in a bunker. Looks like a yolk with sand bunched up around it.

fringe. Same as apron.

frog hair. The short grass that borders the edge of the putting surface.

front side. The first nine holes of an 18-hole course.

gimmie. A putt that is certain to be made on the next shot and will most likely be conceded by an opponent. The opponent, however, must offer the gimmie before it is taken. See inside the leather.

grain. The direction in which the grass on a putting lie grows.

green. The whole golf course, according to the *Rules of Golf*. In popular usage it is just the putting surface.

grip. The part of the shaft where the club is held, covered with leather or other material. Also the manner in which you hold the club.

ground under repair. Any part of the course being repaired. A ball that lands in such an area must be removed without penalty.

gross. The total number of strokes required to complete a round.

guttie or **gutty.** Solid golf ball made of gutta percha, a rubbery substance. It replaced the featherie and was used up until the 1900s.

hacker. An unskilled golfer. Same as duffer.

halved. When a match is played without a decision. A hole is halved when both sides play in the same number of strokes.

handicap. The number of strokes a player may deduct from his or her actual score to adjust to the scoring ability of a scratch golfer.

hanging lie. A ball resting on a downhill slope.

hazard. Any sand trap, bunker, or a specific body of water on the course that may cause difficulty.

heel. The part of the clubhead nearest the shaft.

hole. A 4½" round receptacle in the green that must be at least 4" deep. Also the area between the tee and green.

hole high. A ball that is even with the hole but off to one side.

hole-in-one. Holing out with one stroke. Same as an ace.

hole out. To complete the play for one hole by hitting the ball into the cup.

home pro. A professional who holds a position at a golf club, teaches, and plays only in local events.

honor. The privilege of hitting first from the tee. The privilege goes to the winner of the last hole won.

hooding. Rotating the face of the club inward, which has the effect of reducing the normal loft of the clubface.

hook. A shot that curves sharply to the left of the intended target.

hosel or **hosel offset.** The hollow part of an iron clubhead into which the shaft is fitted.

hustler. A golfer who purposely maintains a high handicap to win more bets.

in. The second nine holes, as opposed to out (the first nine holes).

inside the leather. The distance from the putter's face to the beginning of the grip. A common benchmark for gimmies.

iron. A club with a metal head.

interlocking grip. A grip where the index finder of the top hand is interlocked with the pinky of the opposite hand at the point where the hands meet.

jigger. A utility club once popular for playing chip shots.

juice. Backspin.

jungle. Slang for trees, bushes, heavy rough, or any punishing form of natural growth bordering fairways.

lag. A long putt made with the intention of getting near the hole.

lateral hazard. Any hazard running parallel to the line of play.

lay up. To hit the ball to an area on the fairway that will provide the golfer with a good chip shot to the green instead of gambling, trying to hit the ball directly onto the green. Usually taken because of a hazard or a bunker.

leaderboard. Scoreboard that tabulates the ranking of players during a tournament.

lie. Where the ball is in relation to the ground. A good lie is in the middle of the fairway; a bad lie is in tall grass, the sand, or the woods, with a tree in front of your ball. Also the angle of the clubhead's sole into the shaft.

lip. The top rim of the hole or cup.

lob shot. A shot that goes straight up and comes almost straight down. Useful when there is not much green to play to.

loft. The elevation of the ball in the air. Also the angle at which the clubface is set from the vertical, or the angle of the club-face to the ground.

lofter. An obsolete, highly lofted club that was the predecessor of the niblick.

loose impediments. Any natural object that is not fixed or growing. This can include loose stones, twigs, branches, mole-hills, dung, worms, or insects.

low ball and **total.** A four-ball team bet in which the best ball of each team wins a point, and the lowest total of the partners wins another point.

LPGA. The Ladies' Professional Golf Association.

make the cut. To qualify for the final rounds of a tournament by scoring well enough in the beginning rounds.

makeable. A putt with a good chance of being made.

marshal. A person appointed by a tour-nament committee to keep order and handle spectators. Also a person who patrols the course, often instructing players to move faster or to let others play through.

match. A competition played with each hole's being a separate contest. The team or player winning the most holes, rather than lowest score, is the winner.

medal. The low qualifying score for a match-play tournament.

medalist. The player with the lowest qualifying score in a tournament.

medal play. A competition decided by the overall number of strokes used to com-plete the round. Same as stroke play.

missable. A putt that's easy to miss.

mixed foursome. A foursome in which each side consists of a male and a female player.

Mulligan. Not a legal shot. It is often a second shot that is allowed to be taken in friendly play and, if used at all, should be kept to an extreme minimum.

Nassau. A type of bet where a point is given for the front nine, another for the back nine, and one for the complete eighteen holes.

neck. Where the shaft of the club joins the head.

net. A player's final score after he or she subtracts his or her handicap.

nineteenth. First extra hole to decide a tie.

nineteenth hole. A name often used for the clubhouse bar.

observer. A person who is appointed to assist the referee in a match, to decide questions of fact, and to report any breach of rules.

obstruction. Any artificial object that has been left or placed on the course, with the exception of course boundary markers and constructed roads and paths.

open. A tournament in which both ama-teurs and professionals are allowed to play.

open stance. A stance in which the front foot is placed behind the imaginary line of the direction of the ball. This allows the golfer to face more in the direction the ball is going to travel.

out. The first nine holes of an 18-hole course. The second nine holes are called in.

out of bounds. The area outside the course in which play is prohibited. A player is penalized for stroke and distance. He or she must replay the shot with a penalty of one stroke.

outside agency. Anyone who is not part of the competitors' sides in stroke play or not part of the match, such as observers, forecaddies, referees, etc.

outing. A group of people that reserve time on a course.

overclubbing. To use a club that gives too much distance.

overlapping grip. Also known as the Vardon Grip, the pinky overlaps the index finger where the hands meet to grip the club. It is the most commonly used grip in golf today.

opposing grip. A grip used in putting. Here, the player grasps the club with one palm under the other.

par. The optimal number of strokes a player should take to complete a round with good performance. It is also the standard score for a hole, usually based on its length. Holes up to 200 yards are three pars; up to 475 are four pars; anything longer than 475 is a five par. The occasional golf course does have a six par, but it is not considered a regulation hole. Club committees can vary par when a hole's difficulty warrants and not stick strictly to the distances laid down.

penalty stroke. An additional stroke added to a player's score for a rules violation.

PGA. Professional Golfers Association.

pin. Same as flagstick.

pin high. A ball even with the pin but off to one side. Same as hole high.

Pinehurst. A variation of play in which a partner plays the other partner's drive. One ball is then selected to finish the hole.

pitch. A short shot, usually to the green, with a high arc that lands with backspin. A pitch shot is farther out than a chip shot.

pitch and run. The same as pitch shot but hit with a lower-numbered club to reduce loft and backspin. This allows the ball to travel farther after it lands on the putting green.

pitching wedge. An iron club designed for making pitch shots.

pivot. The rotation of the shoulders, trunk, and pelvis during the golf swing.

play club. An obsolete ancient driver.

playing through. Passing another group of players who are playing ahead.

plus handicap. The number of strokes a player gives to adjust his ability to the common level.

pot bunker. A small, deep sand trap.

preferred lie. Local rules that allow a player to improve his or her lie in a specific manner without penalty.

professional. A player who receives payment for teaching or playing in tournaments.

pro shop. The golf-course shop, usually operated by the head professional, where equipment is sold.

provisional ball. A ball played if the previously played ball is thought to be lost or out of bounds.

pull. A ball that is hit and goes to the left of the target with a little curve.

punch. Low, controlled shot into the wind.

push. A ball that goes to the right of the target with very little or no curve, as opposed to a pull.

putt. The shot made on the putting green.

putter. A club with a straight face for putting.

putting green. The surface area around the hole that is specially prepared for putting.

quest. The goal to shoot par or under.

quail high shot. Extremely low-flying ball.

R&A. Royal and Ancient Golf Club of St. Andrews.

rabbit. A novice player.

roll on a shot. Turning the wrists too much at impact.

rough. Long grass areas adjacent to fairway, greens, tee-off areas, or hazards.

round. A complete game of golf, eighteen holes.

rub of the green. Also known as tough luck, this is when your ball is deflected by agencies beyond your control that are not part of the match or the competitor's side during stroke play, and for which there is no provision under the rules.

run. The distance the ball travels on the ground or when it lands on the ground.

running iron. A club that is used for making short running shots.

run up. An approach shot that is close to the ground or on the ground.

Ryder Cup. Biennial team match between players from the PGA European Tour and the United States PGA Tour.

sand trap. The common name for a bunker. Sand traps came into being back in the old days when foxes and rabbits dug out trails on the golf courses. These trails eventually became hollow. Course owners then filled them with sand so that golf balls wouldn't land in the gullies created by the local habitat.

sand wedge. An iron with a heavy flange on the bottom that is used primarily to get out of sand traps.

scoop. A swing in which the club has a digging or scooping action.

Scotch foursome. A match in which partners alternate hitting the ball. Partners can also alternate driving, regardless of who holed out on the previous hole.

scratch. Par play.

scratch player. A player who has no handicap.

shaft. The part of the club joined to the clubhead. It is surrounded by the grip at the top and connected to the hosel or the clubhead at the bottom.

shank. A shot made with the neck of the club, causing the ball to fly off at a wild angle.

shagging. Picking up golf balls from a practice range.

shooting stick. Walking stick with a collapsible seat on top.

short game. The part of the game that is made up of chip shots, pitching, and putting.

shotgun start. A method of beginning play in which players tee off from different holes at the same time.

side. Can mean the first nine holes (front side) or the last nine (back side) of an 18-hole course. Also two or more players who are partners.

skulling or **to skull a ball.** Hitting the ball at or above its center, causing the ball to be hit too hard and travel too great a distance.

sky. To hit underneath the ball, sending it much higher than intended. Like a pop fly in baseball.

slice. A shot that curves to the right.

smashie. Any club wrapped around a tree.

snake. A very long putt that travels over several breaks in the green.

snipe. A ball that is hooked and drops quickly.

sole. The bottom of the clubhead.

sole plate. The metal plate on the bottom of woods.

splashie. Any club that is thrown into the water.

spray. To hit the ball far off line.

square stance. Placing your feet in a line parallel to the direction in which you want the ball to travel.

stance. The position of your feet when addressing the ball.

Stimpmeter. A device used to measure the speed of a green. Stimpmeter readings in the five-to-six range mean slow greens; seven-to-eight medium; nine-to-ten fast; and above eleven, extremely fast—PGA tournament speeds.

stipulated round. The playing of all holes of a course in the correct order.

stony. To hit a ball close to the flagstick.

stroke. The forward motion of the club-head made with the intent to hit the ball (whether contact is made or not).

stroke play. A competition in which the total number of strokes for one round, or a predetermined number of rounds, determines the winner.

stymie. A rule, now abolished, in which a player whose ball on the green had another one blocking its route had to putt around or loft his ball over the other. Since a ball blocking another ball on the green may now be lifted, the term is used these days to refer to a tree in the way of a shot.

sudden death. When in a match or stroke competition the score is tied after completing the round, play continues until one player wins a hole.

summer rules. Ordinary play, according to the *Rules of Golf*, in which the ball is played where it lies.

sweet spot. The dead center of the face of the club.

takeaway. The beginning of the back-swing.

tee. A peg on which the ball is placed for driving. Also refers to the area from which the ball is hit on the first shot of the hole.

tee box. The starting place for each hole. Its rectangular shape is the size of two club lengths from front to back. The width of the box varies and is defined by the tee markers.

Texas wedge. What the putter is called when used from off the green for an approach shot.

thin. A long, low shot hit with the leading edge of the club blade.

thread. To direct the ball through a narrow opening.

three ball. Three players playing against each other, with each player playing his or her own ball.

threesome. A match in which two players play the same ball and alternate strokes against a single player. Also means three players playing a round together.

Tiger. Golfer of high ability.

Titanic. Making par after hitting a ball into the water.

toe. The part of the clubhead farthest from where it joins the shaft.

top. A shot mistakenly hit with the bottom edge of the club so that the ball is imbedded in the ground before popping up, and in most cases traveling only a short distance.

touch and feel. The ability to judge distances accurately and putt with delicacy.

tournament. A stroke- or match-play competition.

track iron. An obsolete club that was used primarily to hit the ball from cart tracks.

tradesman's entrance. Back or side edge of the hole.

triple bogey. Three shots over par.

turn. The midway point between the first and last nine holes.

twitches. The British term for the yips.

underclubbing. Using a club that does not give the needed distance.

unplayable lie. A lie in which the ball is impossible to play, such as in a thicket of trees.

up. The number of strokes or holes you are ahead of your opponent.

up and down. A high chip shot from off the green that lands near the hole, allowing the player to sink the ball with one putt.

upright swing. A swing that carries the clubhead more directly backward and upward from the ball.

Valley of Sin. Famous hollow in front of the eighteenth green on the Old Course at St. Andrews, Scotland.

waggle. Movement of the hands, hips, or clubhead at the address position to release tension while establishing a sense of feel and rhythm.

water hole. A hole with water, such as a stream or lake, that forces the players to shoot over it.

wedge. An iron that has a high loft, used for short shots.

whiff. To swing and miss the ball completely. Also known as fan.

whipping. The material used to wrap the space where the head and shaft are joined.

winter rules. A local rule that allows a player to improve the lie of the ball on the fairway. Usually used in the off season to protect the course.

wood. A club, which can be made of wood or metal, that has a large head and is used for shots requiring a great distance.

wormburner. A ball that when hit travels down close to or on the surface of the ground.

wry neck. Club with a curved neck.

Wyatt. The course marshal (as in Wyatt Earp).

XXX. Marking on a ball signifying that it should be used on the range and not played on a course.

yardage rating. The rating of a hole's difficulty based on yardage only.

yips. A condition where the player is so anxious about his putting that he can't swing his putter back and his stroke becomes a jerky jab at the ball. Also known as the twitches.

Zen golf. When you and the course are one and you are able to achieve par.